Personality Disorders and Older Adults

Diagnosis, Assessment, and Treatment

Daniel L. Segal

Frederick L. Coolidge

Erlene Rosowsky

WILEY

JOHN WILEY & SONS, INC.

For general information on our other products and services or for technical
support, please contact our Customer Care Department within the United
States at (800) 762-2974, outside the United States at (317) 572-3993 or
fax (317) 572-4002.

Wiley also publishes its books in a variety of electronic formats. Some content that
appears in print may not be available in electronic books. For more information
about Wiley products, visit our web site at www.wiley.com.

ISBN-13: 978-0-471-64983-0 (cloth)
ISBN-10: 0-471-64983-X (cloth)

Printed in the United States of America.

10 9 8 7 6 5 4 3 2 1

In loving memory of my grandfather and hero, Samuel H. Segal,
who always believed in me and my potential.
—D. L. S.

To the newest joys in my life, my grandbabies,
Melissa, Allison, and Ryan.
—F. L. C.

To the memory of my father, William Cohen.
Pa lived to 103 and did old age so very well.
—E. R.

Chapter 2

The Odd and Eccentric (Cluster A) Personality Disorders and Aging 23

General Diagnostic Criteria 24

Cluster A Personality Disorders: Paranoid, Schizoid, and Schizotypal 27

Paranoid Personality Disorder 27

Schizoid Personality Disorder 36

Schizotypal Personality Disorder 44

Chapter 3

The Dramatic, Emotional, and Erratic (Cluster B) Personality Disorders and Aging 55

Cluster B Personality Disorders: Antisocial, Borderline, Histrionic, and Narcissistic 55

Antisocial Personality Disorder 56

Borderline Personality Disorder 67

Histrionic Personality Disorder 81

Narcissitic Personality Disorder 92

Chapter 4

The Fearful or Anxious (Cluster C) Personality Disorders and Aging 103

Cluster C Personality Disorders: Avoidant, Dependent, and Obsessive-Compulsive 103

Avoidant Personality Disorder 104

Dependent Personality Disorder 113

Obsessive-Compulsive Personality Disorder 124

Chapter 5

Other Personality Disorders and Aging: Sadistic, Self-Defeating, Depressive, Passive-Aggressive, and Inadequate 137

Personality Disorders in *DSM-III-R* Appendix A and in *DSM-IV-TR* Appendix B 138

Chapter 6
Epidemiology and Comorbidity   159

Chapter 7
Theories of Personality Disorders:
Cognitive, Psychoanalytic, and Interpersonal   185

Chapter 8
Theories of Personality Disorders: Evolutionary and Neurobiological

Chapter 9
Assessment

Personality disorders (PDs) are among the most complex aspects of human behavior to understand and manage. When the vicissitudes of old age further complicate these disorders, mental health clinicians are faced with immense challenges to their therapeutic skills.

Why is the diagnosis of PD especially important in old age? Adaptation in late life is increasingly challenging, and as this book so expertly describes, PD can impair adaptive capacities in many ways. This impairment has many negative outcomes such as association with several Axis I disorders that are precipitated by or complicated by PD. The interpersonal maladaptive patterns associated with PD in late life can be destructive to elders. In addition, certain maladaptive personality traits such as undue pessimism, a tendency to helplessness, and overreliance on supportive relationships with others—so-called sociotropy—are associated with physiological reactions that may produce severe consequences if they are unrecognized or untreated. These consequences may include predisposition to depression associated with a rise in inflammatory markers such the interleukins, heart disease, and cancer. Although the cause-and-effect nature of these associations is not yet well defined, there is enough data to suggest that understanding and treating PD or trait disturbances could have important physical and mental health benefits. Similarly, other aspects of management of the problems of the elderly by care-givers will be much more challenging in the presence of the primary problem of PD: the associated impairment of interpersonal relationships. Elders, whose PD-based pathology compels them to demean and reject those on whom they must rely, can provoke rejection and abandonment at a time in their lives when they are often most in need of practical support, care, and love. The outcome can be disastrous. Even professional mental health practitioners often shrink from the task of dealing with such patients knowing instinctively or from experience that the treatment can be unrewarding, personally difficult, and complex.

To our rescue have come Segal, Coolidge, and Rosowsky, who are just the seasoned authors we need to guide the profession into this challenging arena of diagnosis, assessment, and treatment of PD in elders. Their important book synthesizes the accumulated knowledge of personality and its disorders in late life, combining the rigor of science with the sensitivity of that indefinable, essential component of practice called clinical art.

As every practitioner of mental health care for older adults will readily know from both experience and epidemiological data, the old retain the capacity to express all the psychopathology of the young including personality disorders. As is true for other disorders, however, old age creates additional clinical features that often obscure the immediate recognition of PD by the clinician who is using criteria of diagnosis created for younger patients. In old age, the many changes in health, intellectual ability, physical capacity, and social circumstance all interact to produce behaviors that, as the authors so well describe, mimic PD; for example, the withdrawal of the schizoid or the clinging neediness of the dependent personality. Similarly age-associated alterations can induce behavioral changes that obscure an underlying personality disorder such as diminishing the expression of the drama of Cluster B symptoms.

In the arena of personality disorder, the iconoclastically inclined reader may question the utility of applying the *Diagnostic and Statistical Manual of Mental Disorders* (fourth edition, text revision; *DSM-IV-TR*) criteria for PD to any age group. Thankfully, this book refreshingly deals with diagnosis by recognizing both the value of the formal criteria and the complexity of the issues. The criteria for each PD diagnosis are well presented and then thoroughly dissected from the perspective of diagnosis of the elderly patient using case histories to enliven the discussion. This careful analysis, supported by clinical cases, should help the framers of the next generation of *DSM* criteria specifically define age-appropriate criteria for PD.

Segal, Coolidge, and Rosowsky not only have established an important clinical and heuristic base for the practical application of PD diagnostic criteria to the elderly but have also highlighted those areas where the clinician must be cautious in applying the standard criteria to aging patients. This is especially true for the more dramatic personality disorders such as the borderline.

The criteria of the *DSM-IV-TR* appropriately rely, wherever possible, on the most observable behaviors to define diagnosis. However, behavior is multidetermined especially in the elderly. To understand the behaviors of personality disorders in elders, the clinician must be guided to elicit the full range of factors that influence behavioral expression—affect, cognition, inner conflicts, and motivations must all be explored systematically with each patient to accurately distinguish which behaviors arise out of personality-based factors and which are precipitated by other age-related problems such as brain pathology or physical limitations. In addition, the clinician must be able to gather the longitudinal data to establish the early evidence in support of habitual aspects of the behavior necessary for diagnosis of PD, a sometimes challenging task when dealing with the lifelong histories of elders. The authors have embraced the tangled diagnostic web and have begun to create a diagnostic map to guide the clinician. Their approach also highlights those areas where empirical and systematic data are lacking and need further research, thereby implicitly suggesting a research agenda for investigating diagnosis of PD in elders in a targeted fashion.

Empirical approaches to diagnosis are further strengthened by the thoughtful discussion of standardized PD diagnostic instruments, emphasizing the strengths and weaknesses of each and in particular emphasizing the utility or lack of it for the elderly. All standardized instruments have the great advantage of systematically eliciting data from the patient. But their focused nature also imposes limitations that should lead to cautious interpretation of results. Some instruments such as the Structured Clinical Interview for *DSM-IV* (SCID-II) simply offer a structured approach for defining the presence or absence of the symptoms used for making a *DSM* diagnosis. Others such as the NEO Personality Inventory (NEO-PI) rely on a theoretical base that arbitrarily restricts the features of human behavior to predetermined categories. Standardized interviews therefore are but one useful approach to understanding the diagnosis of PD in elders.

An important, but as yet unresolved, question is whether maladaptive personality-based behavior can newly emerge in late life. The authors usefully examine this ongoing debate. Firm conclusions cannot be drawn based on the data at this point in time, but clearly, behaviors can change and evolve in late life. The clinician meeting the patient in a cross-sectional fashion, must, among other possibilities, decide on the origin of the symptoms. New, previously unexpressed behaviors can arise when the patient's prior capacity to deal with psychological stress fails. Why might this occur? One possibility is that age-associated life stressors such as loss and grief may selectively assault the patient at points of long-standing personality-based vulnerabilities that were dormant earlier in life when the stresses of life required different strengths and capacities.

One of the most important aspects of this book is the careful interweaving of detailed and well-described case histories. Throughout, the reader is guided by comprehensive cases that acknowledge the complexities of diagnosis and management. The observational perspectives are integrated with the psychological, social, and psychodynamic. In addition, for each case, the authors address the challenge of effective management strategies tailored to the needs of each type of PD. This by itself is worth the price of the book.

The final section deals with the core of the matter for clinicians—what are we, the therapists, to do with these extremely difficult patients; how do we help them? The answer derives from the way in which the problems are conceptualized, and here again Segal, Coolidge, and Rosowsky draw on their well-honed clinical experience integrating it with the existing, and admittedly small, pool of empirical data on effective outcomes. Management of PD must deal with a disorder that has by definition been present for a long time, perhaps lifelong, and that tends to permeate the fabric of the patient's life. The clinician therefore must be able to define and respond to those problems that are amenable to intervention.

The authors recognize that treatment addresses the syndromal (e.g., anxiety or depressive elements requiring medication) and the less well-defined elements of behavioral disturbance. They acknowledge the difficulties of trying to implement intensive psychodynamically oriented techniques in this population although the outcome data in this regard are scarce indeed. Rather they appropriately combine in-depth understanding of the patient and marry it to the most effective environmental, cognitive, and behavioral interventions.

While therapeutic optimism is important in treating any patient, the clinician must be realistic about the extent of change that is possible in certain PDs and be prepared to accept limited gains which, though small, may be significant to the patient's life. In the process, the therapist often endures intensely unpleasant interactions with these patients, who are renowned for their ability to induce some rather untherapeutic feelings in therapists. Therapy is often best when the therapist is highly self-aware during treatment, thereby avoiding being driven away by the patient or responding in an otherwise untherapeutic manner. It is here that the depth of understanding of the psychodynamics and thought patterns of these patients becomes crucial to management. Phenomenology alone will not equip the therapist adequately.

This book is the best of its kind in the field of personality disorder of the elderly. It is a landmark description of the state of current knowledge and a wise guide to move the field forward to the next phase of understanding and intervention.

JOEL SADAVOY, MD
University of Toronto and Mount Sinai Hospital Toronto
Toronto, Ontario, Canada

The inspiration for this book comes out of our combined experience over the past 20 to 30 plus years as teachers, researchers, and clinicians. As teachers, we appreciate the necessity of educating our students to recognize when mental health becomes mental illness and how this might present in later life. Indeed, as the baby boomers move into later life and increase the proportion of the population that is older, this need becomes ever more pressing. The rate of mental illness in the current cohort of older adults is high (estimated at about 20%) and the boomers are bringing even higher rates of illness and greater use of mental health services with them to later life (Jeste et al., 1999). Many more trained specialists in geropsychology are needed to meet the needs of older adults now and in the coming decades (Qualls, Segal, Norman, Niederehe, & Gallagher-Thompson, 2002).

As clinicians, we are called on to assess, diagnose, and treat the spectrum of older adults who come to us for help. They come for relief from suffering and for the hope that their later years might be better, or at least less difficult.

The understanding of personality disorders is limited. Our diagnostic criteria are often reductionistic and likely not adequately relevant to many older adults given the unique context of later life. However, we do need to assess, under-stand, and treat, and we do need a reasonable lens through which to make sense of what presentations and problems we see. Some areas within the field of clinical geropsychology are better understood; there has been more research conducted and more evidence-based treatments suggested especially for the Axis I disorders. The Axis II disorders have always been in the shadow of the Axis I disorders for a number of reasons. Perhaps chief among these is their "reputation" of immutability as well as the difficulty we have in truly understanding that the essence of the individual, the personality, *is* the pathology. To this is added the uncertainty about what are normal age-related changes and what effect these might have on the personality, as well as the implications of the historical moment.

Yet, it is critical, in our opinion, that clinicians and students of clinical geropsychology achieve an understanding of the per-sonality system as well as the symptoms and expressions of per-sonality disorders in the older individual, and how such expressions affect people and systems outside the individual. We wrote this book with the hope of providing some of this fundamental knowledge.

DANIEL L. SEGAL
FREDERICK L. COOLIDGE
Colorado Springs, Colorado

ERLENE ROSOWSKY
Needham, Massachusetts

W e are grateful to have had the opportunity to come together to work on this volume. We represent different
professional emphases—theory, research, clinical—but are
joined by a common interest (some might say passion) in the
area of personality disorders in older adults. We have collab-
orated and worked together on each chapter with the hope of
bringing the material to the reader in an interesting and clinically relevant way. We also hope to encourage interest in this
area among students and trainees who come across this text,
whether by intent or assignment.

No book is created in a vacuum. Therefore, we would like
to gratefully acknowledge those who have helped each of us
along the way. Our mentors—Bennett Gurian, Michel Hersen,
C. Michael Levy, Edward J. Murray, Sara H. Qualls—are
always within us as dynamic introjects, encouraging us to
think clearly and creatively, and to stay the course. We appreciate the institutional support of the Department of Psychology at the University of Colorado at Colorado Springs, The
Department of Psychiatry, Harvard Medical School, and the
Massachusetts School of Professional Psychology. We also
thank the many students we have each trained and worked

with over the years for their valuable contributions to our research and thinking in this area.

A special thank you goes to our friends at John Wiley & Sons, specifically to Peggy Alexander and Tracy Belmont for sharing our vision and supporting the project, to Patricia Rossi, our senior editor, for being understanding and patient throughout the process, and to Isabel Pratt and Katherine Willert for their professionalism and diligence during production. We also wish to thank Brenda Phillips for her research assistance and Tracy Welch for her administrative management, always with a cool head and a warm heart.

Finally, we are deeply appreciative and indebted to our families and friends for their encouragement and support. They understand intuitively how to help us be less "difficult."

D. L. S.
F. L. C.
E. R.

Introduction to Personality Disorders and Aging

Perplexing. Vexing. Bedeviling. Frustrating. Confusing. Maddening. Exasperating! These are just a few of the words clinicians commonly use to describe their interactions with patients who have a personality disorder. Now, on top of this already challenging clinical situation, add in the common stressors associated with aging: physical declines, social losses, reduced independence, financial stressors, and cognitive declines. Adults with personality disorders are woefully ill prepared to meet these challenges of aging. Their interpersonal worlds are characterized by dysfunction, conflict, distance, or chaos, and they often lack the necessary social support networks that help buffer stress. Intrapsychically, they arrive at later life with lifelong coping deficits and, in most cases, diminished self-esteem due to a lifetime of problems and failures. They are often defeated and demoralized. Sadly, they can often be described as "surviving not thriving" with age. They are the "problem" cases that cause considerable consternation on the part of the clinician.

This synergistic combination of personality disorder psychopathology with the stressors of aging creates a host of unique clinical dilemmas. Older adults with a personality disorder are some of the most difficult patients to understand, evaluate, and treat effectively. And because older adults with a personality disorder commonly experience comorbid mental health problems, such as anxiety and depression, treatment is predictably more complicated and less successful for them.

We have written this book for clinicians and clinical students interested in working with older patients and for others who provide services for the difficult older person. Although our professional training is in clinical psychology, we intend this book for all mental health professionals who work with older adults. Our impetus is to provide the reader with a greater understanding of personality disorders within the context of aging and to offer guidelines for assessment and intervention. Our premise is that with increased understanding of this challenging clinical population, we can help personality disordered older adults age more gracefully and successfully, and improve their quality of life.

The Demographics of Aging

Traditionally, 65 years of age has been used as the demarcation of old age or later life. This may be useful for demographic purposes (e.g., to describe the number of older adults in the United States) but it is also limiting because there are wide variations in life experiences, physical challenges, psychological experiences, and social opportunities between the "young-old" (usually defined as those between the ages of 65 and 74), the "old-old" (between the ages of 75 and 84) and the "oldest-old" (85 years of age and older). Regardless of the exact entry point into old age, the demography of aging in the United States indicates that this population is booming, and the trend is similar in most regions around the globe.

As of 2001, almost 13% of the citizenry of the United States was over age 65, representing 35 million people. By 2030, this number is expected to double to over 70 million representing a noteworthy 20% of the population. The fastest growing subpopulation of older adults is the oldest-old group, who are also the frailest. The oldest-old group is projected to increase from the current 4.4 million to 8.9 million by 2030 and to 19.4 million by 2050 (U.S. Bureau of Census, 2003). As of 2000, there were 70,000 centenarians in the United States—by 2050, this number is expected to increase by 10-fold to over 800,000. The aging of the massive baby boomer cohort is a main reason for this bulge in the demographic profile of the United States, but other important factors include decreased birth rates and increased life expectancy (due to better health care, nutrition, exercise, and medical treatments). The culmination of these trends has generated a profound impact on modern society—for the first time in human history, surviving into later life is an expected part of the life cycle.

Mental Health and Aging: The Big Picture

With the reality of the greatly expanding aging population comes pressing challenges to meet the physical and mental health needs of this group. As the actual number of older adults increases, so does the number of older adults with mental health problems (even if prevalence rates for mental illness remain static). Estimates indicate that about 20% of older adults have a diagnosable mental disorder (Gatz & Smyer, 1992; Jeste et al., 1999). Physical illness and advanced age further negatively impact these rates. Dementia is one of the most serious and debilitating illnesses among older adults. Although normal aging does not cause dementia, it is an age-related disease, which means that prevalence rates increase with advancing age. Conservative estimates suggest that 2% to 5% of people over the age of 65 experience some kind of diagnosable dementia, whereas about 20% of people over 85 suffer from dementia. Rates of mild cognitive impairment (but not full-blown diagnosable dementia) are even higher, affecting 25% to 50% of those 85 years old and older (Bachman et al., 1992). Depression is another common mental health problem in later life, with an estimated 8% to 20% of older adults in the community experiencing significant depressive symptoms (Gurland, Cross, & Katz, 1996). Anxiety disorders are an even greater concern among older adults, with their prevalence estimated to be more than double that of diagnosable affective disorders (Regier, Narrow, & Rae, 1990).

A serious and unfortunate consequence of mental health problems (most notably depression) is suicide, and contrary to common perception, older adults have the highest suicide rate of any age group (National Center for Health Statistics, 2000). Older adults constitute about 13% of the population but commit about 20% of all suicides. These alarmingly elevated numbers are due primarily to the exceptionally high rate of suicide among older White males. Settings also impact rates of mental disorders among older adults: Acute medical settings and long-term care settings have particularly elevated rates, ranging from 40% to 50% in hospitals to 65% to 81% in nursing homes (Burns et al., 1993; Lair & Lefkowitz, 1990). A troubling portend for the near future is that the rates of mental illness are expected to increase even more because the baby boomers have higher lifetime rates of mental illness and are expected to carry these problems with them into later life (Jeste et al., 1999). This baby boomer group also has a greater familiarity with mental health services and a higher expectation for services that will no doubt strain the psychotherapeutic community's ability to provide adequate help.

We have provided only a cursory overview of mental health and aging as a context for our specific discussion of one class of mental health disorder: personality disorders. But the reader should appreciate that the field of geropsychology has blossomed in the past 2 decades; as a consequence, several excellent books now provide solid overviews of mental health, aging, and the fundamentals of clinical practice in geropsychology (Duffy, 1999; Knight, 2004; Laidlaw, Thompson, Gallagher-Thompson, & Dick-Siskin, 2003; Lichtenberg, 1998; Molinari, 2000; Nordhus, VandenBos, Berg, & Fromholt, 1998; Smyer & Qualls, 1999; Zarit & Zarit, 1998). The interested reader is encouraged to seek out these resources.

Compared with the amount of research devoted to the cognitive, mood, and anxiety disorders among older adults, personality disorders and aging have received scant attention. This is surprising because personality disorders are among the most problematic and debilitating of all mental health disorders, and individuals with such problems have a particularly difficult time negotiating the challenges associated with aging. Personality disorders are now better understood than ever before, but their impact in later life has not yet been fully explored. Rates of personality disorders in older adults will be discussed in detail later, but between 10% and 13% of persons in the general adult population are believed to suffer from a personality disorder (Casey, 2000; Weissman, 1993), and this rate is generally stable across adulthood.

Overview of Personality and Personality Disorder

To introduce our examination of personality disorder, we need to first understand the nature of personality. The term *personality* can be defined as an individual's pattern of psychological processes, including his or her motives, feelings, thoughts, behavioral patterns, and other major areas of psychological function. Personality is expressed through its influences on the body, in conscious experience, and through social behavior (Mayer, 2006). Thus, personality is roughly synonymous with the major trends in an individual's mental and behavioral functioning, and as such is generally stable over time.

A classic approach to understanding personality is the trait approach, which conceptualizes personality in terms of stable features that describe a person across many different situations. Many people are able to identify the major personality traits in those whom they know well, and similarly many people can identify and describe their own prominent personality traits. What the trait approach emphasizes is one's characteristic way of thinking, feeling, and behaving across diverse life situations, and not atypical ways one may act under especially unusual circumstances. We all have our moments when we do not act like ourselves, but such moments would not define us at the trait level unless those behaviors become persistent and pervasive. To give some simple examples of trait descriptors—some people are characteristically shy, quiet, and reserved; whereas others are typically outgoing, boisterous, and loud. Some are impulsive and churlish, whereas others are thoughtful and measured. Some are caring and selfless, whereas others are cruel and insensitive. Literally thousands of words can be used to describe enduring personality traits; this is an area in the English language where there is particularly great depth and breadth of description.

All people have a mix of some personality traits that are adaptive and others that are less than ideal. In psychologically healthy individuals, however, the majority of personality traits are positive ones that are adaptive and functional for the person in everyday life, whereas the negative traits are displayed either parsimoniously or appropriately. Not all individuals possess a generally adaptive personality style, but instead have prominent maladaptive traits. Some people may be characteristically untrusting, hostile, arrogant, ruthless, rigid, egocentric, labile, shallow, aloof, fearful, or bizarre. Personality traits can be dysfunctional in many ways, and where these dysfunctional traits become rigid and inflexible impairing a person's ability to function successfully, then a personality disorder diagnosis may be warranted.

According to the fourth edition, text revision of the *Diagnostic and Statistical Manual of Mental Disorders* (*DSM-IV-TR*; American Psychiatric Association, 2000), a personality disorder is "an enduring pattern of inner experience and behavior that deviates markedly from the expectations of the individual's culture, is pervasive and inflexible, has an onset in adolescence or early adulthood, is stable over time, and leads to distress or impairment" (p. 685). A part of the formal personality disorder definition is that the traits have to be rigid, maladaptive, and pervasive across a broad range of situations rather than as expectable reactions to particular life experiences or as a normal part of a specific developmental stage. Adolescence, for example, is a developmental stage frequently accompanied by intense psychological turmoil, and as such, a personality disorder diagnosis would not be warranted if the adolescent appears to be going through an expectable and typical developmental process. An important caveat in the *DSM-IV-TR* is that, *although the definition of personality disorder requires an onset no later than early adulthood, a person with a personality disorder may not be diagnosed or treated until later life.*

A possible explanation for this caveat is that the personality disordered individual may have presented clinically with the more obvious and florid signs of a clinical disorder such as anxiety, depression, eating disorder, or substance abuse, and the underlying personality disorder features may not have been examined as closely (Sadavoy & Fogel, 1992). Another important factor is that, in some cases, personality traits can be adaptive at one phase of life but become maladaptive at a later developmental phase. For example, an extremely aloof and reserved man might have functioned successfully in the occupational area by choosing a job requiring little social interaction (e.g., a computer programmer who writes code at home). He managed to live alone, was fiercely independent, and had little use for others during much of his adult life. Imagine the psychological challenges that he would face if, in later life, he became physically frail and debilitated and subsequently was forced to move into an assisted living facility or a nursing home where he had to cope with medical professionals, caregivers, and other residents. In this case, it would only be after the person failed to adjust to his new living situation that his personality traits would become apparent and viewed as dysfunctional (and a personality disorder diagnosis given). Thus, the context in which personality traits are expressed is an extremely important concept in determining their relative usefulness or hindrance. We return to this important idea later in this book.

To conclude this section, we want to highlight the debilitating nature of personality disorders. According to Fabrega, Ulrich, Pilkonis, and Mezzich (1991), nearly 80% of people with personality disorders suffer from a concomitant Axis I disorder. Similarly, between one-half and two-thirds of psychiatric inpatients and outpatients meet the criteria for at least one personality disorder (O'Connor & Dyce, 2001). Thus, anyone doing clinical work is likely to encounter personality disorders, and it is therefore important that they be understood and carefully considered by the clinician.

History of the Personality Disorder Category

The earliest writings concerning personality disruption and problems can be traced to the Greek physician Hippocrates (460 B.C.–377 B.C.). He was also the first physician to postulate that thoughts, ideas, and feelings come from the brain and not the heart as Egyptian cultures had long proposed. Hippocrates described four fundamental body fluids associated with specific personality patterns (e.g., black bile is indicative of melancholia). His theory was physiologically based, but he also associated environmental features like climate and temperature with the exacerbation or even creation of such personality traits as aggression or gentleness (e.g., mild climates produce gentle races, and climatic extremes arouse strong emotions and passions).

With the death of Aristotle in 322 B.C., Theophrastus (372 B.C.–285 B.C.) was recognized as Aristotle's preeminent student, and he assumed direction of Aristotle's teaching traditions. Theophrastus wrote on such topics as marriage, child raising, alcoholism, melancholy, epilepsy, and the effects of various drugs on mental states. Interestingly, he also wrote about people's characters or temperaments. In his relatively short book *Characters,* Theophrastus described 30 different characters or personalities that were differentiated on the basis of such fundamental traits as bravery, aggression, passivity, trustworthiness, friendliness, superstitious beliefs, and vanity. In *Characters,* Theophrastus appears to have established the beginnings of many of the concepts for modern personality disorders. The Greek writer Homer, centuries earlier, had adopted a similar stance by ascribing to some of his characters a single dominant personality trait, such as the "brave Hector" or the "crafty Ulysses." Theophrastus went beyond Homer's single master trait by describing how an individual's character might express itself in varied situations. Each of his 30 characters was typically dominated by a single trait, but related traits were also described. These traits were as diverse as lying, flattering, talkativeness, cheapness, tactlessness, surliness, discontentedness, and rudeness. His description of the cheap person (penurious) overlaps with many of the general and associated features of the modern Obsessive-Compulsive Personality Disorder: stinginess with money, compliments, and affection; excessive devotion to work; rigidity; and inflexibility. His character dominated by superstitious beliefs may be a forerunner of the Schizotypal Personality Disorder; his lying character may herald the Antisocial Personality Disorder; his flatterer may suggest the Narcissistic Personality Disorder; and his discontented character may have features of both Passive-Aggressive Personality Disorder and Depressive Personality Disorder.

In more modern times, an important advance in thinking about personality problems was crafted by the English psychiatrist James Prichard (1786–1848). He noted the distinction between antisocial behavior (e.g., lying, gambling, and drug use), and other types of insanity more typically found in mental hospitals. Prichard (1835) called this behavior "moral insanity" and described its symptoms as including a perversion of feelings, habits, morals, and impulses without any defects of intellect or reasoning and without the presence of hallucinations.

This general category of disorders that Prichard described would much later come to be known as character disorders and still later as personality disorders. According to Millon (1981a), the word *character* is derived from the Greek word for "engraving," which was originally used to "signify distinctive features that serve as the 'mark' of a person" (p. 7). This engraving implies that the behaviors in question are deeply and permanently imprinted so that change is unlikely or extremely difficult. Until the early twentieth century, most character disorders remained largely unstudied entities. Until the mid-twentieth century, the bulk of personality disorder research was focused on the "morally insane," and the term *psychopath* (which is now synonymous with Antisocial Personality Disorder) was used predominately.

Even more influential on the overall structure and nature of current personality disorders has been the work of Kurt Schneider (1923/1950) who first published his taxonomy in 1923. He heralded the present *DSM* Axis II perspective in many respects. First, he did not view *psychopathologic personalities* (his term for personality disorders) as necessary precursors to other or more severe mental disturbances but saw them as coexistent entities. This contribution heralded the multiaxial diagnostic classification system and separate diagnosis for personality disorders that was introduced by the American Psychiatric Association in 1980 in *DSM-III*. Second, he proposed that psychopathologic personalities developed in childhood and continued into adulthood consistent with modern evidence. Third, he described 10 psychopathologic personalities commonly seen in psychiatric settings, many of which have greatly influenced current personality disorder diagnoses, such as his depressive personality (Depressive Personality Disorder), anankastic personality (Obsessive-Compulsive Personality Disorder), attention-seeking personality (Histrionic Personality Disorder), labile personality (Borderline Personality Disorder), and the affectionless personality (Antisocial and Schizoid Personality Disorders).

Modern Conceptualizations

The most modern tradition for the official diagnosis of personality disorders began in 1952 with the publication of the first edition of the *DSM* (American Psychiatric Association, 1952). The descriptions for all 12 main types of personality disorder in the *DSM* consisted of at most two paragraphs and typically four or five sentences. A further advance was shown in the *DSM-II* (American Psychiatric Association, 1968), which contained 10 major categories of mental disorders (up from 7 in the original *DSM*). Section V was entitled "Personality Disorders and Certain Other Nonpsychotic Mental Disorders." In the official coding system, number 301 was given to the 10 specific types of personality disorders. The general description of personality disorders in *DSM-II* was brief (two sentences): "This group of disorders is characterized by deeply ingrained maladaptive patterns of behavior that are perceptibly different in quality from psychotic and neurotic symptoms. Generally, these are lifelong patterns, often recognizable by the time of adolescence or earlier" (p. 41).

The diagnosis of personality disorders took the equivalent of a quantum leap with the publication of *DSM-III* in 1980. The entire manual nearly tripled in pages from 134 in *DSM-II* to 494 in *DSM-III*. The major evolution in *DSM-III* came in the form of an innovative multiaxial approach, in which psychiatric diagnosis was divided into five separate *axes* or domains on which information about several important areas of functioning are recorded. Major clinical syndromes (e.g., Bipolar Disorder, Panic Disorder, Schizophrenia, Alcohol Dependence) were to be coded on Axis I, whereas Axis II was reserved for personality disorders. Also, the number of types of personality disorders expanded from 10 to 11.

Placement of personality disorders on Axis II had a profound effect. Clinicians were now strongly encouraged to evaluate each of their patients for a personality disorder and to appreciate the important role that personality style may play in the development and maintenance of clinical disorders. Because many people seeking treatment for clinical disorders also suffer from personality disorders or personality disorder features, the need for psychometrically sound instruments to assess personality disorders became obvious. In the *DSM-III*, there was a revolutionary development in the descriptions and diagnosis of personality disorders. For the first time in the history of diagnostic nomenclature, a specific list of numbered criteria was presented for each personality disorder. To receive a personality disorder diagnosis, the patient had to meet a specified minimum number of criteria. The set of criteria was considered to be *polythetic*, indicating that no single criterion was considered to be essential or sine qua non.

The *DSM-III* also revised the formal definition of personality disorders:

> *Personality traits are enduring patterns of perceiving, relating to, and thinking about the environment and oneself, and are exhibited in a wide range of important social and personal contexts. It is only when personality traits are inflexible and maladaptive and cause either significant impairment in social or occupational functioning or subjective distress that they constitute Personality Disorders. The manifestations of Personality Disorders are generally recognizable by adolescence or earlier and continue throughout most of adult life, though they often become less obvious in middle or old age. (p. 305)*

With the publication of *DSM-III-R* in 1987, the number of types of personality disorders remained the same at 11, but an official appendix was added to the manual. Appendix A introduced two new personality disorders for research purposes; the Self-Defeating and the Sadistic Personality Disorders. With the publication of *DSM-IV* in 1994, one personality disorder (Passive-Aggressive) was dropped from Axis II, and it was placed in an appendix along with a new personality disorder for research, the Depressive Personality Disorder. The Self-Defeating and the Sadistic Personality Disorders were dropped altogether. The current manual, *DSM-IV-TR*, had no changes to the list of personality disorders or the diagnostic criteria for the disorders. There are 10 official personality disorders on Axis II, with Passive-Aggressive and Depressive Personality Disorders listed as criteria sets for further study in the Appendix. For greater detail on the evolution of the personality disorder diagnostic category, the interested reader is referred to Coolidge and Segal (1998).

The DSM-IV-TR Personality Disorders

In the *DSM-IV-TR*, the 10 standard personality disorders are organized into three superordinate clusters based on presumed common underlying themes. Cluster A groups 3 disorders in which individuals often appear odd or eccentric: Paranoid, Schizoid, and Schizotypal Personality Disorders. Cluster B includes 4 disorders in which individuals appear to be dramatic, emotional, or erratic: Antisocial, Borderline, Histrionic, and Narcissistic Personality Disorders. Cluster C contains 3 disorders in which individuals often appear fearful or anxious: Avoidant, Dependent, and Obsessive-Compulsive Personality Disorders. Two additional personality disorders are not grouped into the clusters but instead are listed in an appendix of the *DSM-IV-TR* for further empirical justification; these are the Depressive Personality Disorder and the Passive-Aggressive Personality Disorder (which is also called the negativistic personality disorder). Importantly, a diagnosis called "Personality Disorder Not Otherwise Specified" is also available for use and is assigned for cases in which the patient has clear signs of a personality disorder but does not fit neatly into one of the specific personality disorder categories (e.g., a patient having three or four symptoms of two different personality disorders but not meeting the threshold for either one).

The *DSM-IV-TR* provides specific diagnostic criteria for each of the personality disorders, with criteria reflecting mostly behavioral manifestations of the disorder. The symptoms are listed in order of diagnostic importance, and a specific number of symptoms must be present to meet the threshold for diagnosis. Like all disorders in the *DSM-IV-TR*, diagnosis is categorical. Similar to Axis I, multiple disorders can be listed on Axis II as long as the patient meets the diagnostic threshold for each one diagnosed. Dysfunctional personality *features* can also be listed on Axis II when symptoms are noteworthy but below the diagnostic threshold. Significant uses of defense mechanisms can also be listed on Axis II although this technique appears uncommon in clinical practice. Little reference to age is made in the features of personality disorders with the exception that a personality disorder requires onset no later than early adulthood.

Next, we provide a broad overview of each of the 10 standard personality disorders and the 2 personality disorders under further review in the *DSM-IV-TR*. In subsequent discussions (Chapters 2 to 5), we provide the full *DSM-IV-TR* diagnostic criteria for each of the personality disorders, discuss potential problems in applying the criteria to older persons, and include another additional but often neglected feature—the clinical presentation seen in the older adult (which in many cases differs markedly from that seen in younger persons) and the typical ways that specific personality disorders are affected by the common challenges associated with growing older (e.g., retirement, widowhood, physical illness, changes in appearance, and increased dependency).

The definitions of the personality disorders provided next are adapted from the *DSM-IV-TR:*

Cluster A Personality Disorders

- *Paranoid Personality Disorder:* A pattern of pervasive distrust and suspicion of others such that the motives of others are perceived as malevolent
- *Schizoid Personality Disorder:* A pervasive pattern of detachment from social relationships and a restricted range of emotional expression
- *Schizotypal Personality Disorder:* A pervasive pattern of social deficits marked by acute discomfort with close relationships, as well as eccentric behavior and cognitive and perceptual distortions

Cluster B Personality Disorders

- *Antisocial Personality Disorder:* A pervasive pattern of disregard for, and violation of, societal norms and the rights of others, as well as lack of empathy
- *Borderline Personality Disorder:* A pervasive pattern of instability in interpersonal relationships, self-image, and emotions, as well as marked impulsivity
- *Histrionic Personality Disorder:* A pervasive pattern of excessive emotionality and attention-seeking behavior, with superficiality
- *Narcissistic Personality Disorder:* A pervasive pattern of grandiosity, need for admiration, and lack of empathy and compassion for others

Cluster C Personality Disorders

- *Avoidant Personality Disorder:* A pervasive pattern of social inhibition, low self-esteem, and hypersensitivity to negative evaluation
- *Dependent Personality Disorder:* A pervasive and excessive need to be taken care of and a perception of being unable to function without the help of others leading to submissive and clinging behaviors
- *Obsessive-Compulsive Personality Disorder:* A pervasive pattern of preoccupation with orderliness, perfection, and control at the expense of flexibility, openness, and efficiency

DSM-IV-TR Appendix B Personality Disorders

- *Depressive Personality Disorder:* A pervasive pattern of depressive cognitions, feelings, and behaviors
- *Passive-Aggressive Personality Disorder:* A pervasive pattern of negative attitudes and passive resistance to demands for performance in social and work situations

Challenges Associated with Personality Disorder Psychopathology

Besides causing significant problems for the person so afflicted, personality disorders pose extensive difficulties to the mental health clinician. It is fair to suggest that the personality disorders are perceived as among the most challenging forms of psychiatric illness. Some clinicians, in fact, attempt to avoid treating them (Lewis & Appleby, 1988), although this is practically impossible. A complicating feature of personality disorders is that by their very nature they are *chronic* conditions, which can make treating clinicians feel ineffective and even hopeless.

Another important part of the challenge is that the personality disorders differ from the clinical disorders (coded on Axis I) in a fundamental way. In many cases, clinical disorders are perceived as illnesses, sicknesses, or diseases that "happen to people." In the case of depression, for example, a relatively healthy person may experience a series of losses that temporarily overwhelm his or her ability to cope, and classic signs of depression may subsequently emerge (e.g., tearfulness, loss of interest in activities, lethargy, sleep and appetite disturbance, poor concentration). In this case, the person may then be diagnosed as suffering from major depression.

With treatment, the depression may remit and the person might have the perception, "I was depressed before, but I am not depressed now." Because the person was not depressed before the episode began and is no longer depressed after it ends, it would be reasonable for the person to see the depression as an illness that came upon him or her and then went away. The person might view the depression as having little to do with him- or herself personally and to be the result of external factors such as overwhelming life stressors. In short, being depressed can easily be distinguished from one's normal nondepressed state. This same type of "illness" analogy can readily apply to a host of Axis I clinical disorders that seem episodic in nature and are easily discriminated from one's normal functioning.

This distinction is not easily made with personality disorders. Because personality disorders are defined by personality traits that are labeled as maladaptive and inflexible, the disorders in this category do not seem like illnesses that come from outside the person (e.g., as in depression). Rather, what is "wrong" is the person's personality, which is not subject to easy change. The personality disorder construct signifies a pathological development of the self, at the person's core. As such, those who endorse a disease model of mental illness find it difficult to understand and conceptualize the nature and meaning of personality disorders because the disease metaphor does not readily apply.

This concept of personality disorders also affects those who suffer from them. A classic hallmark of the category is that those who have a personality disorder typically lack insight into it or are unaware of having the disorder. Many people with a personality disorder perceive their symptoms as *ego-syntonic* (meaning congruent with their self-image) in contrast to seeing the symptoms as *ego-dystonic* or something outside the self to be fought, altered, addressed, or gotten rid of by some means. An unfortunate consequence of the poor insight associated with the personality disorders is that most patients with a personality disorder do not identify the need for treatment per se because they do not see any signs of having a problem. In contrast, it is axiomatic for individuals with a personality disorder to come to treatment seeking relief for the overt signs of clinical disorders they are also experiencing or for problems they are having with others although they typically see little of their own role in the conflict. Our case examples in the coming chapters emphasize this ego-syntonic quality of personality disorder.

This distinction between the clinical disorders and the personality disorders is also made explicit by the *DSM* classification system in which, as noted, the conditions are coded on different axes as part of the multiaxial diagnostic format. Of course, this division is artificial, as many Axis I disorders certainly represent problems at the level of personality. Dysthymia is defined as chronic low-level depression that lasts for at least 2 years. Pessimism is part of the common conceptualization of dysthymia although pessimism reflects a stable part of personality. Anorexia Nervosa, an eating disorder, is another example of the intermingling of clinical disorders and personality styles because anorexia is highly associated with perfectionism and a strong need for control, both of which represent dimensions of personality. Nonetheless, at present, clinical disorders and personality disorders are defined as separate diagnostic categories, and an important outgrowth of this distinction is the high probability of comorbidity between the clinical disorders and the personality disorders. This comorbidity is commonplace among older and younger persons in the clinical setting and provides a considerable challenge to the treating clinician.

An issue related to the distinction between Axis I clinical disorders and Axis II personality disorders is the stability and constancy of Axis II disorders. Defining hallmarks of Axis II conditions have been their presentation by early adulthood and their stability. The maladaptive trait patterns for each of the personality disorders have been posited to endure through time and across venues. This stability is the major distinguishing criterion from Axis I conditions, which are suggested as being adventitious and episodic. It appears that, as Axis II disorders become better understood (and, indeed, Axis I disorders), this essential distinction is neither so clear nor pervasive. The challenge to what has clinically been accepted as a robust heuristic comes from several sources of inquiry:

- Many Axis I conditions present early in life, are established by young adulthood, become chronic, and do not remit fully enough to no longer meet criteria for the diagnosis. Schizophrenia is a good example of this (Shea & Yen, 2003).

- Although other Axis I conditions, such as mood and anxiety disorders, present with distinct episodes, there are subgroups that go on to incomplete remissions or rapid cycling so that the presence of the disorder, while not the degree of symptom display, evidences significant stability (Judd et al., 2002).

- The state of the Axis I condition can affect whether a personality disorder can be diagnosed (Shea & Yen, 2003). During personality disorder assessment, clinicians must evaluate the usual or typical personality functioning of the patient, which may be impaired during a period of clinical disturbance. A depressed patient who may be excessively negative and hopeless during the mood episode is a good example of this.

- The high comorbidity rate between Axis I and Axis II conditions suggests that they may share the same predisposing factors, be continuum phenomena, or are in some other highly significant relationship (Shea & Yen, 2003).

- Looking at the Axis II disorders, there are data as well as anecdotal evidence of change affecting the pattern of one's personality traits, thereby worsening or diminishing the degree of the disorder to where it can or cannot be diagnosed as a formal personality disorder. Thus, the posited temporal stability of the personality disorders has been questioned (Shea et al., 2002).

- Important confounds inform the diagnosis. There is a question of whether the diagnostic criteria for personality disorders in general, or for specific personality disorders capture the presentation of personality disorders in older adults, missing the so-called "geriatric variants" of the disorders (Rosowsky & Gurian, 1991; Sadavoy & Fogel, 1992; Segal, Hersen, Van Hasselt, Silberman, & Roth, 1996). We return to this theme later in the book.

A final challenge concerning the personality disorder category is that sufferers (young and old) rarely present with the signs and symptoms of just one personality disorder. Rather, a person with one personality disorder is likely to present with significant signs and symptoms of other personality disorders (Oldham et al., 1992; Segal et al., 1996). Or a person may have signs of several personality disorders but does not meet full diagnostic threshold for any one disorder. In most cases, occurrence of personality disorder features from more than one personality disorder appears to be the rule rather than the exception across the life span. A part of the problem is that prototypes of the personality disorders were created in the *DSM* system to maximize discrimination among the types, although this procedure has led to the impression that pure types are regularly seen in clinical practice, which they are not.

Conclusions

We want to highlight a final important point about personality disorders: By their very nature, these disorders manifest as disruptions in the interpersonal sphere. All personality disorders reflect interpersonal difficulties, and while their exact nature will differ across the disorders, these social problems appear robust over the life course (Rosowsky & Gurian, 1991). Although most people with a personality disorder do not see themselves as having a problem, they almost always identify having problems relating to others in their social world (Rosowsky, 1999). These others may include caregivers, neighbors, relatives, employers, and health care professionals, but the interpersonal dysfunction is particularly enhanced in intimate relationships, for example, with children, spouses, and romantic partners. We are emphasizing this chronic and characteristic social impairment because it becomes particularly salient for the aging individual. Interpersonal problems affect sufferers in their ability to handle stressors associated with growing older. There is a large body of literature on the buffering effects of social support: Close and supportive relationships can help people adjust to and cope with difficult life experiences. But social problems across much of adult life typically leave the personality disordered older adult with little or no remaining social support at a time in life when it is critically needed. This aspect of personality disorder makes patients particularly vulnerable to the challenges of aging. The social ineffectiveness of older adults with personality disorders also affects their ability to form an appropriate therapeutic relationship with the mental health clinician. Patients with personality disorders typically evoke strong feelings in their clinicians (Rosowsky, 1999), just as they do with other important people in their life. How clinicians use their emotional reactions to the patient and how they understand what the individual engenders in close relationships with others are important parts of the diagnostic and treatment process, and we return to this theme later in this book.

About This Book

In subsequent chapters, we provide a clinical description and the official diagnostic criteria for personality disorders grouped by the official clusters of the *DSM-IV-TR*. These include Cluster A (Paranoid, Schizoid, and Schizotypal Personality Disorders; in Chapter 2), Cluster B (Antisocial, Borderline, Histrionic, and Narcissistic Personality Disorders; in Chapter 3), and Cluster C

(Avoidant, Dependent, and Obsessive-Compulsive Personality Disorders; in Chapter 4). Chapter 5 examines personality disorders that have been part of the official diagnostic nomenclature in previous versions of the *DSM*. In Chapters 2 through 5, we discuss potential problems applying the diagnostic criteria for the personality disorders to older adults, provide a theorized pattern of each personality disorder in later life, examine the potential impact of aging on each of the personality disorders, and offer numerous extended case examples. We then present information about epidemiology and common comorbid disorders (Chapter 6); an analysis of theories of personality disorders (Chapters 7 and 8), with special attention to the manner in which aging is addressed in the theories; and an overview of assessment issues (Chapter 9). We conclude with two chapters that address intervention, including an overview of general issues and models of intervention (Chapter 10) and a model of goodness of fit (Chapter 11).

The Odd and Eccentric (Cluster A) Personality Disorders and Aging

2

Chapter

In Chapters 2 through 5, we focus on a clinical description of the specific personality disorders according to *DSM* conceptualizations, organized by clusters (Cluster A in Chapter 2, Cluster B in Chapter 3, Cluster C in Chapter 4, and other personality disorders in Chapter 5). The diagnostic criteria for each personality disorder are reviewed with particular attention to possible age-biases, age-relevance, and problems with the suitability of the criteria to older individuals. Theorized patterns of the personality disorders in later life are discussed in each chapter as well as the typical ways that they are affected by common challenges associated with aging. Case examples are offered throughout. Age-related stressors are addressed, including retirement, spousal loss, physical illness, changes in appearance, and increased dependency. In Chapter 6, we turn to the epidemiology of personality disorders and the challenges of comorbidity.

The personality disorders described in these chapters are listed in Table 2.1. Before turning our attention to the personality disorders in Cluster A, we first examine the applicability and age appropriateness of the *DSM*'s General Diagnostic Criteria for personality disorders overall.

Table 2.1   **Personality Disorders Grouped by Clusters in the** *DSM-IV-TR* **and Other Personality Disorder Conceptualizations**

DSM-IV-TR Cluster A
Paranoid, Schizoid, and Schizotypal Personality Disorders

DSM-IV-TR Cluster B
Antisocial, Borderline, Histrionic, and Narcissistic Personality Disorders

DSM-IV-TR Cluster C
Avoidant, Dependent, and Obsessive-Compulsive Personality Disorders

Other Personality Disorders
Sadistic Personality Disorder (*DSM-III-R* Appendix A)
Self-Defeating Personality Disorder (*DSM-III-R* Appendix A)
Depressive Personality Disorder (*DSM-IV-TR* Appendix B)
Passive-Aggressive Personality Disorder (*DSM-IV-TR* Appendix B)

Adapted from *Diagnostic and Statistical Manual of Mental Disorders,* third edition, revised, and fourth edition, text revision, by American Psychiatric Association, 1987 and 2000, Washington, DC: Author.

General Diagnostic Criteria

The *DSM-IV-TR* (American Psychiatric Association, 2000) embodies a pragmatic approach to diagnosis that intentionally deemphasizes specific theoretical perspectives on psychopathology. Rather, the approach focuses on making diagnoses in a reliable and valid fashion, based largely on behaviorally operationalized criteria (Segal & Coolidge, 2003). Regarding personality disorders, the first step in diagnosis is to gauge whether the patient shows a broad pattern of personality problems that meets a general diagnostic threshold. Only after the general criteria are met should the clinician determine which specific personality disorder or personality disorders are present.

The general criteria provided by *DSM-IV-TR* (American Psychiatric Association, 2000) are listed in Table 2.2. Several features from this description are informative. First, the description of a personality disorder (Criterion A) begins with an implicit definition of personality, this is, "an enduring pattern of inner experience and behavior" in conjunction with psychopathology in that the pattern "deviates markedly from

Table 2.2   *DSM-IV-TR* **General Diagnostic Criteria for a Personality Disorder**

A. An enduring pattern of inner experience and behavior that deviates markedly from the expectations of the individual's culture. This pattern is manifested in two (or more) of the following areas:
   (1) cognition (i.e., ways of perceiving and interpreting self, other people, and events)
   (2) affectivity (i.e., the range, intensity, lability, and appropriateness of emotional response)
   (3) interpersonal functioning
   (4) impulse control
B. The enduring pattern is inflexible and pervasive across a broad range of personal and social situations.
C. The enduring pattern leads to clinically significant distress or impairment in social, occupational, or other important areas of functioning.
D. The pattern is stable and of long duration, and its onset can be traced back at least to adolescence or early adulthood.
E. The enduring pattern is not better accounted for as a manifestation of consequence of another mental disorder.
F. The enduring pattern is not due to the direct physiological effects of a substance (e.g., a drug of abuse, a medication) or a general medical condition (e.g., head trauma).

Source: From *Diagnostic and Statistical Manual of Mental Disorders,* fourth edition, text revision, American Psychiatric Association, 2000, Washington, DC: Author. Copyright 2000 by American Psychiatric Association. Reprinted with permission.

the expectations of the individual's culture." Recognition of the influence of culture was first introduced in *DSM-III-R* (American Psychiatric Association, 1987) and refined in *DSM-IV* (American Psychiatric Association, 1994) and *DSM-IV-TR*. Further, this pattern must be demonstrated in at least two important areas of functioning, including one's thinking patterns (cognition), emotional reactions (affectivity), social relationships (interpersonal functioning), or ability to moderate desires (impulse control).

As implied in the definition, cultural sensitivity and an understanding of the nuances of the individual's cultural frame of reference are important in avoiding diagnostic mistakes, especially the overpathologizing of normal variations in beliefs and behaviors consistent with an individual's culture (American Psychiatric Association, 2000). Because cultures vary widely in conceptions of selfhood, coping, and communication styles, applying personality disorder criteria across diverse cultures may be particularly challenging (American Psychiatric Association, 2000). For example, an individual from a cultural group that values interdependence and deference to others should not be viewed as having a Dependent Personality Disorder in the classic sense. Some cultures value dramatic personal expressions, not necessarily implying a histrionic personality. Two aging issues regarding Criterion A are that emotions (both positive and negative) typically become somewhat leveled or muted with age, and people are generally less impulsive in later life. These changes reflect normal aging, and therefore these aspects of Criteria A do not apply well to some older people.

Other general criteria indicate that the personality pattern must be inflexible and manifested in several areas of life (Criterion B), the pattern leads to clinically meaningful distress or impairment in the individual's functioning (Criterion C), and the pattern is relatively stable and can be traced back to adolescence or early adulthood (Criterion D). The last two criteria are the exclusionary rules included in almost all diagnoses. It must be ascertained that the disordered (personality) pattern cannot be better accounted for by another (primary) mental disorder (Criterion E) or by the direct effects of a substance or an underlying medical condition (Criterion F; American Psychiatric Association, 2000).

Criterion D may be problematic among some older adults because it can be difficult to identify exactly when a personality disorder originated, and this problem is confounded even more by the difficulties with retrospective reporting over many decades. Finally, Criterion F may be problematic in an aging context because older adults are likely to have health problems, both chronic and acute, and to be taking medications for these problems. Thus, diagnostic consideration must take into account the effects of physical illness and medications on one's everyday functioning. In summary, it is apparent that some of the General Diagnostic Criteria may fail to take into account normal changes that are associated with the aging process and in some cases fail to capture aspects of personality disorder pathology as it is expressed in later life. With these general issues in mind, we now examine several specific personality disorders.

Cluster A Personality Disorders: Paranoid, Schizoid, and Schizotypal

The core thematic features of the personality disorders in Cluster A include unusual, odd, eccentric, and sometimes even bizarre personality features. Based on the odd nature of these personality disorders, it should not be surprising that these patients are typically withdrawn and isolated and that there is a link between Cluster A personality disorders and the psychotic disorders, most notably Schizophrenia. Cluster A personality disorders are more common in relatives of schizophrenics than in the general population (O'Connor & Dyce, 2001). However, individuals with Cluster A personality disorders are not blatantly and persistently psychotic (or may not be psychotic at all), and they generally maintain contact with reality. The *DSM-IV-TR* diagnostic criteria for the three Cluster A disorders are listed separately in the following subsections.

Paranoid Personality Disorder

Clinical Description
This disorder manifests itself as a pervasive pattern of distrust and suspiciousness of others without appropriate or adequate justification. People with this disorder easily perceive malevolent, malicious, and deceitful intent in others and maintain the suspicion that others are out to do them harm. They are easily slighted and dwell on the loyalty and trustworthiness of others.

The pervasiveness of suspicion is such that benign comments by others or innocuous events are often interpreted as threatening personal attacks. Their hypervigilance against attacks from others results in the chronic scrutiny of others. During such scrutiny, paranoid persons tend to find spurious evidence to distrust others and, as a consequence, they typically feel persecuted. The famous writer William S. Burroughs revealed this tendency in his famous quote: "Paranoia means having all the facts."

People with Paranoid Personality Disorder often become involved in hostile disputes and aggressive confrontations with others. Counterattacks are common as a perceived way of self-protection. Due to their chronic suspiciousness, people with Paranoid Personality Disorder tend to neither confide in others nor share personal information because doing so would open them up for attack. They believe that they cannot openly or authentically relate to others because anything that they share can and will be used against them. They bear grudges and are frequently obsessed with jealousy and perceived infidelity of romantic partners. Paranoid individuals often go through life extremely isolated and alone. The very nature of the paranoid person can be compounded by social isolation. Others tend to recoil and to be leery of interacting with the cold and suspicious paranoid person. Thus, their isolation intensifies their already paranoid beliefs because they are not afforded the reassurance and corrections that may happen in healthier relationships. Further, paranoid individuals are highly vulnerable and feel that they must constantly "keep their guard up" to prevent interpersonal exploitation. In many cases, their isolation can be extreme. In one of our cases, a 67-year-old woman with Paranoid Personality Disorder reported a lifetime history of never having even one close friend or confidant due to her profound concern that if she revealed personal information, the acquaintance would use the knowledge to hurt the patient. She also avoided sexual intimacy for the same reasons. Table 2.3 provides the *DSM-IV-TR* diagnostic criteria for Paranoid Personality Disorder.

Table 2.3   *DSM-IV-TR* **Diagnostic Criteria for Paranoid Personality Disorder (Code: 301.0)**

A. A pervasive distrust and suspiciousness of others such that their motives are interpreted as malevolent, beginning by early adulthood and presenting in a variety of contexts, as indicated by four (or more) of the following:

    (1) suspects, without sufficient basis, that others are exploiting, harming, or deceiving him or her

    (2) is preoccupied with unjustified doubts about the loyalty or trustworthiness of friends or associates

    (3) is reluctant to confide in others because of unwarranted fear that the information will be used maliciously against him or her

    (4) reads hidden demeaning or threatening meanings into benign remarks or events

    (5) persistently bears grudges, i.e., is unforgiving of insults, injuries, or slights

    (6) perceives attacks on his or her character or reputation that are not apparent to others and is quick to react angrily or to counterattack

    (7) has recurrent suspicions, without justification, regarding fidelity of spouse or sexual partner

B. Does not occur exclusively during the course of Schizophrenia, a Mood Disorder With Psychotic Features, or another Psychotic Disorder and is not due to the direct physiological effects of a general medical condition.

Source: From *Diagnostic and Statistical Manual of Mental Disorders,* fourth edition, text revision, American Psychiatric Association, 2000, Washington, DC: Author. Copyright 2000 by American Psychiatric Association. Reprinted with permission.

Potential Age-Bias of Criteria

Two Paranoid Personality Disorder criteria may be problematic for older adults. Criterion A1 (suspects, without sufficient basis, that others are exploiting, harming, or deceiving him or her) may not apply well to some in later life because older adults with certain risk factors (e.g., impaired physical or cognitive status; family social isolation) are known to be at heightened risk for elder abuse (Wolf, 1998). A further complication to this issue is that older adults in the present cohort are increasingly being targeted by unscrupulous people who are trying to scam or swindle them. In these cases, it makes sense that older adults should be *more wary* of others to reduce their risk of abuse. Criterion A2 (is preoccupied with unjustified doubts about the loyalty or trustworthiness of friends or associates) may not fit as well for those in later life who have to form new social connections to replace lifelong relationships that have been lost. In many cases, new friendships may not have the same level of trust and security as those forged over many years.

Theorized Pattern in Later Life and Possible Impact of Aging
The primary aging issues relevant to the paranoid type include physical illness, sensory decline, and increased dependency. Regarding sensory impairments, older adults who experience declines in hearing and vision may incorrectly think that others are talking about them or threatening them in some way. Evidence suggests that sensory deterioration is a primary cause of certain psychiatric disorders, most notably late-onset paranoia (Almeida, Forstl, Howard, & David, 1993). Among those with Paranoid Personality Disorder, these types of sensory impairments may make the underlying paranoia more pronounced. The emergence of cognitive dysfunction due to a dementing illness may also trigger paranoid thinking or may worsen premorbid paranoid traits.

Increased dependency on others will also be problematic for paranoid older adults who are not used to and are uncomfortable with accepting help from others. In cases where professionals (e.g., home health care workers) need to provide services in the home, the paranoid person may react with distrust and agitation due to perceiving the workers as being intrusive and untrustworthy, or deny them entry to the home altogether. The paranoid person may voice complaints of being abused, victimized, or taken advantage of, and the clinician must carefully evaluate his or her concerns and the situation to make sure that, in fact, no harmful acts are occurring. Because older people with Paranoid Personality Disorder are often experienced as being distrustful, argumentative, and hostile, their level of social support may be poor. Whereas they are likely to be highly isolated, they are equally rejecting of needed social support. In fact, Butler, Lewis, and Sunderland (1998) suggest that the paranoid type has the most problems of all the personality disorders in later life, due to the loss of the few relationships they may have developed earlier in life and the subsequent increasing isolation.

The Case of Albert: Paranoid Personality Disorder

Albert M. contacted the psychologist for an appointment stating, "I think I am depressed and I'd like to get your opinion about this." The initial telephone intake conversation revealed that Albert was 72 years old and had recently experienced new physical health changes in addition to his chronic health problems. He announced, at the outset of the conversation, "You'll have to speak slowly and clearly. I have a hearing problem and even though I have one of those phone adaptors, I have trouble hearing people who mumble or talk too fast. I don't trust this gizmo anyway. It never worked right." The psychologist, familiar with the more frequently occurring problems of older adults presenting to his outpatient practice, quickly formulated a likely differential diagnosis. Albert could be presenting with an adjustment disorder with depressed mood or perhaps he was experiencing an episode of major depression. Quite possibly, his health problems and/or medications prescribed to treat them were contributing to his dysphoria as well.

On the day of the appointment, Albert arrived early. When the clinician greeted him, it was apparent that Albert had been passing the waiting time by carefully observing the physical space including brochures and other reading materials set out for patients to peruse and take home. He was reading the clinician's credentials, framed and hanging along a sidewall, when the psychologist ushered him into the interview room.

The clinical interview began quite easily, although the psychologist noticed that Albert had difficulty sustaining eye contact, instead glancing around the room, appearing to want to take it all in. Albert was appropriately forthcoming about his chronic health problems, including cataracts, hearing loss, and osteoarthritis, and the medications he was currently taking. However, he was noticeably reluctant to describe the most recent health problem which presumably had preceded his depression. When the clinician began to inquire about his family of origin, Albert straightened himself in his chair and challenged this line of questioning. "What do you need to know about that for? You're going back a long ways, you know." The clinician was able to coax a little more information before Albert resisted even more vigorously. "Look. I don't like where this is going. I don't know what you're getting at. I came to see you for your opinion about my depression. I just need your opinion. Now can you do that or not?"

The clinician agreed to go where Albert wanted, and returned to guiding the interview toward clarifying the precise events that led up to the patient seeking this appointment. The patient revealed that 4 months earlier his primary care physician (PCP) noticed a change in lung sounds, which was of concern. A chest film was ordered, and a suspicious shadow was noted. The PCP referred the patient to a pulmonary specialist for a consultation. Given Albert's age, medical history, and current condition (former smoker and clinically obese), the specialist was also concerned and admitted Albert to the hospital for further diagnostic refinement. The specialist's diagnosis, as the patient told it, was that Albert had a pulmonary embolism, which was serious and indeed life threatening. He would therefore start treatment immediately, even before all the tests were completed.

Ultimately, on further evaluation, an embolism was ruled out. The diagnosis then was made of a small calcification (the shadow initially seen), which was a benign finding and had likely been there a very long time. They attributed the change in the lung sounds his PCP had noticed as a temporary sequela of a recent upper respiratory infection.

Immediately following his discharge from the hospital, Albert felt greatly relieved that his life was not, after all, in jeopardy. But then his thinking changed. "Don't you think I know that these local docs get something a little extra when they refer people to these fancy specialists?" He caught himself and modified his tone. "I've been with this doc for years, but you know I'm getting up there. Who questions if there's something new that's not quite right? And you know what hospitals get for every day someone's in a bed there? This specialist is on the hospital staff there. Don't you think he has to fill some of those beds, too? And you have to have a diagnosis to get in, otherwise the insurance company won't pay." When asked how he thought this might relate to his depression, Albert did make eye contact, hard eye contact: "Who wouldn't get depressed when they thought they were going to die because some fancy doctor told them that so he could get the extra bucks? You're darn right I got the depression. They caused it and they're going to pay for that."

Albert divulged that he had engaged an attorney to sue both the specialist and his primary care doctor. When asked how he felt about severing the long-term relationship with his PCP, Albert responded, "He was always nice enough; friendly. But to tell you the truth, I never trusted the guy." He let it slip that he had used this attorney before for several lawsuits. He reported that instead of taking the law into his own hands, it was far better to take the law to the lawyer's hands. "It's a mean world out there, and if you don't watch out and take care of things, they can do real damage."

The psychologist conducted the usual diagnostic interview and determined that Albert was not experiencing an episode of major depression. He didn't meet *DSM* criteria for dysthymia or even for an adjustment disorder. But he was angry and nearly delusional, and he was seeking the psychologist's confirmation of a clinical condition to get back at his enemies, in this instance, the two physicians. He was diagnosed on Axis II with Paranoid Personality Disorder.

One of the benchmarks of the paranoid personality is to misperceive and misattribute others' behaviors and reactions. Inevitably, others are put on the defensive, further confirming their guilt or at least their adversarial, frequently threatening, posture. These personalities twist, misconstrue, and reconstruct reality in an effort to confirm their idiosyncratic reality, ever scanning for more support and confirming evidence. They do not trust the "system" or others and they cannot be honest, especially in more intimate relationships. Albert embraced many of the dominant personality traits lying at the core of Paranoid Personality Disorder: steely coldness while being controlling, humorless, intimidating, critical, mistrustful, rageful, and uncompromising. They make very difficult therapy patients. Understandably, they are suspicious of directness and honesty and do not do well with confrontation. They construe any interpretation that challenges or is even inconsistent with their own point of view as evidence of potential victimization by the clinician. When enough such evidence is accrued, the clinician is summarily relegated to the enemy camp, and the helping relationship is over.

Interpersonal distance regulation is also a challenge for the treating clinician. As those with Paranoid Personality Disorder maintain distance from the clinician, they mirror their disconnection and aloofness, thereby disallowing the necessary joining, or closeness, necessary to achieve a therapeutic alliance. Moving too close will be countered by their withdrawing, pulling away, intensifying an intellectualization defense and becoming more critical and suspicious. Some with this personality disorder will identify themselves as a patient and try to join with the clinician in a treatment dyad. If enough trust (or more accurately the absence of distrust) is present, patients can come to entertain the possibility of alternative interpretations and meaning makings other than their own. But the tightly held, erroneous but self-confirming beliefs cannot be directly or too aggressively challenged. To do so nearly guarantees the clinician will be inducted into the camp of the "other," with whom it is necessary to keep up one's guard.

Primary care physicians have an especially difficult time managing these patients and quite likely dread seeing their names on the day's patient roster. These are among their most problematic patients. They can be difficult by demanding too much time, questioning the doctor's questions, withholding information if they do not trust the reason the doctor would need to know, and rejecting treatment suggestions. Most of all, they feel distant to the physician, aloof, with little capacity for empathy or mutual regard. Although PCPs are sometimes impressively alert to the signs and symptoms of Axis I disorders, personality disorders (which apply to approximately half of their difficult patients) are often missed and poorly understood. This is especially so when they co-occur with an Axis I disorder. Mental health clinicians can help their medical colleagues to recognize likely personality disorders (or at least serious traits) as well as to understand how these will inform the treatment and guide its course without excessive frustration. Many individuals with personality disorders present with somatic complaints that often meet criteria for an Axis I somatoform disorder, anxiety disorder, or alcohol or substance abuse condition.

Albert, however, told his PCP that he was depressed and that this was a direct result of the trauma he endured secondary to the erroneous (and negligently so, in his opinion) diagnosis. What the PCP did not consider was how his patient made sense of the world and interpreted events. In the mind of Albert, not only were the doctors' actions negligent, they were intentional and probably collaborative and in line with some greater medical scheme or scam. The PCP took the patient's self-diagnosis at his word, or perhaps felt the need for an outside professional to make sense of what was going on. The PCP was probably feeling uncomfortable and a little threatened. So he referred Albert to the psychologist for a clinical opinion and diagnostic clarification.

During the consultation with the psychologist, Albert did not lie about his symptoms, and he revealed his primitive character in a number of ways. In this case, the patient was not seeking therapy with the psychologist, but only his opinion. This is an important distinction, especially for patients with personality disorders. The psychologist could not ethically diagnose a condition (in this case, depression) that he did not believe existed, just because the patient wanted this. Without challenging Albert's belief system directly, and provoking a head-on collision, the psychologist could consider the following talking points: Join with Albert around his experience as having been extremely unpleasant, even frightening, to really believe that much of it could not have been avoided. If it was not avoided, then perhaps it was intentional (his irrational view). Or perhaps it was because the doctors were especially caring and thereby overly cautious (the competing view).

Either way (with the psychologist modeling how to hold both competing views), it was clear that Albert had suffered, and his feelings were understandably strong, whether they were feelings of sadness, anxiety, or anger. It was generous of him to want to correct the system so that others wouldn't go though what he did (introducing altruism as a mature defense). Using the law is certainly one way to do this. It was important to help the client understand that his convictions, even his best intentions, would have a price. There would be the price of legal fees and also the price of his own time and effort. There was also the price of letting go of the long-standing relationship with his doctor, who had been good enough for many years, and had cared for him—maybe too well this one time. A lawsuit would end their relationship, and Albert would need to decide how much he wanted to pay out and pay back.

Finally, the clinician might suggest that sometimes short-term psychotherapy can be useful. It can help patients sort out strong feelings and decide on a course of action, while decreasing the chances of a true clinical depression setting in. It would be up to Albert to decide whether he could tolerate, perhaps even consider, the feedback and perspective of the treating clinician.

Schizoid Personality Disorder

Clinical Description

The hallmark features of this disorder are a complete detachment from social relationships and restricted emotional responses to others. Such people are often perceived as aloof, cold, detached, and emotionally flat, but most notably they seem to have no desire for close relationships, and they tend to have no connections with others outside of close family members. In lay terms, they fit the classic profile of a "loner" or "hermit," who neither needs nor wants contact with others. Their social detachment is often so acute that they seem immune to the criticism or praise of others. They consistently prefer and choose solitary activities, experience little or no pleasure in life, and have minimal or no interest in sexual activities with others.

As a result of their style, people with Schizoid Personality Disorder lack close relationships. They are indifferent to the emotional lives of others, seem oblivious to social nuances, and rarely marry (although if they do marry, they tend to be passive during the courtship and afterward). Schizoid individuals may have a fantasy life that far exceeds their actual existence. Among schizoid older adults, it is important to understand that their lack of relationships has been a lifelong characteristic and is not simply a function of age-related losses. Because people with schizoid features experience little or no concern about their lack of relationships, they infrequently seek psychotherapy and experience little distress as long as their fiercely independent style is not compromised. They tend to resist help offered, especially when a relationship would be involved. The extreme detachment of the schizoid personality was demonstrated in one of our cases in which an adult daughter of a schizoid father requested help to deal with her father's increasing aloofness, especially since the death of his wife who had previously orchestrated his minimal social contacts. According to the daughter, her father even expressed objection to the family's request for an annual phone call let-

Table 2.4 *DSM-IV-TR* **Diagnostic Criteria for Schizoid Personality Disorder (Code: 301.20)**

A. A pervasive pattern of detachment from social relationships and a restricted range of expression of emotions in interpersonal settings, beginning by early adulthood and present in a variety of contexts, as indicated by four (or more) of the following:

   (1) neither desires nor enjoys close relationships, including being part of a family

   (2) almost always chooses solitary activities

   (3) has little, if any, interest in having sexual experiences with another person

   (4) takes pleasure in few, if any, activities

   (5) lacks close friends or confidants other than first-degree relatives

   (6) appears indifferent to the praise or criticism of others

   (7) shows emotional coldness, detachment, or flattened affectivity

B. Does not occur exclusively during the course of Schizophrenia, a Mood Disorder with Psychotic Features, another Psychotic Disorder, or a Pervasive Developmental Disorder and is not due to the direct physiological effects of a general medical condition.

Source: From *Diagnostic and Statistical Manual of Mental Disorders,* fourth edition, text revision, American Psychiatric Association, 2000, Washington, DC: Author. Copyright 2000 by American Psychiatric Association. Reprinted with permission.

ting the family know where he is and how he is faring. Table 2.4 provides the *DSM-IV-TR* diagnostic criteria for Schizoid Personality Disorder.

Potential Age-Bias of Criteria

Criterion A3 (has little, if any, interest in having sexual experiences with another person) is inappropriate for many older adults, not due to emerging schizoid tendencies, but rather due to the lack of suitable partners as well as normal age-related declines in libido among some older people. Criterion A5 (lacks close friends or confidants other than first-degree relatives) may also be problematic for older adults who have outlived their friends and in their later years rely primarily on relationships with their children. In fact, psychologist Laura Carstensen's famous theory of socioemotional selectivity suggests that with advancing age, many individuals reduce the range of their relationships to maximize the social and emotional rewards of the relationships and reduce risks associated with relationships (Carstensen, 1987; also see Carstensen, Isaacowitz, & Charles, 1999). As such, older adults increasingly prefer to spend time with people who are close to them, especially family members, instead of meeting new people. Hearing impairment, which is common in later life, can also restrict one's social network, and in these cases, reduced social contacts should not be perceived as being due to maladaptive personality traits.

Finally, Criterion A7 (shows emotional coldness, detachment, or flattened affectivity) may not fit well with older individuals due to their enhanced abilities to (a) regulate their emotions, (b) control the way they express their emotions, and (c) understand their emotional experiences, each of which is a trend commonly associated with normal aging (Carstensen & Turk-Charles, 1994; Carstensen et al., 1999; Labouvie-Vief & Hakim-Larson, 1989; Lawton, Kleban, Rajagopal, & Dean, 1992).

Theorized Pattern in Later Life and Possible Impact of Aging
The aging issue most threatening to the schizoid type is the increased dependency on others (usually due to loss of mobility, loss of financial resources, and/or physical declines). Because the older schizoid's socially disconnected style is ego-syntonic, it causes marked distress when the person must by necessity depend on relationships with others for his or her care. Schizoid people prefer to be alone and independent and will typically react poorly if they must be in regular contact with others, for example, in an assisted living situation or a nursing home.

Sensory decline is also an important issue especially as it relates to reduced independence and the need for closer contact with others. In contrast, retirement would not seem to be particularly challenging to the older schizoid. In fact, in cases where the work environment precipitated contacts with other people, retirement may be a welcome change in life. Widowhood may also be less stressful to the older schizoid because the attachment to the marital partner likely was less intense compared with healthier older adults, and the subsequent loss less meaningful. The older schizoid's grief over spousal loss is much more likely to occur for practical reasons such as the loss of a cook or laundress than because of an emotional attachment loss. Typically, the lifelong recluse becomes more reclusive with advancing age for as long as the person can manage being alone (i.e., until changes that often accompany aging require increased contact with others).

The Case of Dom: Schizoid Personality Disorder

Dom D. came to the United States as a young boy, together with his parents and two older brothers. They settled in a large metropolitan area where his father worked as a skilled laborer in a factory and his mother as a homemaker. Dom was an easy child for his overwhelmed mother to raise. While she counted on her older sons to ease her way in this new country, she relied on Dom to help her with domestic chores, which he did dutifully, if not willingly. He did not appear to anticipate or even to react to his mother's expressions of sadness or explosions of anger—but he did do what he was told and never appeared especially concerned or moved to exhibit emotional responses, whether of happiness, sadness, irritability, or anger.

He attended school regularly but was an indifferent student. He did not relate to his teachers or to the other students. His work was most often minimally executed, without any reflection of what he thought or felt inside. On the playground, he typically stood off to the side, not showing much interest in what the other children were doing. It was as if the whole concept of play was extraneous and foreign to him. On those occasions when participation in team sports was required, he was often the last one chosen to be on a team. This was less because others viewed him uncoordinated (which he was not), but more because he was unknown, making the other children feel uncomfortable in his presence.

When he became a student in a large city high school, Dom became even more invisible. When he dropped out of school shortly after his 16th birthday, few noticed or cared. It was as if the enthusiasm, passion, and self-presence lacking in him was reflected in his lack of connection to and effect on others.

His mother was aware that he was very different from her two older boys. They were good students and had been energetic, ambitious, and occasionally volatile adolescents. Each had moved on to a community college, and the eldest was completing a bachelor's degree at a university. After Dom dropped out of school, his mother could no longer provide him with enough chores to keep him from appearing idle to her. To complicate matters, he was not willing to do things that required socializing, or even more than the briefest communication with others. In time, she appealed to her husband to use his connections through his job to provide Dom with a position and a future.

The father knew very little about his sons. He had never been involved with the children, leaving that to their mother. He worked very hard, often doing double shifts at the factory, to support the family. He considered his hard work to be good enough parenting. When he allowed himself time for his own pleasure, it was with one or two coworkers from the plant. He was neither abusive nor demanding of his wife or sons, nor did he offer them much beyond financial support. He was both proud and resentful of his "college boy" sons, but had never given thought to any alternatives. When he was made aware that this same scenario would not apply to his third child, he was perplexed. What did he know about this boy, this young man?

One thing he did know was that Dom was "good with his hands" and naturally adept at electrical work. He seemed to have great patience doing minor electrical repairs around the apartment. The few books he borrowed from the library were manuals of circuitry and wiring that he would take off to his bedroom and read over and over. His father spoke to someone he knew in the office at work, and the company was able to hire Dom as an electrician apprentice. Dom learned quickly. His work ethic was excellent. He made no friends on the job, but just attended to his work. Fortunately, the man assigned to train him made no demands on Dom to be sociable; therefore, Dom's lack of social skills did not have negative occupational consequences. For his boss's part, he was happy to train an extra pair of hands and relished the shared solitude.

Dom engaged in few activities outside of work. He rented his own small apartment a short distance from where he had been raised and lived there all his adult life. He saved his money, not because he had any plans or goals that it might support, but because he did not especially want anything. His major personal expense was on magazines related to his interest in gadgetry and electronics. His living room was piled high with back issues of *Popular Mechanics*. Dom's hygiene and appearance were marginal. He looked "okay" for the machine shop at work (just barely), but was always a bit disheveled in public. Dom did not appear to be someone a passerby or fellow shopper would want to smile at or exchange pleasantries with, and this suited him well.

His daily routine changed little over the years. During the work week, he worked. On Sundays, he had dinner with his parents. After they died, he took Sunday dinner with one or the other of his brothers and their families. Dom never evidenced any sexual interest or desire to create a family of his own. His nieces and nephews came to understand Uncle Dom as a loner. He was not lonesome and not especially weird, but he was remarkably detached—a solitary man living out his life.

Dom developed no bad health habits, as he pursued no pleasures. He did not take up smoking or drinking, and his diet was plain and simple. He walked to and from his work each day, and he avoided doctors, beyond the cursory health checkups required by the company. He remained at his job well into his 60s. One winter morning as he left his apartment to head to work, he noticed a tin can at the bottom of the building's steps. As he went to pick it up, he missed a step and tumbled in such a way as to incur severe compound fractures of his pelvis and thigh. He was transported to the hospital where he endured several surgical procedures to stabilize the fractures. He was bedridden for a time, then wheelchair bound; and ultimately he was transferred to a rehabilitation facility for intensive physical therapy as well as the tincture of time. It was there that his personality disorder became evident.

He was assigned a bed in a three-bed room, sharing the room and the lavatory with two other men. He took the third bed, as the other two men had already been at the facility for several weeks. They had already struck up a nice friendship, offering one another encouragement and considerable good-natured bantering. They were eager to show the ropes to their new roommate and to welcome him as a friend and fellow traveler though the rehabilitation process.

Dom had been sent to an excellent rehabilitation facility. The physical therapists on staff were all dedicated and knowledgeable professionals, offering good therapy and much encouragement. They had many tricks and techniques to cajole the patients, frequently older adults, past discomfort and fatigue to do the necessary exercises and maintain a positive outlook. They welcomed Dom and introduced him to the professional staff and their assistants, all of whom warmly greeted and welcomed him.

By Day 2, the social worker and the head dietician had visited with Dom. The social worker tried to learn about what he enjoyed and who was in his friendship and kinship network and might be involved during his stay at the facility. The dietician also visited, wanting to know his food preferences and what might make his experience in the dining room most agreeable.

By Day 3, a pleasant volunteer came to visit, introducing herself as "a friendly visitor." The social worker had noted that Dom had indicated no friends and a small family, and had notified the volunteer office. By Day 4, Dom refused to participate in his therapy, or to go to the dining room for meals. By Day 5, he refused to get out of bed, and screamed at the morning aide "Get the hell away from me!" A mental health consultation was then ordered.

The consulting clinician read the record and interviewed a number of staff before meeting with Dom. It became apparent that the demands of the system were what had pushed Dom to the edge, not the requirements and challenges of the physical therapies. Dom was an absolute loner and did not have the skills nor the desire to get close to others. He had been used to living alone, and his personal space was violated by the accommodations in the facility. The warmth and friendliness of the system functioned well, and the employees were respected and satisfied. This is admirable and generally bodes well for patients, but it does not suit everyone. Dom was an example of a poor fit with the environment.

The consultation plan was developed with three main goals:

1. *The staff* would deviate from the system's culture and their own need to offer patients warmth and support in addition to direct care and physical therapy. They would understand that their feelings of being ignored, dismissed, or not valued did not reflect their deficiencies, but rather the personality structure of this particular patient. Their good and compassionate care was directly serving to exacerbate expressions of Dom's psychopathology. The consultant "introduced" them to the person who was Dom, reviewed his history, and identified his dominant personality traits. These traits included being purpose driven and industrious, with marked preferences for routine and minimal interpersonal involvement. What had been toxic to Dom was staff attempts to connect, express, or demand affect, touch, sustained prox-

imity, and intimations of intimacy. He did not require praise or encouragement and would prefer to keep this to a minimum. His goal was the most expedient, least intrusive return to his former life. The staff discussed how this made them feel, touching on how the richness of their work was in large part derived from the interpersonal context. They agreed that while they would try to understand Dom's character, they were glad that most patients were not like him, but rather thrived in their loving care.

2. *The staff* was asked to identify the specific goals that Dom would ideally need to meet to be discharged to home. They were also asked to design an ideal aftercare plan.

   At the next meeting with the consultant and staff, each goal was discussed and appraised as either being ideal/optimal or absolutely necessary for his discharge. The "absolutely necessary" goals were then each discussed in terms of what minimal amount of interpersonal contact would be required. The staff were creative in generating ideas. For example, Dom would be set up with a piece of equipment to do 30 repetitions. Typically, the therapist watches and cheers the patient on, especially toward the end of the cycle when weakened muscles become fatigued. Instead, Dom would have a bell to ring when he had completed the repetitions, and then the therapist would transfer him to the next therapy activity. No coaching, cheering, praise, or even conversation would be necessary.

   The aftercare plan was discussed and reduced to a weekly home visit rather than two per week, if Dom would contract to document executing the assigned routine. The therapist who paid home visits would be encouraged not to chat, but only to go over the physical program, make the necessary adjustments, review the documentation, and respond to any questions Dom might have. No friendly visitors allowed!

3. *Dom* would agree to meet with the consultant to determine how he and the facility could speed up his rehabilitation and discharge to home. Dom would shower and dress and they would meet in a private room where it would be quiet and free of interruptions. They would sit at a table a reasonable distance apart. The consultant would sit to the side to avoid

direct eye contact with Dom when he looked up from his notes from his sessions with the staff.

It was explained to Dom that the staff knew that he was a man who was used to being on his own, by himself, and that this experience in the rehabilitation facility was a difficult one. There were a lot of things that understandably bothered him. The staff was responsible for patient care and for getting patients back on their feet as well and as quickly as possible. The consultant explained that he had met with the staff to learn what exactly Dom needed to be able to do before he could safely return home. They went over each of the rehabilitation goals. It was then explained how each would be addressed so as to not bother Dom any more than was necessary. Dom was asked if he had any suggestions and if he would agree to this contract. This procedure was carried out again with each of the aftercare goals. Dom wanted to know how many weeks someone would have to come to his house for therapy visits after he went home. The consultant said that he would ask the staff and get back to Dom with this information.

The final product was a brief, written contract signed by the Director of Nursing and Dom and witnessed by the consultant. Each side kept up its half of the bargain, and Dom was discharged to his home in a few weeks. The contract was able to serve the functions of binding Dom's acting out (in this case, an exacerbation of his tendency to withdraw, isolate, and disallow interpersonal cooperation), and unlinking the kindness culture of the facility from the necessary, technical aspects of care.

Schizotypal Personality Disorder

Clinical Description

Individuals with this disorder are characterized as bizarre or eccentric with odd perceptions and cognitions. Their eccentricities are typically not confined to an isolated area; rather, schizotypal people often combine a peculiar style of dress or appearance, strange uses of language, unusual behaviors, and odd thought patterns. Their hygiene may be also poor. As such, schizotypal people are often identified easily and quickly by others, even nonclinicians. The schizotypal type is the classic oddball often fitting the characterization from relatively early in life as "marching to the beat of a different drummer."

People with Schizotypal Personality Disorder experience extreme discomfort with interpersonal relationships, lack close friends or confidants apart from relatives, and appear socially inept and withdrawn. They may be drifters and rarely date or marry. They often have ideas of reference, peculiar superstitions, and magical thinking that are so extreme as to be inconsistent with their culture or subculture. They may report beliefs in magical powers such as clairvoyance or telepathy, bizarre fantasies, and mystical experiences. Whereas some normal people may endorse some of these beliefs, those held by the schizotypal are often more extreme and interfere with typical social and occupational functioning. Perceptual and somatic distortions are also common, but are not as extreme as those experienced by people with a psychotic disorder. Importantly, people with Schizotypal Personality Disorder do not evidence overt psychosis and have less deterioration of their functioning, which further discriminates the personality disorder from a psychotic disorder.

Emotionally, people with Schizotypal Personality Disorder are likely to show a restricted range of expression and in some cases, inappropriate affect. They have high levels of social anxiety with the themes of suspiciousness and paranoia contributing largely to the social deficits. Striking examples of unusual thought processes and emotions were shown in one of our patients, an 80-year-old woman, who during a relatively nonthreatening part of the initial intake suddenly burst into tears and sobbed uncontrollably for several minutes. When asked what prompted her intense feelings, she replied that she was not sad, but rather that her sister (who was her only close relationship and who was living in another state) was crying at that very moment and the patient could always "feel her sister's feelings." Later in the same interview, the patient began laughing hysterically and reported that "her sister was having a good time" at that moment. Table 2.5 provides the *DSM-IV-TR* diagnostic criteria for Schizotypal Personality Disorder.

Table 2.5   *DSM-IV-TR,* **Diagnostic Criteria for Schizotypal Personality Disorder (Code: 301.22)**

A. A pervasive pattern of social and interpersonal deficits marked by acute discomfort with, and reduced capacity for, close relationships as well as by cognitive or perceptual distortions and eccentricities of behavior, beginning by early adulthood and present in a variety of contexts, as indicated by five (or more) of the following:

  (1) ideas of reference (excluding delusions of reference)

  (2) odd beliefs or magical thinking that influences behavior and is inconsistent with subcultural norms (e.g., superstitiousness, belief in clairvoyance, telepathy, or "sixth sense"; in children and adolescents, bizarre fantasies or preoccupations)

  (3) unusual perceptual experiences, including bodily illusions

  (4) odd thinking and speech (e.g., vague, circumstantial, metaphorical, overelaborate, or stereotyped)

  (5) suspiciousness or paranoid ideation

  (6) inappropriate or constricted affect

  (7) behavior or appearance that is odd, eccentric, or peculiar

  (8) lack of close friends or confidants other than first-degree relatives

  (9) excessive social anxiety that does not diminish with familiarity and tends to be associated with paranoid fears rather than negative judgments about self

B. Does not occur exclusively during the course of Schizophrenia, a Mood Disorder with Psychotic Features, another Psychotic Disorder, or a Pervasive Developmental Disorder.

Source: From *Diagnostic and Statistical Manual of Mental Disorders,* fourth edition, text revision, American Psychiatric Association, 2000, Washington, DC: Author. Copyright 2000 by American Psychiatric Association. Reprinted with permission.

Potential Age-Bias of Criteria

Like the problems associated with criteria for Schizoid Personality Disorder, Criterion A6 (inappropriate or constricted affect) and Criterion A8 (lacks close friends or confidants other than first-degree relatives) may confound normal aging with illness because people become less affectively charged with age, and they are more likely to experience catastrophic but real social losses with advanced age, which can severely limit their social network beyond immediate family.

Theorized Pattern in Later Life and Possible Impact of Aging
Like the schizoid, the central aging issue for the schizotypal personality is increased dependency on others. Because of acute social anxiety, older schizotypal patients will likely become agitated if physical infirmities force them to endure relationships with health care professionals, staff, and residents in congregate living settings or long-term care facilities. Their bizarre behaviors and beliefs will likely make the schizotypal older adult an easy target for social rejection in communal living settings. Like the paranoid type, schizotypal older adults may react to declines in hearing and vision by becoming even more paranoid and suspicious, further lowering their social effectiveness.

Another aging issue affecting the Schizotypal Personality Disorder has to do with the way people perceive bizarre behaviors in others across the life span. Among younger people, particularly adolescents, there is often a period when they try out a host of beliefs and styles of dress and appearance, some of which may be unusual or socially nonconforming. Some young adults intensify their eccentricities as a way of expressing themselves and perhaps making a social statement. Picture a young person with multiple body piercings, a Mohawk haircut, and bright tattoos. Now imagine an 85-year-old man with the same appearance. It is likely that his social standing would be greatly diminished compared with that of the younger person.

A problem facing schizotypal older adults is that their eccentricities are often perceived as more pathological than among younger adults. Individuals with this personality disorder are also at risk for being marginalized and discounted by others, being easily dismissed due to the overt "weirdness." One of our patients, an elderly schizotypal woman, was easily identified by others as being unusual (e.g., she wore a large fur hat, even indoors, and ill-fitting biker shorts). When she complained to her family doctor about having miniseizures throughout the day, he was dismissive, possibly attributing her experience to her psychiatric disorder (he was very familiar with her history and problems). Over time, her seizures worsened and played a role in an accident in which she wrecked her car and injured herself and two passengers in the other car. Only after that accident was a seizure disorder diagnosed and treated properly.

An interesting pattern is that of the older adult with Schizotypal Personality Disorder who is found by a visitor (e.g., utility company worker, health department worker) to be living in a deteriorating house (inside and out). Numerous neglected pets often cause putrescent conditions (e.g., one of our patients had 40 uncaged ferrets who urinated and defecated throughout the home). In the absence of an organic condition such as dementia or a history of psychotic disorder, an older adult who has a constellation of eccentricities (e.g., is unkempt, dressed inappropriately, malodorous, suspicious, paranoid, bizarre, and has few friends) likely is suffering from Schizotypal Personality Disorder.

Finally, a more optimistic view of aging and the Schizotypal Personality Disorder is offered by Butler et al. (1998) who propose a context in which the schizotypal type may do somewhat better in later life. They suggest that because such individuals are "insulated against the experiences of life" (p. 109), they may be less unnerved about some of the isolation and difficulties common in later life. However, these authors also note a competing pattern of increased reclusivity and isolation with age. We have seen this latter pattern in many cases, with the detrimental consequence of increased bizarreness due to the complete or near-complete lack of social contact.

The Case of Doreen: Schizotypal Personality Disorder

Doreen G. is a 68-year-old woman who has come to the attention of mental health professionals only twice in her life. The first time was early in high school when the teachers were concerned about the degree of her introversion and lack of connection to her classmates, and about her sometimes bizarre facial expressions, which did not seem to match the events going on around her. She was a bit peculiar and significantly withdrawn and detached. Her parents were called into school to discuss these concerns, and apparently Doreen (by her own report) told the teachers to "leave me alone. I am like my Uncle Jake, and he needed to be left alone, too." The school complied, and Doreen was graduated from high school with her class; still disconnected, somewhat peculiar, but left alone.

She had been in the business curriculum in high school, and after graduation she enrolled in a program to improve her general office skills, which at that time included typing, filing, and basic bookkeeping. She did not want to study shorthand because, as she put it, "I don't like sitting with someone for so long and having to think about what they are saying and writing it all down."

With the business program completed, she needed to get a job. Doreen was still living at home with her parents; an older brother had completed college and was living out of state on his own. Her parents suggested that she try to get a job at a large insurance firm, and her father was able to arrange a contact for her there. She got an entry level office job and remained with that same company for over 20 years. During most of that time, she remained living at home with her parents. Between ages 32 and 38, however, she lived by herself in a small apartment near her work in the city. This period marked her most independent level of functioning. At the end of these 6 years, the rent increased to where she could no longer afford it on her salary, so she returned home to her parents. When she was just over 40, she lost her job at the insurance company because the requirements, technologically and interpersonally, exceeded her ability to perform. She says that she did not especially miss the job, nor did she maintain contact with any coworkers.

She lived at home and says, "I did nothing for a while and it was okay. My mother would take me out with her to see her friends, and I didn't like that, so I wanted another job." Again her father knew someone in management at a nearby chain supermarket and arranged a job interview for Doreen. She accepted a job in the bakery section working 20 hours per week. Her job consisted of monitoring the preparation orders and display stock. She was a reliable and consistent worker, valued by the store. According to Doreen, her "off hours" were mostly spent in solitary pursuits, except when her mother "made me go on visits with her." A few times during these years, one or the other parent would suggest that Doreen join a group (e.g., through their church), so that she might socialize with others around her own age. Eventually, they gave up. She was indeed like her father's older brother, Jake; an odd soul, disconnected but "regular as a clock." Doreen liked saying this about herself.

Her favorite activity was dancing to rock-and-roll music in her bedroom with the stereo turned up "pretty loud" and watching herself "in the big mirror on the wall. I could feel like I was dancing in this big ballroom and there were other dancers, too."

As her parents aged, and their health and level of functioning began to decline, Doreen assumed more of the household tasks. "I like cleaning, but not cooking. But someone has to do it." Always on the heavy side, Doreen became obese as the years went by. She favored snack foods and eating out by herself, at local fast-food restaurants. "I'm a burger and fry person." Sometimes her father would join her for lunch, but she says she liked it better when he did not. "I don't like talking when I'm eating."

After her mother died, Doreen assumed the cooking duties for herself and her father. She would accompany him regularly to visit the cemetery where her mother was buried. She said "I didn't like that, but he made me go. I knew my mother wasn't there." When asked where she believed her mother was, she looked away, smiled slightly, and answered "I know, but I'm not saying."

With the exception of a semiannual visit with her father to her brother's home, Doreen did not vary her routine. Her weight ballooned, and it became more difficult for her to walk any distance. Despite her father's pleas, she refused to see a doctor, stating, "I don't like doctors. They ask too many questions."

When Doreen was in her mid-60s, her father died following a sudden, massive stroke. Her brother invited her to move to an assisted living complex near him, but she adamantly refused to make the change. Her mobility became increasingly limited, and her food choices worse and more stereotypic. She spent her days dancing, eating "junk" food and watching television. Her brother now visited her, as she could not travel by herself. During one such visit, about 3 years following their father's death, her brother realized that Doreen could not continue to live alone. Despite her protests against leaving the house or altering her familiar routine, he made arrangements for her to move to an assisted living facility (ALF) near where he and his family lived. Her brother, himself an older adult, cleaned and reconstituted the house, which was in great disarray. He then sold the house, packed his sister's belongings, and accomplished the move. Doreen was most concerned about moving her stereo and substantial record collection.

Although her brother had told the administration of the ALF about Doreen's peculiarities, they were not prepared for the experience of having her as a resident. Such facilities typically offer specific amenities well suited to older adults who have become less able or less willing to continue responsibility for certain regular, domestic chores. In addition, ALFs offer the older adult a community context, including activities and opportunities for socialization, thus addressing the common complaints of isolation and loneliness.

Housekeeping services were offered, and Doreen's one-bedroom apartment would be thoroughly cleaned once per week. This typically took the cleaners one to two hours, depending on the size of the unit. Doreen's unit was small, but it was always such a mess that the cleaning staff needed to spend half a day cleaning it. Food remains (garbage) were left all over the apartment, becoming odiferous and attracting bugs. Her dirty clothing was left lying around as well, and she used the laundry hamper to store her record albums. Sometimes during the cleaning sessions, Doreen would become visibly agitated, and dance in front of the cleaning staff, waving her fingers before their faces as if trying to scare them off. The cleaning help complained to the management and ultimately refused to enter her apartment. Doreen accepted this as a victory.

Another ALF offering was two daily meals in the dining room, breakfast and dinner. Dinner could be taken either at midday or in the evening, as the resident chose. For the third meal, it was assumed that the resident would prepare either lunch or a light dinner in the apartment. After moving, Doreen quickly discovered several local fast-food shops that would deliver. She became a frequent customer. The result of this was that she grew even more obese, and her apartment was littered with cartons and take-out bags that she used to store music tapes.

That the ALF provided opportunities for companionship was more than lost on Doreen; she ignored or avoided these efforts. During the first several weeks, the dining room staff tried, as they did for all new residents, to introduce her and seat her with others at meals, observing which pairings or groupings appeared to work best. Doreen passively accepted being seated anywhere, with anyone. She voiced no complaints. Other residents, however, did have complaints. Her eating behavior was most unattractive. She made no attempt at conversation, and between courses when she wasn't eating, she would stare at her tablemates, as if they could not see her stare. At times, she would become engaged in a tune that was being played as background music, and "dance" to it with her hands and fingers. Her odd behaviors, poor manners, and nonexistent social skills ultimately led the other residents to ignore Doreen and to refuse being seated with her for meals.

The ALF repeatedly called her brother to meet with the staff about his sister's unacceptable behavior. His efforts to help were to no avail. He bought her a new, larger clothes hamper, which she proceeded to use for storing more record albums. He bought a chest to hold her music tapes, but she still preferred to keep them in bags from the fast-food shops. He hired an outside cleaning service to come in biweekly to preclean the apartment for the ALF cleaners. Her untidiness easily kept pace with this new challenge.

Doreen was at the point of being evicted. A psychologist who had consulted with the ALF in the past was called for a consultation to see if there was a way Doreen could stay on as a resident. The psychologist interviewed Doreen, her brother, the staff, and read her resident file.

Doreen's diagnosis was Schizotypal Personality Disorder. The major benchmarks of this personality disorder as exhibited by Doreen included odd beliefs, bodily illusions, constricted affect, alignment with paranormal phenomena, peculiar behaviors, and a lack of interpersonal relationships. The absence of relationships reflected feedback from others who responded to her oddness in ways that contributed to it and isolated her further. A paranoid thread also ran underneath, and the inherent suspiciousness was effortful and anxiety provoking, thereby reinforcing the wish to stay clear of others or to behave as if they were not there.

The consultation challenge in this case was to ascertain what the facility could offer and would accept that would enable a compromise between the facility and Doreen. What did each party want, and what would each be willing to give to get it?

The facility wanted to maintain reasonable cleanliness in the units and to avoid complaints by workers and residents. Doreen wanted not to have to move again, to have the food she likes, access to her music, and to not be required to socialize beyond a minimum, other than with her brother. (She has always been comfortable with his visits, and eagerly looks forward to them.)

A meeting was arranged with the psychologist, the ALF director, the ALF social worker, and Doreen's brother. The psychologist, with information from her brother, gave a detailed overview of Doreen's history. He emphasized that when she had the roles and relationships to buffer her, she did well. She held two jobs, each for many years, and was regarded as a most reliable employee at each. She was a very involved and responsible family member, gradually assuming care and household responsibilities for her parents, until one and then the other died. Because of technological changes in her job requirements, she was let go; not an unusual experience for older adults these days. And finally, after living nearly her entire life in the same small town, she was moved to a different living environment in a different state where she had no landmarks for continuity, other than the visits from her brother.

It is easy to identify Doreen's weaknesses and limitations, but the psychologist highlighted a number of her strengths, thereby reframing some of her maladaptive behaviors as adaptive. Four issues were important to her and provided her with necessary continuity to feel like herself, and the psychologist noted how Doreen managed to secure them.

First, Doreen quickly learned where in the local area she could order and have delivery of the foods she preferred. She not only loved the food, but these were reminders, "transitional objects," of her former life. Fast food was not only a comfort, but also a constant. To remind her of this, to provide comfort to savor after the food was gone, she kept the paper bags emblazoned with the logos. Second, she nestled her other love, music, in these bags. Third, while she did not have the social or communication skills to state her strong preference to eat alone, and did not outwardly object to being seated with others, she managed to behave in such a way to get what she needed by having others withdraw from her. She was able to keep her apartment "free of intruders" by making it nearly impossible for the cleaners to work there. When they redoubled their efforts, she increased her bizarre behavior and "warded them off."

Finally, her limited affiliative needs are met by the one living person whom she trusts and feels commutable and comfortable with, her brother. His routine had been to visit Doreen every other week; twice each month. She felt the need for more frequent visits from her brother since moving to this new environment, which she perceived as potentially threatening. She did not have the skill or even a clear idea of what she felt she was missing and needed to ask for. What frequently happens with personality disorders is that such unformed thoughts and unnamed feelings get acted out. Doreen acted out, misbehaved, and got her brother to be called in by the facility, and therefore she was able to see him more frequently. In addition, he brought her gifts, such as a new hamper for her records.

A meeting was scheduled that included Doreen, the psychologist, the ALF director, the ALF social worker, and Doreen's brother.

A contract mutually developed at the meeting included the following points:

- Doreen could remain at the ALF (recall, she did not want to move again) if she kept the apartment clean of leftover food. This was presented as a public health hazard, and neither the facility nor she would want public health strangers snooping around her apartment. She was asked to vacate the apartment weekly while the cleaning people worked in her apartment. It was explained that they liked to work alone, just as Doreen did. And finally, she could order food as she liked and from where she liked. But it would need to come through the front desk. They would mark each delivery and Doreen would bring the garbage in the delivery bags to the front desk for disposal after the meal. If she did not comply, she would not be allowed to order food from outside.

- From the facility's end: They would be willing to be the fast-food gatekeeper and monitor. They would allow the cleaning staff to spend whatever reasonable time was needed to clean her apartment; they would direct the dining room host to seat Doreen by herself, stating that she preferred to eat alone and was entitled to do so.

- The brother would agree to visit Doreen weekly, unless he had been contacted by the facility with a problem related to this contract.

- And finally, this same group would be reconvened regularly to address problems and acknowledge successes. They agreed that they were all equal players, and all would have a voice.

The Dramatic, Emotional, and Erratic (Cluster B) Personality Disorders and Aging

Cluster B Personality Disorders: Antisocial, Borderline, Histrionic, and Narcissistic

3

The four personality disorders in Cluster B are grouped together because they share similar core features of dramatic, theatrical, emotional, or erratic behavior, often with intense interpersonal strife as a result. Compared with the odd and withdrawn personality disorders in Cluster A, the Cluster B personality disorders often present with tumultuous and chaotic relationship histories and marked impulsivity. People with these personality disorders typically affect others with whom they are in close relationships, sometimes in highly destructive ways. The themes in psychotherapy often center around interpersonal dissatisfaction, conflict, and turmoil. One could argue that the antisocial type is a poor fit for this particular cluster. Whereas the impulsivity of the antisocial type matches that of the other disorders in this grouping, especially the borderline type, the antisocial type is set apart by the striking *absence* of most normal emotional reactions (with the exception of intense anger). In contrast, the other three personality disorders in this assemblage are generally *overly* emotional and affective. The *DSM-IV-TR* diagnostic criteria for the four Cluster B personality disorders are described in the following subsections.

Antisocial Personality Disorder

Clinical Description

As the term *antisocial* implies, individuals with this disorder are "against society." Indeed, the hallmark feature is a pervasive pattern of disregard for, and failure to comply with, societal norms. Among people with Antisocial Personality Disorder, the rights of others are never a consideration, and when individuals with this disorder hurt, deceive, manipulate, abuse, or victimize others, they fail to experience remorse, guilt, or shame. When caught, antisocial types may weep "crocodile tears" but real feelings of remorse are notably absent, and they appear to lack a conscience. People with Antisocial Personality Disorder are often aggressive, ruthless, and interpersonally exploitative with a poor sense of responsibility. They take what they want, when they want it, with no regard for the impact that their actions have on others. They lack empathy and can be dangerously indifferent to the rights of others. Lying, cheating, stealing, and fighting appear to be part of their nature. Societal rules do not apply to them. In many cases, people with Antisocial Personality Disorder commit criminal acts (often habitually), and as a consequence, the disorder is overrepresented in prison populations (rates range from 30% to 70%; Widiger & Rogers, 1989) and is responsible for a markedly disproportionate amount of societal misery.

Other features of Antisocial Personality Disorder include a host of impulsive, reckless, and erratic behaviors. In some cases, the crimes these people commit seem aimless, random, or impulsive. They appear not to be motivated by any rational purpose, but rather are perversely impetuous. They typically show an inability to learn from experience and to avoid negative consequences. People with Antisocial Personality Disorder often present as charming and ingratiating, and they are well skilled at hiding their true intentions. As such, many victims are known to have been misled and conned by the superficial charm of antisocial criminals. Another feature is that they lack a capacity to genuinely care about others. Their relationships, therefore, tend to be superficial, shallow, and exploitative. Others are seen as objects to be manipulated and used for the antisocial individual's personal gain. They lack a capacity for love, intimacy, and sustained attachment and are generally unresponsive to trust, kindness, or affection. They lie shamelessly and can easily take advantage of those who have trusted them.

Whereas the inner lives of people with Antisocial Personality Disorder are flat and emotionally empty, and their personal suffering muted or nonexistent, contact with antisocial personalities may be dangerous because many of them are outright criminals. A saying we have used illustrates the deceptive nature of the antisocial: "The most dangerous criminals are not those who break down your backdoor but those whom you let in the front door." An important diagnostic feature of Antisocial Personality Disorder in the *DSM-IV-TR* is that it must have originated in childhood or early adolescence in the form of Conduct Disorder, which is diagnosed on Axis I. Antisocial Personality Disorder is diagnosed if the pattern continues into adulthood. Historically, one of the earliest views of people with Antisocial Personality Disorder was that they were morally insane. Other descriptions of the disorder have included the terms *sociopath, psychopath,* and *dissocial personality.* The term Antisocial Personality Disorder became the official diagnostic label in the *DSM-I.* Interestingly, the term psychopath still persists in popular media and is often used synonymously by the public with the term psychopathic killer (e.g., to describe notorious serial killers such as Ted Bundy, John Wayne Gacy, Gary Gilmore, and Charles Manson). Use of the term in these contexts gives the false impression that all psychopaths are murderers. Table 3.1 lists the *DSM-IV-TR* diagnostic criteria for Antisocial Personality Disorder.

Potential Age-Bias of Criteria

Two Antisocial Personality Disorder criteria seem to be problematic for older adults. Criterion 4 (irritability and aggressiveness, as indicated by repeated physical fights or assaults)

Table 3.1   *DSM-IV-TR* **Diagnostic Criteria for Antisocial Personality Disorder (Code: 301.7)**

A. There is a pervasive pattern of disregard for and violation of the rights of others occurring since age 15 years, as indicated by three (or more) of the following:
   (1) failure to conform to social norms with respect to lawful behaviors as indicated by repeatedly performing acts that are grounds for arrest
   (2) deceitfulness, as indicated by repeated lying, use of aliases, or conning others for personal profit or pleasure
   (3) impulsivity or failure to plan ahead
   (4) irritability and aggressiveness, as indicated by repeated physical fights or assaults
   (5) reckless disregard for safety of self or others
   (6) consistent irresponsibility, as indicated by repeated failure to sustain consistent work behavior or honor financial obligations
   (7) lack of remorse, as indicated by being indifferent to or rationalizing having hurt, mistreated, or stolen from another
B. The individual is at least age 18 years.
C. There is evidence of Conduct Disorder with onset before age 15 years.
D. The occurrence of antisocial behavior is not exclusively during the course of Schizophrenia or a Manic Episode.

Source: From *Diagnostic and Statistical Manual of Mental Disorders,* fourth edition, text revision, American Psychiatric Association, 2000, Washington, DC: Author. Copyright 2000 by American Psychiatric Association. Reprinted with permission.

and Criterion 5 (reckless disregard for safety of self or other) require physical strength and agility. It is likely that these aggressive, impetuous, uncontrolled, and reckless behaviors diminish as the person's stamina, impulsivity, and energy levels decline naturally with age (Kroessler, 1990; Zarit & Zarit, 1998). For many persons, however, even externally imposed limitations (e.g., jail) and age-related physical declines do not assure that antisocial behavior will remit since the underlying psychological processes are known to remain constant (a point that is discussed further in Chapter 6). There is no reason to think that empathy, genuine concern for the welfare of others, and a conscience will meaningfully develop in people with Antisocial Personality Disorder as a mere function of growing older.

Theorized Pattern in Later Life and Possible Impact of Aging

An important issue in the study of aging individuals with Antisocial Personality Disorder is that some of them do not survive into old age because of a lifestyle of risky behaviors. Substance abuse often compounds the characteristic recklessness and impulsivity of the antisocial type and can lead to early mortality. Those who reach later life typically have poor social support systems in place, with the exception of those who have integrated into a "fellowship of thieves." A pattern among some aging individuals with Antisocial Personality Disorder is that they have been rejected and completely cut off by family members and peers who have had enough of the person's deceitful, manipulative, self-centered, and aggressive ways. In these cases, each of the specific stressors of aging is likely to be difficult for aging antisocial individuals because they lack appropriate supports. Perhaps most important, what one can expect to see in the aging antisocial type is a person who is unlikely to be acting out in the extreme and physical manner of his or her youth, but the underlying psychological processes (e.g., lack of concern for the welfare of others, deceitfulness, exploitative approach, emotional coldness, and irresponsibility) will likely remain (Harpur & Hare, 1994).

Physical disability, sensory decline, and cognitive impairment can be particularly problematic for incarcerated older individuals with Antisocial Personality Disorder because their limitations make them especially vulnerable to exploitation from other prisoners. The prognosis for treating individuals with this personality disorder is generally bleak across the life span largely due to their limited personal distress and limited awareness that something is wrong with their attitudes and behaviors. They tend to seek treatment only under duress from others (e.g., court mandated) or when it is in their best interest to do so (e.g., when applying for parole). Thus, should the aging antisocial type seek therapy, it is important to fully explore and understand the ulterior motives for seeking help. Because the antisocial type has difficulty forming meaningful relationships with others, it likely will be difficult to achieve any semblance of an honest, collaborative working relationship. Instead of helping the patient develop empathy or concern for others, the interventions might focus on helping the patient to think through the consequences of his or her actions, plan constructive behaviors (or minimize the extent of destructive behaviors), and discover strategies to stay out of trouble.

The Case of Mickey: Antisocial Personality Disorder

The ambulance doors opened, and the male figure on the stretcher was flailing and fighting the attendants as they attempted to wheel him into the emergency room. "Lie still, Mister. You'll be okay. Everything will be okay. Just take it easy."

"You son of a bitch! Get me the hell out of here! Oh, crap, it hurts. My chest hurts like hell."

The new ER (emergency room) admission, now a patient, is a 71-year-old man named Mickey H. He has been transported to this inner-city hospital from a nearby bar, where he is known as a regular. Late into the night, and after much drinking, things turned ugly and an altercation began between Mickey and another man at the bar. Blows were exchanged to the amusement of the other patrons. Suddenly, Mickey let down his guard and clutched his chest. Crumpling to the floor, he hit his head on the metal base of the barstool. At first his opponent and nearby onlookers thought "Old" Mick was pulling a fast one on them, as he was known to do. But it soon became apparent that his chest pains and falling to the floor were real. At least the blood flowing from a gash to his forehead and down his nose was real. So the police were called, and they in turn called for the ambulance.

The ambulance attendants were no strangers to this bar. They were called to it fairly regularly, especially late into weekend nights. They were used to responding to near comatose patrons, and to those who were surly and belligerent. They knew how to talk them down while applying pressure to a wound and starting an IV line. They were not, however, familiar with Mickey. While a regular at the bar, he was not one of the emergency medical technicians' (EMTs) regulars. Mickey was known to throw a good punch and then walk away. He could stay and fight if he had to, but he seldom had to. He was savvy about who he took on. He took care of the cuts and bruises himself. He never clutched at his chest or got transported to the ER. When he did go to the ER, it was under his own steam and for his own purposes, either to get drugs or to avoid being followed or apprehended. At those times, he would convincingly feign severe upper abdomen pain and nausea, accurately describing the symptoms of acute pancreatitis. Admitting to being alcoholic, he was rewarded with IV pain relief. When the acute attack subsided, he was usually discharged with a refillable prescription for a painkiller.

At other times he would present with severe signs of alcohol withdrawal (delirium tremens) and win a hit with a benzodiazepine and a prescription for the road, as he promised this time to follow up with attendance at AA meetings.

Kicking and screaming, literally, Mickey announced his intention as he was being transferred from the stretcher to a gurney in the ER. "Get me the hell out of here! Clean me up and get me the hell out of here!" However, having collapsed at the bar and complained of chest pains, facts the EMTs had conveyed to the ER staff, Mickey would require a cardiac workup in addition to sutures for his lacerations. It appeared he would also need to be detoxed.

He calmed down enough for the nurses to clean his wounds and deliver an injection to assure he would stay calm. The attending physician was then able to suture his head and face wounds. Mickey was resting after the procedure, still under the effect of the medication, when it was decided to transfer him to a medical floor for a thorough cardiac workup. He dozed through the transfer, and that was the last of quiet and calm on the unit.

Mickey grew up in the city, born to a single mother who worked, when she was able to work, as a hairdresser. She was addicted to street drugs and would spend her money on drugs as often as on food. Hunger and malnourishment were constant companions for her and her son. She often did not notice, but little Mickey did. When times were especially rough for his mother, and she took off, leaving her young child alone and unattended, her own mother would take the boy in. A sick woman, a heavy smoker and chronically short of breath, Lil was not happy with her daughter's lifestyle nor with being too regularly burdened with rescuing her grandson. Although she couldn't run after him or watch him carefully, she did at least provide enough food. So Mickey spent his early years between the two apartments; one with his mother and one with food.

By the time he was in grade school he had developed a pattern of behaviors that defined him as a troubled kid and a school problem. He was untrustworthy and lied excessively; he was aggressive and he was destructive. He became the playground bully, beating up on smaller kids, and threatening others, forcing them to be his accomplices. A natural leader, he would create opportunities for vandalism and get others to go along with his ideas. When a street sign near the school went missing, right or wrong, Mickey was the first one the authorities suspected. If a kid were naive enough to show Mickey money he had brought from home, he would be relieved of it in a flash. If the child threatened to tell, Mickey would threaten to beat him up. If the child then broke down and cried, Mickey would laugh and walk off.

Perhaps most troubling was a behavior that the school did not know about and that Mickey did not share with the other kids, but did alone. If he came across an injured animal, or a baby animal separated from its littermates, he would take that animal to a special spot in his neighborhood, a private alleyway with the unusual distinction of not being regularly used by people from the streets, and he would set the little animal on fire. Killing it, watching it die a horrible death, felt just about right to Mickey, just about how he felt inside. This was as close to empathy as Mickey would ever get.

By his early adolescence, Mickey was frequently truant from school, and would run away from home, especially when he was under Lil's watch. The first few occasions she reported his absence to the police, but over time, she stopped reporting these disappearances. Mickey dropped out of school the day after his 16th birthday. He got a job as a commercial cleaner and supplemented his paycheck with money taken from Lil's pocketbook after she cashed her Social Security check. Thinking about his mother, and hating what she had become, he stayed away from street drugs, but developed a taste for alcohol and took up smoking, regularly relieving Lil of her smokes as well as her cash.

Mickey also developed a taste for, and then an addiction to, gambling of all sorts. This brought Mickey into a new network of associates, from the seamier side of the streets and from the organized underworld. He was identified by them as a potentially useful character, who had no respect for property, person, or feelings, and who disregarded rules and social convention. And if someone had to get hurt, that didn't bother him either. He was in the job for the paycheck and to do what he liked. A fairly good-looking guy, now with cash in his pocket, he enjoyed the company of any number of women. Smooth talking, he exploited them all for his own purposes, taking their money and using them not only for sex but also for protection. When the law came looking for him, a woman would often be his alibi. He had been with her at the time.

He didn't drink on the job, but he did at night and bar brawls became a regular social event. When, at some point in his 40s or 50s (his memory was hazy and his reporting was unreliable), Mickey began to supplement the alcohol with a little stuff, which was easily procured through his work associates.

He remained remarkably healthy and his need for doctoring was negligible. His major health problems were trauma related. He believed, to the extent that he thought about the future at all, that he would die on the streets, probably in a fight he had miscalculated or by being blindsided in a payback act. When he did require medical attention, such as to get an occasional antibiotic, he would use the hospital ER as his private health center, pushing his way past others to get at the head of the line. He always knew what he needed and could size up the attending staff member quickly and swing into one of his two dominant modes of getting it. He could act tough, cool, and efficient, with the tacit message of "This is what we both know I need. Give it to me and I'll get out of your space and your face. You wouldn't want me in your face." Or he'd turn on the charm and wheedle what he needed out of the staff. When the staff member was a woman, he knew how to sexualize the encounter or pull for a maternal response or a rescue fantasy. He was highly skilled at assessing situations quickly, and being who he needed to be.

This time, however, he could really be ill. The chest pains were different for him and were probably real, but he would not cooperate with the medical staff on the floor as they attempted to do a cardiac workup. They had his name and hospital number, as well as the information about the bar brawl, but that was it. He responded to their questions either with a caustic comment, an obvious lie, or the directive to "Get the hell away from me unless you're here to spring me from this place." They were not able to determine how much he'd been drinking, what drugs he was currently using, or any medical history that could possibly have implications for his heart. When asked about his parents' health history, Mickey snorted loudly and then looked away. The only procedure he would cooperate with was the start of an IV to prevent the DTs, a condition he knew enough about to want to avoid, and the promise of a drug infusion that he liked. He was verbally abusive to the pulmonary resident, a gentle young fellow trying to explore possible shortness of breath episodes. When the sedating drug would start to wear off, Mickey would scream and become especially abusive to the staff. It was a tough hour's wait before the next drug dose could be administered. Terms and phrases entered in his chart by the nursing staff included "obnoxious," "demanding", "unreasonable expectations," "will not obey rules," and "nasty to anyone trying to help." The institutional and individual countertransference to this horrendously difficult patient was frustration, then anger, and fantasies of how to get rid of him. It took all their collective and individual will not to lose their temper or professional demeanor, and not to do bodily harm to Mickey. The staff responded in a passive-aggressive way in not facilitating the workup either by reducing the number of steps and procedures or by speeding up the evaluation schedule. Ultimately Mickey left the hospital against medical advice with an incomplete workup. It was never determined if his cardiac symptoms were in fact real, or another ruse to end a bar brawl he was losing without losing face. This act also would have the secondary gain of getting some legal and legitimate drugs, at the taxpayers' expense.

Mickey H. can be diagnosed with Antisocial Personality Disorder (ASPD). Individuals with this disorder consistently live outside the law and social convention. They abuse and misuse others, typically without remorse. They behave as if without a conscience, expressing this through the lack of empathy, not feeling remorseful or guilty when they hurt others. According to psychoanalytic theory, the conscience (or superego) normally develops before 5 years of age as the child resolves his (or her) Oedipal (or Electra) complex. Negotiating this requires stable parents, at least a mother figure, who can provide a safe holding environment for the conflict resolution and superego development. The history of most antisocial characters is noteworthy for the absence of such parental consistency and opportunity for healthy attachment.

Individuals with ASPD habitually lie, cheat, and steal, are aggressive and impulsive, and live in the moment, with little or no thought of future consequences. A clinical assessment usually reveals the history of Conduct Disorder, beginning before the age of 15, and a stormy adolescence with significant disregard of social norms and the feelings or well-being of others.

These individuals do not come into treatment voluntarily to work on their personalities, but are frequently encountered in hospital ERs and in prisons. Individuals with ASPD often experience dysphoria, anxiety, and rage attacks, and they typically respond to these affects by acting out or self-medicating with alcohol or drugs, or both. Trying to take a reliable clinical history is nearly impossible as these characters lie and withhold information to advance their cause, whether to appear more frightening and dangerous or more benign, bending the facts so that past behaviors can appear almost reasonable. Individuals with ASPD may claim or fake an Axis I disorder as a "cover" for their antisocial exploits. However, comorbid Axis I conditions are prevalent with ASPD, including Major Depression, Bipolar Disorder, Panic Disorder, and Posttraumatic Stress Disorder (PTSD). Mood disorders are especially likely to develop as the individual reaches middle age. In addition, approximately 70% of people diagnosed with ASPD have a comorbid alcohol or substance use disorder (Black, 2001).

There is no treatment plan for Mickey H. because, once he has left the hospital, he is no longer a patient of any one or of any system. However, as long as he lives, he will be a member of society where he will continue to disregard, and often flout, its rules. While aware of the rules and laws, he does not feel they apply to him. If you or a system is bothered by his behavior, according to Mickey "then it's your problem, not mine." If he meets challenge or resistance, he will fight back, and he can be dangerous. This is why individuals with ASPD make up such a high percentage of the recidivist prisoner population.

Individuals with ASPD are no match for the average mental health clinician. An adequate assessment is nearly impossible. As they lie and do not cooperate with the process, a therapeutic alliance cannot be established. They lie easily because there is no conscience to keep them from lying. Whatever comes out of their mouth is their truth at the moment. It is also difficult to secure collateral or informant data, as they typically do not have a history of intimate or long-standing relationships, either personal or professional. Often their cohort is as socially impaired as they are. Even potentially treatable Axis I conditions are hard to diagnose as they might be faking positive or faking negative to advance their own agenda. Common agendas include securing controlled substances, someone else's money, or avoiding responsibility for their actions, criminal culpability, and apprehension by authorities.

We know nothing about Mickey's father. We do know something about his mother and certain features of ASPD can be seen in her, if not the full disorder. Although the disorder is far more prevalent in men, it presents in women as well. Clinical evidence suggests that there is a strong genetic contribution to this disorder. One major study of twin pairs found that there is a 69% likelihood of a second twin being diagnosable with ASPD if the first twin was so diagnosed (Fu et al., 2002). A meta-analysis of twin and adoption studies of the development of ASPD suggested that the disorder is more strongly influenced by genetic than by environmental and social learning factors (Rhee & Waldman, 2002).

Appropriate treatment options for Mickey H. are between few and nonexistent. If he would agree, the next time he presented at the ER it might be helpful to transfer him from the hospital to an inpatient facility specializing in the treatment of alcohol and substance use disorders. He might agree to this if he needed a safe haven at that time. It is doubtful he would cooperate with the program, but it would be worth a try. He is reaching old age, and some of these characters mellow a bit, becoming less hostile, violent, and impulsive. This could provide a window of opportunity where a previously rejected treatment might now be accepted. An inpatient setting would also enable a diagnosis of any Axis I condition and the implementation of reasonable treatment. Pharmacological treatment is very complicated for the individual with a substance abuse history. Certainly the social factors that contribute to and sustain his antisocial behaviors need to be identified and environmental engineering strategies applied where feasible. Are there socially acceptable ways for him to meet his needs? We know that having a personality disorder means having a limited and rigid repertoire of responses. Perhaps his being older might be used to convince him that things aren't going well for him now and that they can go better and he can get more if he does things differently. Then the challenge would be to help him learn how to do this.

Borderline Personality Disorder

Clinical Description

In trying to understand Borderline Personality Disorder, one may wonder what is the "border" to which the name of the disorder refers. Historically, and from a primarily psychoanalytic perspective, people with the disorder were theorized to be on the boundary—the borderline—between neurosis and psychosis, reflecting the severe nature of the syndrome (Stern, 1938/1986). Borderline Personality Disorder has also been referred to as *borderline personality organization* (Kernberg, 1975), *pseudo-neurotic psychosis,* and *pseudo-neurotic schizophrenia* (Hoch, Cattell, Strahl, & Penness, 1962), suggesting that underneath the overt neurotic-like symptoms was a much more profound thought disturbance. The terms also implied that people with the disorder often have the same profound and deleterious effects on the family as a blatantly psychotic person. In the original *DSM* (American Psychiatric Association, 1952), the concept of borderline psychopathology was officially named the "emotionally unstable personality," which, in our estimation, is a more accurate description of the core feature of the psychopathology (and is free of the psychoanalytic connotations) than the current name Borderline Personality Disorder. In a sense, it is ironic that the name of the disorder is as unstable as the people who suffer from it.

Borderline Personality Disorder is notable for extreme instability in interpersonal relationships, self-image, behaviors, and emotions. Sufferers are also extremely impulsive, which usually results in high risk, dangerous, and self-destructive behaviors, such as substance abuse, sexual promiscuity, reckless driving, compulsive spending, shoplifting, gambling, eating sprees, self-mutilation (e.g., cutting on the self but without the intent of killing oneself) and suicidal threats and behaviors (often with a history of multiple suicide attempts; Widiger & Trull, 1992). The dangerous and chronic self-mutilating nature of the borderline pathology was demonstrated by one of our patients, a 77-year-old woman, who blithely reported at intake that she had "tried to kill herself 76 times in the past 5 years" and wanted help to "get the job done right." She further reported a chronic history of parasuicidal and self-mutilating behaviors since her teen years, having had over 30 psychiatric hospitalizations and been treated by numerous outpatient clinicians, none of which were perceived by her as helpful.

People with Borderline Personality Disorder often feel chronically bored or empty and are perceived by others as manipulative, mercurial, demanding, and exasperating. They have a poorly defined or unclear sense of self and have the perception that they "do not know who they are" with concomitant uncertainty about their values, goals, loyalties, and career aspirations. There is little sense of meaning in life. Due to an often intense emotional dysregulation, their moods shift rapidly. It is common for the borderline individual to be angry, rageful, and hostile. They tend to rely on splitting as a defense mechanism, regarding themselves, the world, and others in black-or-white terms (e.g., "all good" or "all bad") and they can shift their perspective with alarming alacrity. This cognitive tendency toward dichotomous, "black-or-white" thinking leads the borderline individual to either idealize or demonize others. People with Borderline Personality Disorder are known to have intense and chaotic relationships: They can also be extraordinarily charming and tend to "suck people in" and then "spit them out" just as rapidly. This chronic vacillation between the idealization and devaluation of others often results in the severe and frequent social rejection of the person with the disorder.

In the clinical setting, it is common for borderline patients to present in a state of crisis, usually interpersonal in nature, with volatile and changing moods demonstrated throughout the session. Unsure of who they are at their core, and unable to tolerate and regulate negative emotions internally, they desperately seek the attention and support of others, and frantically seek to avoid real or imagined abandonment. However, because of a chronic inner conflict between fusion with others and abandonment, they may easily reject or become hostile toward the person whom they just pulled in closer, pushing the person away only to demand his or her attention and nurturance soon after, in a vicious cycle. Individuals with this disorder are typically experienced by others as compellingly painful to relate to. An additional feature is that those with this disorder may have brief periods of paranoia or dissociation when stressed, but otherwise their contact with reality is generally well maintained.

People with Borderline Personality Disorder are typically high users of psychiatric services (both inpatient and outpatient; Serin & Marshall, 2003) and can be a drain on mental health systems. Hollywood portrayals of Borderline Personality Disorder have appeared in several popular films including *Fatal Attraction* and *Single White Female*, demonstrating the often dramatic and severely dysfunctional nature of this disorder. Certainly, this disorder is among the more florid, provocative, and evocative of the personality disorders, and the pathology can be highly seductive. The *DSM-IV-TR* diagnostic criteria for Borderline Personality Disorder are shown in Table 3.2.

Potential Age-Bias of Criteria

Several experts have suggested that Borderline Personality Disorder is the most difficult personality disorder to accurately identify and diagnose in later life due to limitations in the diagnostic criteria to capture the manifestations of the disorder among older adults. In fact, there is considerable debate whether the disorder declines with age. Cross-sectional studies documenting lower levels of Borderline Personality Disorder in older versus younger persons (e.g., Coolidge, Burns, Nathan, & Mull, 1992; Segal, Hook, & Coolidge, 2001) may indicate a veridical decline in borderline symptomology across the life span. A competing explanation, however, is that the diagnostic criteria are inadequate in detecting manifestations or signs of the disorder in older adults (Rosowsky & Gurian, 1991, 1992). Reflecting on the lower prevalence of the disorder in older adults, Rosowsky and Gurian (1991) have suggested that this "could reflect more the lack of fit of our existing diagnostic yardsticks than the lack of Borderline Personality Disorder in old age. If there are individuals with Borderline Personality

Table 3.2   *DSM-IV-TR* Diagnostic Criteria for Borderline Personality Disorder (Code: 301.83)

A pervasive pattern of instability of interpersonal relationships, self-image, and affects, and marked impulsivity beginning by early adulthood and present in a variety of contexts, as indicated by five (or more) of the following:

(1) frantic efforts to avoid real or imagined abandonment. Note: Do not include suicidal or self-mutilating behavior covered in Criterion 5

(2) a pattern of unstable and intense interpersonal relationships characterized by alternating between extremes of idealization and devaluation

(3) identity disturbance: markedly and persistently unstable self-image or sense of self

(4) impulsivity in at least two areas that are potentially self-damaging (e.g., spending, sex, substance abuse, reckless driving, binge eating) Note: Do not include suicidal or self-mutilating behavior covered in Criterion 5

(5) recurrent suicidal behavior, gestures, or threats, or self-mutilating behavior

(6) affective instability due to a marked reactivity of mood (e.g., intense episodic dysphoria, irritability, or anxiety usually lasting a few hours and only rarely more than a few days)

(7) chronic feelings of emptiness

(8) inappropriate, intense anger or difficulty controlling anger (e.g., frequent displays of temper, constant anger, recurrent physical fights)

(9) transient, stress-related paranoid ideation or severe dissociative symptoms

Source: From *Diagnostic and Statistical Manual of Mental Disorders*, fourth edition, text revision, American Psychiatric Association, 2000, Washington, DC: Author. Copyright 2000 by American Psychiatric Association. Reprinted with permission.

Disorder in old age, as clinicians know there are, then we need to adapt our yardsticks to be able to identify them" (pp. 39–40). Several of the specific *DSM-IV-TR* criteria seem awkward or inappropriate in the context of later life and these are discussed next.

Criterion 1 (frantic efforts to avoid real or imagined abandonment) makes little sense in the case of physically frail older adults who must rely on care from others to meet their basic needs. Abandonment in this context can have catastrophic consequences, and as such, efforts to avoid it can reasonably reach frenzied proportions. We have seen the pattern in which aging individuals with Borderline Personality Disorder are extremely fearful of abandonment by their caregivers, constantly checking in with them and upping the ante of dependency. Criterion 3 (identity disturbance) does not apply well in cases when, for example, older adults (primarily women in the current cohort) seek psychotherapy because their lifelong role as a caregiver (to their spouse and children) no longer is necessary (e.g., after the spouse has died and the children have left the family home). We have seen many cases wherein older women in this situation have felt as if they "do not know what to do with themselves" and that they no longer have a strong sense of identity, direction, or purpose. What distinguishes this case from Borderline Personality Disorder is that the struggle to define oneself makes sense in the developmental context of role loss and does not reflect a core lifelong deficit in identity formation.

Criterion 4 (impulsivity in at least two areas that are potentially self-damaging) and Criterion 5 (recurrent suicidal behavior, gestures, or threats, or self-mutilating behavior) may also be a poor fit among older adults. As noted, impulsive behaviors naturally decline with advancing age. As such, some aging individuals with Borderline Personality Disorder may not show this particular sign. In an interesting study, Stevenson, Meares, and Comerford (2003) did indeed find diminished impulsivity in older patients with Borderline Personality Disorder compared to younger patients with the disorder. Another issue about these two criteria is that of mortality effects: People with severe expressions of these dangerous behaviors are at increased risk for early death. Thus, the lower prevalence rates in cross-sectional studies may not reflect declines in the symptoms over time but rather selective early mortality for some severe cases. These particular symptoms are also of concern in the clinical context as such behaviors in frail elderly can be fatal, even if the person did not intend to hasten death.

Finally, Criterion 6 (affective instability due to a marked reactivity of mood) and Criterion 8 (inappropriate, intense anger or difficulty controlling anger) may not apply well to some individuals in later life because of the natural tendency for older adults to become better at regulating and controlling their emotions. However, the available data suggest that, throughout the life span, affective instability and poorly controlled anger continue to be diagnostic benchmarks. These two features seem to be robust across the life span and effectively discriminate Borderline Personality Disorder from other personality disorders, even in later life (Rosowsky & Gurian, 1991).

Given the apparent problems with many (but not all) the criteria for Borderline Personality Disorder, some later-life borderlines will not be detected through routine application of the current diagnostic criteria. This puts the mental health field in a precarious catch-22 situation in forming a diagnosis: Disorders are defined by the diagnostic criteria, but if the criteria do not fit a particular group or subgroup (older adults in our examples), then those with proxy signs of the disorder cannot be formally diagnosed with the disorder, preventing further study of the phenomena and hampering treatment efforts. However, there are ways around this issue. When a patient meets four of the nine criteria for Borderline Personality Disorder (not five of nine as is required for formal diagnosis), then *Personality Disorder Not Otherwise Specified* may be indicated if the symptoms are pervasive and result in some impairment. A final point to understand is that because we treat people with problems (and not problems per se, in a vacuum), treatment can logically proceed and target the symptoms of personality pathology regardless of whether any diagnostic threshold is met.

Theorized Pattern in Later Life and Possible Impact of Aging

As noted, selective premature mortality due to risky behaviors and completed suicide serves to reduce rates of Borderline Personality Disorder in later life. Among those with this disorder in later life, however, a commonly observed pattern is for some of the symptoms to be significantly attenuated or "burned out" over time. One can imagine that the intense rage, physical fights, substance abuse, sexual acting out, self-mutilation, and other impulsive and physically punishing and taxing behaviors will be muted among many older adult sufferers. These behaviors seem to be either transcended or transmuted somewhere between early adulthood and old age (Rosowsky & Gurian,

1991). An example of a core symptom hypothesized to manifest differently in later life is anorexia, which may be a substitute for more obvious and provocative forms of self-mutilation seen in younger patients. Other geriatric variants of self-harming behaviors may include self-prescribed polypharmacy, refusal of needed medical attention, or sabotage of medical care (Rosowsky & Gurian, 1992). Changes in the phenomenology of identity disturbance manifest in later life as an inability to formulate future plans or pursue goal-directed behaviors (Rosowsky & Gurian, 1992). In contrast to expressions of the disorder likely to undergo age-related metamorphoses, some symptoms may be expressed similarly throughout life. Indeed, it seems unlikely that the effects of aging alone will have much impact on Borderline Personality Disorder features including chronic feelings of emptiness, unstable and intense interpersonal relationships, emotional lability, anger dyscontrol, and the reliance on splitting and other primitive defenses. Without intervention, these features will likely persist into later life. In some cases, the symptoms may even become more pronounced.

Increased dependency is a particular challenge likely to impact the aging individual with Borderline Personality Disorder. Older adults with the disorder are known to cause havoc on their move to assisted living facilities, rehabilitation hospitals, or skilled nursing facilities. They may intensely attach themselves to unsuspecting residents only to turn against them in a brief period. The borderline type is expert at turning people against each other (including staff) and generally creating chaos in relationships.

Older adults with this disorder will also likely have trouble negotiating relationships with caregivers. We have often seen the pattern where these individuals identify one or two professionals as the "good ones" and vehemently complain about and reject help from others, the "bad ones." To make matters worse, their preferences may change abruptly, which can confuse and anger the staff. Due to their underlying difficulties regulating interpersonal distance, older adults with Borderline Personality Disorder are also likely to struggle between wanting closeness and angrily rejecting it from caregiving staff. Another pattern may be attempts at manipulation of caregiving staff by distorting information about their past medical history or their compliance with medical and rehabilitative regimens. Their angry entitlement may serve to engender anger in the caregiving staff, or alternatively, helpless frustration (Rosowsky & Gurian, 1992).

A final aging issue is that many older adults with Borderline Personality Disorder come to later life with a minimal (or nonexistent) social support network. Many of them have worn out family members during a lifetime of crises and poor boundaries. Thus, aging in general can be viewed as extremely challenging for those with Borderline Personality Disorder. Individuals with this personality pathology perhaps are the least prepared to cope with the usual changes and stressors that accompany the late-life stage. Sadly, their relationships with psychotherapists are at great risk for mirroring the unstable and tumultuous patterns they enact with others. They are likely to foster splitting and specialness, and evoke negative countertransference reactions (Rosowsky & Gurian, 1991). A general tenet for the clinician is to be a model of stability, neither moving in too close to rescue patients who appear helpless and lost nor withdrawing and rejecting patients even when they seem to be asking for it.

The Case of Lenore: Borderline Personality Disorder

The consultation request came as a message left on the psychologist's answering machine, which began: "Hi, Doctor. This is Jane, the nurse over at Ashton Manor. There's a patient here whom I'd really like you to see. Her name is Lenore, and if you can't come and do something with her soon, I'll probably murder her."

The psychologist was able to stop by the skilled nursing facility on her way home, intending to look over the resident's chart and to set up an appointment for the assessment and consultation. As this was late in the day, a new group of nurses and aides had arrived for the evening shift. The charge nurse greeted the psychologist warmly and asked whom she had come to see. When told the resident was Lenore, and that the call to come in had seemed quite urgent, the nurse responded incredulously: "Lenore? I don't understand it. She hasn't been here that long, but she seems to be a sweetie; no bother. I don't know why you'd be called in about her."

The defense of splitting is central in the repertoire of those with a personality disorder in Cluster B, especially for those with Borderline Personality Disorder (BPD). The reality of the individual with BPD is notable for affective and cognitive experiences and distortions, which shift with remarkable alacrity to the extremes. There is no gray. People and events are experienced as all good or all bad. The splitting transcends multiple relationships and venues, typically wreaking havoc.

Many, perhaps most, individuals who develop a personality disorder have themselves experienced a seriously disordered childhood. Lenore's early history was no exception. She and her identical twin sister, Maureen, were their parents' only children, born when their parents were in their late 30s, considerably older parents than the norm in the 1920s.

Their parents had developed a strong relationship pattern over the more than 12 years of their marriage. The pattern was dysfunctional but comfortably familiar. Lenore's father was tough and distant, having poor regard for women. While always holding a job, he was a weekend drunk, becoming more argumentative and nasty as the weekend progressed. Most of his ire was taken out on his wife, but as the girls got older, they were included as objects of his frustration and rage. Lenore's mother would tolerate her husband's abuse, knowing that by Monday morning he would "clean up and fly right" again. She tried intermittently to protect the girls, but mostly she modeled helplessness and despair. On a few occasions when Lenore's father got especially out of control and the physical violence escalated, their mother took the twins to a cousin's house nearby for a day or two until the situation at home cooled off, at which point they would return home. The tacit rule was that no one would speak about their father's drinking or abusive behavior, or about the fear and inconsistency that permeated their lives. So the girls came to act this out, each in a very different way.

When the twins reached adolescence and became visibly sexual beings, their father's rage would be as easily directed at them as at their mother. As destructive as this was, by taking it, they felt they were in some way protecting their mother in a way that she was never able to protect them.

Lenore's way of dealing with her internal anguish and the helpless victimization at home was to run away, which she began doing at the age of 14. She would stay out of the house for 1 or 2 days, ultimately 3 or 4, and then return, tired and bruised, from the streets or from her own hand. By this time she had started to smoke cigarettes and to burn herself with the lit end. Her forearms and upper arms were marked by blisters, receding into small red circles. This behavior served as a release valve for her feelings of rage which were often threatening to explode. Feeling pain was a way to stop feeling pain.

When she was on the streets, she would engage in sex with anyone who offered to buy her a meal, give her smokes or whiskey, or tell her he loved her. When she would return home, her mother would most often ignore her. At other times, she would yell hysterically, wailing about the worry and concern Lenore's absence had caused. These emotional outbursts would often follow an especially brutal weekend at the hands of her husband.

Maureen's way of handling her pain was very different from her twin's. She did not physically run away. Rather, she learned to stay very still and not flinch, even when her father molested her, which he came to do. But she ran away inside, withdrawing to a point of dissociation, to a place where she felt no pain. In time, the memories became blurred as though through gauze, and in yet more time, vanished altogether. Intermittently she would refuse to eat, starving herself with the magical promise of retreating into a little child's frame.

When Lenore was 17, she left home for the final time. She took a job at a deli shop, waiting on tables and serving behind the counter. She was intelligent and learned fast and was calmed by the repetitive structure of the work. The older couple that owned the shop liked Lenore and allowed her to occupy a room in an apartment above the shop for little rent. And of course she was able to eat very well at no cost. Occasionally she would feel the need to run, and would stay out all night, but the couple was willing to indulge her little slips as they increasingly came to count on her as an employee and a young all-around helper. On the occasions when they would challenge her behavior, she would fly into a rage and threaten to kill herself if they in any way implied that they might dismiss her. Of course her threats kept them in line, precisely what they were intended to do.

Lenore had many boyfriends, but none lasted. Initially she was agreeable, actually quite charming to suitors, but in time they would say or do something to induce panic in her, which she would act out in rage to save her life; accusing, threatening, and always inducing chaos into the relationship. After several such episodes, most of her lovers would cut and run, but one stayed. This was Jack, who came to work as the short-order cook, in time becoming the manager and ultimately the owner of the deli.

They courted briefly and were married. This began a relatively settled period for Lenore. Her impulsivity, affective lability, and self-harming behaviors became calmed in the steady presence of Jack and their work together at the deli. Indeed, Lenore's passionate and enthusiastic tendencies were put to good use as the couple modernized the deli and developed a thriving business. They had two children, a girl and then a boy who died shortly after his birth. Lenore would have no more babies after that. Her mothering was inconsistent, alternating between being overly close and attentive, and being remote and unavailable. Fortunately for their daughter, Jack's temperamental evenness served as a counterbalance to Lenore's erratic behaviors. Their daughter grew up well with the support of the jovial ambience at the deli where she spent much of her childhood.

Lenore was stable until her twin's suicide at age 35. Maureen had been in and out of psychiatric institutions for much of her adult life, leaving Lenore feeling painful survivor's guilt, which overwhelmed her when her twin died. Her profound grief was experienced as blinding rage evolving into a psychosis, which was transient and resolved quickly. She was hospitalized and received shock treatments, which were a major psychiatric treatment at that time. A lengthy stay in the hospital, and perhaps the treatments, appeared to quiet her demons and to contain her. When she returned home, she appeared thinner, weary, and noticeably less animated.

Things changed dramatically after her husband's death and the sale of the deli, which soon followed. Lenore's somewhat subdued demeanor now deteriorated significantly. She became irritable, critical, and demanding. She would call her daughter numerous times during the day to complain about anything and everything, often directing the conversation to provoke a squabble that she ended by slamming down the receiver, or by accusing her daughter of not caring and being unconcerned about her welfare. "What difference does it make to you? You don't care if I live or die."

A smoker all her life, Lenore ultimately developed emphysema. This, in addition to hypertension and coronary artery disease made her life become more circumscribed. She began to drink more in the evenings alone, which did not mix well with either her multiple medications or her impulsive tendencies. Lenore's daughter, a career woman in a responsible position, would visit her mother infrequently because the visits were marked by angry hostility, manipulativeness, and veiled threats of self-harm. When, during one visit, it became apparent that Lenore was at real risk, her daughter, through the family physician, arranged for Lenore to be hospitalized for evaluation and stabilization. This was not a courtesy admission, as Lenore actually was at risk. She was smoking while using oxygen, was drinking alcohol abusively, and was not taking her medications reliably. The hospital determined that because of hardening of the arteries, her mental status was mildly compromised. This, in conjunction with her aggressive outbursts and emotional lability, led to the recommendation that she be discharged to a nursing home where she could be monitored and provided a constant level of skilled care. Lenore was furious but agreed to go for a while, actually feeling somewhat relieved to be spared the isolation of living alone. At least in the nursing home there would be company and new people to care for her and to love her.

Initially she was pleasant to the staff and other residents. She would ask questions about their lives and expect that they would do the same. But quickly events began to irritate her. She would become angry if an aide cut her stories off or attention to her seemed too brief. She became very aware of who among the staff were really interested in her, and who didn't like her and couldn't wait to get away from her. These quickly became the good guys and the bad guys.

Lenore became very jealous of other residents who, she perceived, got more attention, better service, or more food than she did. In time, this jealousy escalated to rage and acting out. Lenore began to take food from these residents' plates, resulting in her being banned from the dining room for the next meal or the next day. Soon she was eating most of her meals in her room. This made her even more angry to the point where she would throw her food tray across the room or, on one occasion, physically lash out at the dietary aide when she came to remove Lenore's tray.

Her favorite nurse and aide were on the same late afternoon shift. For them, she had a smile and was charming. They were both baffled by the report from the other shifts and did not agree with the punishment of barring Lenore from the dining room. At mealtimes when they were on duty, Lenore was allowed to eat with the other residents, who mostly ignored her and gave her wide berth.

Lenore demanded to be taken out several times a day for a cigarette break. This was an inconvenience to the nursing home as it required that a staff member be assigned to Lenore to disconnect her from the portable oxygen and accompany her to an outside, screened-in area where smoking was permitted. Lenore was allowed three such breaks each day. She would, in anticipation of these, place herself in front of the nursing station and verbally, loudly, harass the staff if they were a minute late to take her outside. While waiting, she would make lewd and derisive comments to other residents who were speaking with staff at the station. She was especially likely to pick on the more cognitively impaired residents, calling out terrible things to them. Her repeated verbal abuse of one such resident—a gentle, meek woman favored by the staff—became the active precipitant of the call for a consultation: "If you can't come and do something with her soon, I'll probably murder her."

The consultant began by meeting with the staff to identify Lenore's problem behaviors, defined as those behaviors that were most disturbing to the staff and caused most interference with her care. Staff initially identified the following behaviors:

- She rarely had any visitors because her daughter disliked coming to see her and was often angry at her mother for excessive, angry phone calls. This put pressure on the staff to socialize with her.
- She was a food stealer.
- She was verbally abusive to staff and to other residents.
- She yelled if her needs weren't met immediately.
- She split the staff, so that they argued among themselves about her care.

The next phase identified the antecedents and consequences of these problem behaviors. When she got angry with staff, she placed angry phone calls to her daughter. The consequences of this were that Lenore's daughter avoided visits and became angry with the staff for not being more attentive to her mother and making sure

Lenore didn't make excessive calls at inappropriate times. The staff then became angrier with Lenore and less likely to want to attend to her. The maladaptive pattern was identified and discussed.

The next aspect of the consultation was to share Lenore's story (her personal history) to encourage staff to get to know her and how she might feel and think. This knowledge would provide a context for her behaviors, even the most irritating ones. What might be the message of such behaviors? For example, stealing food might mean, "I need to be fed. I'm hungry for attention and love. If you won't offer it, I'll take it. I need sustenance to survive."

The next aspect of the consultation served to explore the effect of Lenore's behaviors on the system of the nursing home. The staff was encouraged to identify those resident traits that they most valued, and alternatively those that made their jobs most difficult. How did they feel about these residents? What was the effect of these feelings on their behavior? The concept of splitting was discussed, including its adaptive and maladaptive functions.

The consultation then moved toward an intervention/treatment plan. The staff was asked to note everything that had been tried with Lenore. The effect of these attempts was appraised as either having helped, worsened, or had no effect at all on the behavior. The tendency to do things over again, only more vigorously, when not successful, was talked about as being universal. Understanding this opened up staff to trying something new and to discontinuing responses to Lenore that had not been helpful in the past.

Last, the problem behaviors were reviewed and ranked in terms of their negative effect. The questions to the staff about each specific behavior were addressed. How would you know if this gets better? How would improvement be identified?

These then become the intervention goals. Each goal was then operationalized and its probability of success anticipated. A goal was selected to work on and a treatment intervention was delineated and agreed on. Staff understood that all staff had to be on board, and that the response to Lenore's behavior had to be consistent among staff and across shifts. The first goal selected for Lenore was food stealing.

The intervention was outlined as follows: Lenore would be seated at a table with other residents who were sufficiently cognitively intact to support appropriate socialization and conversation. A staff member would sit at the table. The presence of a staff member would serve three functions: To model appropriate communal dining skills (including eating off one's own plate only, and asking for extra food if desired), to facilitate conversation at the table, and to talk with Lenore directly, asking her questions to draw out what she could positively and literally bring to the table. When this was successful (operationalized as 4 successive days with no food stealing), the staff member would then just accompany Lenore to the table and connect her conversationally with her dining mates. When this was successful (a week without food-stealing incidents), the staff member would then simply bring Lenore to the table, settle her, and withdraw.

In addition, after each successful meal, the staff member would give Lenore positive feedback, complimenting her on her behavior and rewarding her with a few extra minutes of conversation and attention.

Although the intervention would be somewhat labor intensive for the short term, all agreed that it would be worthwhile if successful. A follow-up meeting with the consultant was scheduled to review the effect of the intervention on Lenore's behavior and on the staff.

The interventions for the other goals followed this same pattern: goal selection, operationalization of its effectiveness, implementation, assessment, and feedback. With each achieved success, the staff became more unified, proficient with the protocol, and committed to behavioral interventions. Staff came to appreciate that, especially with the more intractable personality disordered residents, the greatest positive change is often most readily achieved through a small change by the system.

Histrionic Personality Disorder

Clinical Description

The essential features of this personality disorder are excessive emotionality and attention-seeking behavior. These individuals are uncomfortable when not the center of attention and characteristically engage in overly dramatic, excessive, exaggerated, and affected emotional displays for which the primary goal is to secure attention and admiration from others. They may present themselves in a sexually seductive, flirtatious, and provocative manner and are concerned with their physical appearance. Their dress and speech are often flamboyant to maximize the attention they receive. They frequently have a long history of drawing attention to themselves and of engaging in excited emotional displays with overstated theatricality as if they are playing to an audience. Their speech is often vague, excessively impressionistic, and lacking in detail.

When they are not successful at maintaining the social spotlight, people with Histrionic Personality Disorder typically respond with anger and frustration. In the clinical setting, they may try to sexually engage the clinician with dramatic stories of their sexual escapades. In general, they try to sexualize the professional relationship and keep it superficial. During the early course of treatment, one of our older patients wore provocative outfits to her sessions, flirted openly and regularly, and shared details of her sexual prowess and current conquests. In later sessions, however, she revealed that she derived little real joy from sex, had been celibate for several years, and was scared of intimacy.

Underneath their bubbly, outgoing, and superficially charming facade, people with Histrionic Personality Disorder tend to be shallow, self-centered, and have a strong need for social approval. They are adept at forming new relationships and often create positive first impressions, but lasting and deep relationships are less likely to occur. Their relationships usually crumble because they turn out to be superficial, are one-sided, and lack true intimacy. Their emotional expressions are shallow, frequently changing, and overblown. They often become needy, dependent, childlike, and demanding with others, which can result in their rejection. They are easy suggestible and influenced by others, likely as an attempt to secure affection. Sadly, they tend to perceive their relationships to be more intimate than they actually are, and often provide exaggerated accounts of their social successes. Their flamboyancy and superficial charm were demonstrated by one of our patients, an elderly woman, who had some occupational success as a greeter for a large retail store. Whereas she described providing dramatic and theatrical welcomes that reportedly thrilled visitors to the

Table 3.3　*DSM-IV-TR* **Diagnostic Criteria for Histrionic Personality Disorder (Code: 301.50)**

A pervasive pattern of excessive emotionality and attention seeking, beginning by early adulthood and present in a variety of contexts, as indicated by five (or more) of the following:

(1) is uncomfortable in situations in which he or she is not the center of attention

(2) interaction with others is often characterized by inappropriate sexually seductive or provocative behavior

(3) displays rapidly shifting and shallow expression of emotions

(4) consistently uses physical appearance to draw attention to self

(5) has a style of speech that is excessively impressionistic and lacking detail

(6) shows self-dramatization, theatricality, and exaggerated expression of emotion

(7) is suggestible, i.e., easily influenced by others or circumstances

(8) considers relationships to be more intimate than they actually are

Source: From *Diagnostic and Statistical Manual of Mental Disorders*, fourth edition, text revision, American Psychiatric Association, 2000, Washington, DC: Author. Copyright 2000 by American Psychiatric Association. Reprinted with permission.

store, her social life, in reality, was replete with failed relationships and superficiality. The *DSM-IV-TR* diagnostic criteria for Histrionic Personality Disorder are shown in Table 3.3.

Potential Age-Bias of Criteria

Criterion 2 (interaction with others is often characterized by inappropriate sexually seductive or provocative behavior) may be a poor fit for many in later life because of the reduced number of potential sexual partners, especially among older women who greatly outnumber older men. Nonetheless, older adults may still meet this criterion if they are inappropriately provocative and seductive despite any real intention of creating a sexual relationship. Criterion 7 (is suggestible, that is, easily influenced by others or circumstances) may be problematic especially when cognitive impairments are present (e.g., poor planning and impaired judgment) and in cases where very frail older adults do not have much actual control over their environments. Being easily influenced ("going with the flow and not causing any problems") may, in fact, be encouraged and rewarded in some long-term care settings. Care must be taken to evaluate whether the suggestibility reflects a lifelong deficit or is an expectable reaction to their present circumstances (cognitive and social).

Theorized Pattern in Later Life and Possible Impact of Aging
Older adults with Histrionic Personality Disorder are often described by their adult children as "acting like spoiled children." Their self-centeredness and shallowness do not appear to diminish with age. Older individuals with this disorder are particularly intolerant of the physical changes that come with age (e.g., wrinkles, hair loss, sagging body parts) since their self-worth is based largely on superficial characteristics such as physical appearance. Because of their lifelong reliance on their physical attributes to attract attention, older histrionics may respond to normal physical changes by becoming excessive users of plastic surgery and other antiaging techniques. One of our older patients spent down her entire savings on surgery to prevent becoming "an icky old lady."

Similarly, we have seen many cases in which older individuals with Histrionic Personality Disorder have a poor adjustment to aging when their flirtatious and seductive style becomes less rewarded. Comorbid depression frequently occurs. Because seductiveness has been part of their social role for so long, aging individuals with Histrionic Personality Disorder are often baffled about how to relate to others without "attracting them." They often perceive the reductions in their sex appeal as catastrophic because they have established little other means to garner attention and affection from others.

Retirement may be a particular source of distress for the older histrionic type especially if the person used the work environment as the stage on which to perform. In cases in which the histrionic person married and maintained the relationship, widowhood may be notably damaging because the individual will have great difficulties cultivating new relationships and sources of support. Increased dependency (due to physical or cognitive problems) is likely to also result in significant problems for the aging histrionic. Whereas they may be perceived initially as warm, friendly, and entertaining by other residents and caregiving staff, their self-centeredness will eventually be discovered, resulting in negative responses and shunning. The resulting petulance and irritability on the part of the histrionic individual often makes matters worse.

The Case of Thelma: Histrionic Personality Disorder

Thelma E. swept into the office carrying a large blue shopping bag from Tiffany's in one hand and an oversized alligator handbag in the other. Her petite frame was dwarfed by them. With a great sigh, she unloaded her burden. Placing the bags on the floor, she scanned the office, trying to decide which seat to claim, finally deciding on a large recliner situated across from the therapist's chair. She proceeded to push the chair closer to the therapist's, sat down, pulled the lever to extend the footrest, and began.

"Whew. I am so glad to be here. I absolutely need to talk with someone. I'm having such problems and I'm driving my daughter nuts. She was the one who told me I absolutely had to talk to someone. She's tired of listening to me. She probably thinks I'm crazy. Anyway, she can't give me the advice I really need. But I'm counting on you. I really don't know what to do. I'm like a kid, but this is really serious." She takes a breath and continues.

"I brought you pictures," pointing to the blue bag on the floor, "so you could see him. He's really a doll. And maybe you can help me understand what's going on and tell me what I should do."

Thelma is a 71-year-old woman who appears to be in her mid-50s, and dresses as if she were in her 20s. She is very pretty in a doll-like way. Her hair is an unnatural shade of red. She wears it sleek and smooth with bangs just barely touching her eyebrows. When she speaks, she often sweeps the bangs aside in a little girl gesture. She bats her eyes and giggles, especially when she becomes excited or anxious. Good genes, cosmetic surgeries, extravagant self-care, and skill with makeup enable her youthful appearance. She and her daughter, in her 40s, are typically taken to be sisters. This error is consistently pleasing to Thelma.

Thelma, growing up, was always considered a dramatic child. She was prone to tantrums, petulance, and great gushing tears at the least provocation. She was also adorable. Her high spirit and passion were expressed with hugs and kisses that would make people feel warmly toward her. As an adult, she came to give lavish gifts and to acknowledge every event with cards and flowers. She was especially fond of sending balloon bouquets when these were popular. Balloons were favorites of hers as a child.

As a young child, Thelma lost her mother suddenly in an automobile accident. One night she went to bed and awoke the next morning without a mother. Her father was overcome by grief following the loss of his wife and soothed himself by further throwing himself into his work and consuming considerable alcohol at home after work. Thelma was mostly cared for by her maternal grandmother. A nice and well-intentioned woman, she was dealing with her own grief at the loss of her daughter. While she loved her granddaughter, she was also resentful at being called on to be responsible for a child at this stage of her life.

As adorable and outgoing as Thelma appeared, underneath she was a lonely little girl who was unattached at a deep level and terribly fearful of again being abandoned by whomever she loved, as she had been by her mother. To counter this she became more endearing to engage the overt expressions of love, and more demanding, to test that love. She danced, hugged, and tantrummed her way around the hearts of others.

A second wounding abandonment came just as Thelma began adolescence. Her father became involved with and then married a divorced woman with a son 3 years older than Thelma. Bruce was a lanky adolescent. He was as quiet and careful as Thelma was outgoing and impulsive.

Thelma, hungry for the love and attention of a mother, tried to get this from her stepmother by doing what she knew best how to do: smile, prance, hug, and giggle, but to little avail. Her stepmother was indifferent to Thelma's charms, valuing instead the quiet centeredness and studiousness of her son. She was in no way cruel to Thelma, but mostly just tolerated her. When she did show positive regard, it was for the benefit of her husband's approval as she was determined to make this second marriage work.

Thelma's father was predictably oblivious to her presence, let alone to her maturation. He was unaware of Thelma's shift away from him and his wife toward seeking the attention of her older brother. Bruce was initially flustered by her attention and flirtatiousness, then engaged by it, and ultimately aroused.

Thelma remains unclear about what actually transpired between her and her stepbrother. What is clear is that something did transpire. Although the duration and precise specifics of their involvement are vague in her memory, Thelma did get from Bruce the love and attention she sought. She reports she was "a happy teenager" and claims to have missed her brother very much when he went off to college, marking the end of their special relationship.

From this relationship, Thelma refined her skills at attracting the attention of boys, and later men, to reassure herself that she could procure the love she needed, and that the resources would not be depleted. She was not an apt student, but completed a junior college course in retailing. She took a position after graduation as an assistant manager of a cosmetics section in a department store. She worked for only a few years before marrying a hard-working, somewhat withdrawn, and slightly older man who thought he had won the prize of his life with Thelma's acceptance of his marriage proposal.

Thelma was content being a housewife and staying at home to raise her only child, a daughter, Elaine. She had a broad circle of friends and was considered the life of parties, her own and others. Her relationship with friends was, however, notable for her often being in conflict with someone. Thelma would become furious at any slight or mildly critical comment, and fly into a rage, talking against one person to others, and calling the offending individual and letting him or her have it. When the world turned mean and ugly, Thelma turned to her husband for comfort and support, engaging him as his little girl, weeping and trembling. He would respond, soothe her panic, and, after the crisis had abated, she would return to essentially ignoring him. He would await the next crisis, which could be counted on to arise.

When her husband was in his mid-60s, he suffered a major heart attack, and spent some months recovering in Florida. Thelma felt chained to him during that period, unused to sustained proximity and not liking it. They owned a small condominium in Florida that they had used during the winter months. Thelma would spend most of the winter there, preferring the sun to the snow. Their pattern was for her husband to join her for a 2-week vacation sometime during the season. The rest of the time, they would stay in contact by phone.

Thelma quickly established herself at the center of the social life of the Florida community. Playing tennis and bridge, she was a welcome addition to the condo complex and the country club. She was younger, and appeared even younger, than many of the residents. She was attractive and dressed provocatively. Thelma aroused the jealousy of some of the women, and the attention of some of the men.

Soon after her husband had recovered and returned to work and their customary geographically separated relationship, Thelma began an affair with a recently widowed man that continued over several winter seasons. This was a secret from her husband, but not from most others. When her lover found a new partner, and became engaged to be married, he broke off the relationship with Thelma. She became absolutely enraged, feeling at once both abandoned and humiliated by the rejection. She had never considered that her lover might, in time, want something more than a winter affair. Thelma had her first major depressive episode around that time. She was treated by her internist who prescribed initially a tricyclic antidepressant. As the episode resolved, she was prescribed an anxiolytic (described by Thelma as a "mother's little helper") that was popular at the time. Psychotherapy or counseling was not suggested to Thelma.

Other brief affairs followed. None were serious, but collectively they served to reestablish Thelma's confidence in her ability to attract the attention of men and to heal her wounded self-esteem. When her husband suffered a second heart attack, which he did not survive, Thelma found herself a grieving wife and an available widow. She sold the family home in the suburbs and bought a small condo in the city. She sold the small condo in Florida and bought a larger unit in the same community. At this point, she began to live in Florida for 9 months of the year, and in the city for 3 months, using it also for occasional weekends to visit her daughter, now married and the mother of two children. Thelma did not envision herself as a grandmother, but frequently sent the children gifts and cute cards signed, "With love from Thelma."

Life was easy. Thelma was sparkly and popular and had lots of activity. Between tennis and bridge and dinner parties, she was busy and content. Then she met a man at the club who, as she recounts, "Just blew me away. He was so handsome. I got tongue-tied just making small talk with him. I felt like a kid all over again."

His name was Mark, and he and his wife owned a condo in a nearby community and had recently joined the country club. His wife never appeared at the club. Thelma pursued Mark vigorously, and soon they would be playing mixed doubles tennis and having postgame and predinner drinks at the club bar.

In time, Thelma learned that Mark's wife was seriously ill. She was homebound and required 24-hour care. Mark had hired care for her during the days and cared for her himself at night. Soon a sexual affair developed. They would meet at Thelma's home during the day. As Mark was unavailable in the evening, Thelma maintained her usual social network and activities. She says about Mark, "He's the love of my life. I waited all my life to really fall in love. He is so sexy, and we like the same things. We even have the same favorite restaurant. We're so perfect together. I just don't get it."

They kept in touch by phone during the summer months when each lived in a different city, an airplane trip distance apart. During the second summer, Mark's wife died. Thelma says, "This put me in a strange spot. I tried to be supportive. I sent him nice cards with sweet messages, but he didn't seem to want to talk to me. I started having trouble even reaching him. I'd get the damn machine, and he wouldn't return some of my calls; most of my calls, really. First when I heard she died, I thought that after a decent period we could come out as a real couple. I knew we were perfect together. I thought we'd get married. I'm not sure about that, but at least we'd be a couple. We never talked about it, of course, because his wife was still alive. But I knew he felt the same way I did. So I couldn't understand why he didn't seem to want my support. I figured he needed time. So I damn well gave him time, and then I really got mad. So I left a few messages on the answering machine that I shouldn't have. He called me once and said for me to back off, please. If I really cared, I would leave him alone for now. So I hung on to that, for now like it was a lifeline." At this point she broke into tears and curled herself into a ball in the big recliner.

Thelma has presented with a lifelong pattern of thinking, feeling, and behaving consistent with a diagnosis of Histrionic Personality Disorder (HPD). Her presentation, while reflecting the unique contexts and relations of different life stages, continues to reflect the pathology and causes her and others with whom she in relationship considerable distress. Consider the following diagnostic criteria for HPD, and how these are expressed by Thelma.

She is melodramatic and requires being the center of attention. Only when all eyes are on her, can she connect with others and, even then, it is often for the purpose of attracting attention to herself or endearing them to her.

Although not grossly inappropriate, her physical presentation and clothing choices are patently seductive. As she has aged, her sense of style, fashion, and makeup have not kept up. She continues to dress and present herself in a flirtatious, overly youthful manner.

She is emotionally labile, shifting rapidly in her emotional expressions. Her face and body are hyperexpressive, continually in motion exhibiting joy, sadness, disbelief, emotions easily read like shifting sands. This is mirrored by her speech and language—colorful and notable for hyperbole.

Most relevant perhaps to her current crisis is a propensity to imbue relationships with much greater intimacy and value than is warranted.

The psychotherapy treatment plan needs to focus on consideration of the specific stressor, or precipitant. In this case it is her perceived rejection by Mark. The realities are that Thelma and Mark have been in a sexual relationship for 2 years and that Mark's wife of more than 45 years has recently died. His relationship with Thelma, while meeting his needs for companionship during this trying stage of his own life, held no promises of future plans. He enjoyed Thelma, they were easy and comfortable with each other and enjoyed good times. However, Mark could not envision life beyond his wife's death, and certainly not what he might want in a life partner at some future time.

Although never discussed directly with Mark, Thelma adopted her fantasy as reality, and planned for the two of them to emerge as a committed couple following a reasonable period after his wife's death. Until that time, Thelma envisioned herself as his life support; waiting patiently in the wings until he was ready to come forth to proclaim his love and fidelity. However, Mark did not behave in accordance with her fantasy script. His grief for his wife was real and deep. Their relationship had been far more intimate than the one he believed he could develop with Thelma.

Thelma responded to his rejection initially with anger and then depression. She developed neurovegetative symptoms including loss of appetite and weight, trouble sleeping, and loss of pleasure and initiative. She was also tearful, and alternated between periods of agitation and lethargy.

The treatment incorporated psychopharmacology. Her anxiolytic was gradually discontinued and an antidepressant medication was introduced. Thelma was also prescribed a nonbenzodiazepine to help her sleep. The aim of the talking therapy included four sequential segments.

The therapist would serve as a reliable presence for comfort and support, and to diminish her sense of helplessness. This would enable Thelma to restore her self-esteem through reviewing past competencies, strengths, and successful relationships.

To revisit the events leading to and comprising this crisis, as both a specific occurrence and as an exemplar of a pattern, Thelma would be encouraged to consider how she shifts fantasy to reality and to achieve some appreciation of another's phenomenology, in this instance, Mark's. She would be led to understand that while another's experience could affect her, it was not about her, and usually not intended to hurt her.

Thelma would be coached around recognizing the different depths and qualities of relationships, and how she might distinguish between them. She would also be coached to recognize her escalating affect and check it against the reality of experience.

Another essential aspect of the treatment would be to help Thelma achieve a sense of control when she feels her feelings are controlling her behaviors. To that end, stress management techniques would be introduced into the sessions and as lifestyle change homework between sessions.

The frequency of the therapy sessions was established in accordance with Thelma's clinical needs, but the frame of the therapeutic contract was held firm. This is especially important in work with patients with personality disorders. As her feelings of helplessness and anxiety receded, her sense of self-cohesion and efficacy became restored, and the between-session intervals were extended. In time, she planned to return to Florida and a last session was scheduled. Rather than a good-bye, a check-in visit was scheduled for during the summer when she would next be in the area. At this time, she would be able to report back to the therapist about how she was faring and how she was using her new learning. At this time, she appeared well and fit and said "I'm feeling like myself again, only better. Maybe a little more grown up. Anyway, thanks for your help. You've been a doll."

Narcissistic Personality Disorder

Clinical Description

The narcissistic personality is characterized by an exaggerated or grandiose sense of self-importance and an illusion of being unique or "special" that lead to feelings of entitlement. Such persons overestimate their abilities, popularity, and power, frequently coming across as self-centered, conceited, and boastful. They are typically preoccupied with themselves and their self-affirming fantasies of unlimited success, fame, intellectual sophistication, power, and beauty. Sadly, their excessive self-regard is equaled only by their cavernous misperception—they think and expect that others should recognize their superiority, special talents, and uniqueness. Underneath, it is presumed that the narcissist feels inadequate and dependent, with fragile self-esteem (Kernberg, 1975). The narcissistic type often responds to negative feedback with intense rage and attempts to degrade those who were critical, presumably in an attempt to bolster fragile self-esteem.

Another feature is that the narcissistic type has a strong need to be admired by others and frequently fishes for compliments. They also lack sensitivity and compassion for others and have difficulty understanding the needs, feelings, and perspectives of others. Interpersonally, they are exploitative, chronically seeing others as unimportant and unworthy. As such, they are prone to take advantage of others because they see their own needs as primary. They choose to associate only with the "best" doctors and the most gifted professionals and peers. When they find themselves in situations where they are not surrounded by people they perceive as being as special, high status, and privileged as themselves, they respond with demeaning, arrogant, and haughty behaviors. Their entitlement is often expressed as expecting especially favorable treatment (without earning it) and having others comply with their requests, no matter how unreasonable. They expect that the world and others "owe them" without assuming reciprocal responsibilities. As such, their near-total preoccupation with themselves massively disturbs interpersonal relationships and their occupational opportunities. The *DVM-IV-TR* diagnostic criteria for Narcissistic Personality Disorder are shown in Table 3.4.

Table 3.4   *DSM-IV-TR* **Diagnostic Criteria for Narcissistic Personality Disorder (Code: 301.81)**

A pervasive pattern of grandiosity (in fantasy or behavior), need for admiration, and lack of empathy, beginning by early adulthood and present in a variety of contexts, as indicated by five (or more) of the following:

(1) has grandiose sense of self-importance (e.g., exaggerates achievements and talents, expects to be recognized as superior without commensurate achievements)

(2) is preoccupied with fantasies of unlimited success, power, brilliance, beauty, or ideal love

(3) believes that he or she is "special" and unique and can only be understood by, or should associated with, other special or high-status people (or institutions)

(4) requires excessive admiration

(5) has a sense of entitlement, i.e., unreasonable expectations of especially favorable treatment or automatic compliance with his or her expectations

(6) is interpersonally exploitative, i.e., takes advantage of others to achieve his or her own ends

(7) lacks empathy: is unwilling to recognize or identify with the feelings and needs of others

(8) is often envious of others or believes that others are envious of him or her

(9) shows arrogant, haughty behaviors or attitudes

Source: From *Diagnostic and Statistical Manual of Mental Disorders,* fourth edition, text revision, American Psychiatric Association, 2000, Washington, DC: Author. Copyright 2000 by American Psychiatric Association. Reprinted with permission.

Potential Age-Bias of Criteria

Most of the criteria for Narcissistic Personality Disorder seem to apply reasonably well in the later-life context although some minor issues are worth noting. Criterion 6 (is interpersonally exploitative, that is, takes advantage of others to achieve his or her own ends) may be somewhat problematic because of the actual reductions in power and influence experienced by many in later life, especially those who had high-powered occupations from which they are removed. With real reductions in control and power come reduced opportunities to exploit others, especially in work settings.

Criterion 8 (is often envious of others or believes that others are envious of him or her) may also be somewhat concerning, especially when the aging individual experiences serious financial and health problems. In this context, common to later life, being somewhat envious of others who are healthier and financially secure would not be unreasonable. Conversely, older adults still meet this criterion if they habitually think that others are envious of them, especially if this belief lacks merit. Sadly, there is little reason to think that the core features of the disorder (exaggerated sense of self-importance, arrogance, need for admiration, and limited capacity for empathy) will improve simply as a result of aging.

Theorized Pattern in Later Life and Possible Impact of Aging

The narcissist type has a particularly poor prognosis with advancing age. In fact, a host of aging issues impinge negatively on the individual with Narcissistic Personality Disorder. They sometimes come to later life alone, isolated, and bitter about their lack of success. One of our patients lamented, "Life never gave me the special treats I deserved." In other cases, they come into old age with great histories of accomplishment, although they often can no longer maintain that success. Alienation of family members is common due to a lifetime of perceived callous disregard for and purposeful manipulation of others in their family. Relationships with spouses and friends are usually impaired due to the narcissistic individual's lifelong patterns of being demanding, insensitive, and self-centered.

With advancing age, people with Narcissistic Personality Disorder frequently suffer narcissistic injuries when they lose power and prestige and receive messages from society that devalue older persons. Aging narcissists typically cannot handle usual, age-related changes in their appearance (e.g., hair loss, wrinkles, shrinking muscle mass) because they perceive signs of age as detracting from their superiority over others. Similarly, physical illness and bodily deterioration impact the narcissist's view of the self as better than others and not subject to the kinds of problems that many others experience. One of our older narcissistic patients bemoaned in therapy that he "thought he could beat aging" and became despondent when he showed physical signs of aging and also developed a limp due to severe arthritis.

Another problem is that the continuous streams of praise required by the narcissist usually diminish with advancing age, frequently leading to severe depression. This pattern is especially noteworthy in cases where the narcissistic person did manage to achieve some measure of prestige and success in the occupational sphere. At an earlier stage in life, the person may have been bolstered by the ability to wield power over subordinates and also to reap praise from them. With retirement, the aging narcissist often begins to feel powerless and deflated, and in reaction, responds with even greater demands for admiration which often go unheeded. Imagine the loss of prestige and power likely to be experienced by Donald Trump, who in later life, will no longer be able to espouse his business acumen; fire people on his television show, *The Apprentice;* and direct his massive conglomeration.

Increased dependency on others also results in problems for the narcissistic type. Throughout life, individuals with Narcissistic Personality Disorder see themselves as a "cut above the masses" and do not see the need for help or even collaboration from others. Instead, others are seen as objects to be taken advantage of. When narcissists find they need care and support from others (clearly indicating having lower social status), rageful reactions are common that result in increased negative feedback and further reductions in the sense of self.

In the clinical setting, it can be expected that therapy with the older narcissistic patient will be challenging. Perhaps the greatest issue is the patient's perception that the problem resides in other people who do not seem to recognize the patient's talents. A lifetime of relying on others' admiration, respect, and awe can be challenging to address. Another problem is that, stylistically, such patients devalue therapy and the therapist, so development of an alliance is often thwarted. Narcissistic patients often demand special consideration (e.g., seeing the therapist at their convenience, reduced fees) and move from therapist to therapist, trying to find one who is exceptionally well qualified and unique to treat them, but forever being disappointed.

The Case of Blanche: Narcissistic Personality Disorder

Blanche E. is a 77-year-old woman who resides in a skilled nursing facility (SNF), where she has been living for the past year and a half. She is dependent on the staff for her full care. At this time, her only independent functions are those involving the use of her hands, with which she still has limited movement. She is cognitively intact, however, and able to use her mind and her verbal skills to reach far beyond the limited confines of her bed. Her sharp tongue has become her weapon, with the effect to slash and cut down those who provide her care. Her family has mostly been spared these attacks, but they have also responded to their own conflicts and struggles with Blanche.

A mental health consultation was requested because the facility had run out of staff who were willing to care for Blanche. The head nurse, in charge of staffing assignments, had exhausted her supply of bargaining chips for her staff. Being assigned the care of Blanche became not worth the value of whatever was being offered in exchange. Absenteeism and actual loss of staff became a major problem on this floor at the facility. An all-staff meeting was called, and chief among the staff complaints was Blanche E. She had managed, despite being nearly bedbound, to shake up a historically solid and well-functioning facility.

Blanche had been raised in an upper-middle-class family where she was the fourth child but first, and only, daughter. She was elevated to princess status at her birth. Her mother raised her to be a miniature replica of herself, and her father unabashedly adored her. Blanche was given everything. She seldom cried or complained as her wishes were anticipated before they were expressed. Blanche reports, "I walked late because my feet never touched the ground. I was always carried around in someone's arms."

Her academic career in a small private girls' day school was unremarkable. Although intelligent, she was never encouraged to work hard at her studies. It was assumed that she would marry well and that her husband would take over from where her father left off in terms of financial care and adoration.

Blanche attended a prestigious private college, achieving admission not on the strength of her application, but rather on the strength of family contacts and the promise of a major donation. Again her academic record was unremarkable, but she graduated with a major in general studies. This major was meant to provide young ladies with a broad basic knowledge of history, literature, and the arts.

In addition, Blanche's college years allowed her to further identify with young women of a high social class; those who descended from fine lineage, which she did not. She came to understand their experiences, their ways of thinking, feeling, and talking about life. Not being the prettiest, fanciest, most intelligent, or athletic—not standing out in any potentially competitive domain—Blanche was acceptable in all. This position made her an ideal dear friend, which Blanche became to many of her classmates.

College graduation ushered in the marriage season, and Blanche was an honored attendant at many weddings. Much of her time was spent shopping for the perfect dress or being fitted to an attendant's gown. Some she liked and others she loathed. But through this process, she became highly knowledgeable about fashion for the fashionable. Attendance and participation at these high society weddings reinforced her keen observations of the structure and meaning of these events to the participants.

Not especially romantic, she did, however, feel a pressure to marry from her family and friends. Her one beau had been a fellow her age from her hometown. He had been smitten by Blanche since their young teens. After college, he landed a job with an insurance company where it was anticipated he would rise in the managerial ranks. On Blanche's 22nd birthday, he proposed to her and she accepted the proposal. Blanche put off looking for a position, as the preparation for her wedding now consumed all of her time, and much of her mother's time. No detail was left unattended and each was considered an important decision. Blanche's recent experience with many weddings allowed her to reflect on what worked well and what did not. She gave far less attention to her marriage beyond the wedding. She expected that there would be little real change in moving from her parents' home to her own; from her father's adoration to her husband's. The rest of life, she assumed, would simply unfold. And it did. It unfolded and also developed; ultimately Blanche would be able to take responsibility for much of how it evolved.

The facts that organized her life for the next many years were the following. Her husband did not rise as far in the company as expected. He came to be regarded as a solid midlevel manager with no special creativity. He continued to adore Blanche; he put her on a pedestal and catered to her every wish. For her part, she was respectful and tolerant of his presence in her life. They had two sons. Blanche was fond of them, but did not care to be responsible for their daily care. The household was thus run by housekeepers and nannies. In time, the boys went off to boarding school and ultimately to prestigious colleges. They are now each married, with children and faring well. One lives nearby, the other out of state.

When the boys were very young, Blanche decided to work outside the home for the first time in her life. She had her fill of club work, and she knew she did not want to stay home and take on more domestic responsibility. She also recognized that she was not being included in the better social events of the society ladies. Although she had the social skills to be included, she did not have the genealogy.

Her career began with work at the Ladies League Thrift Shoppe, where society women came to donate their cast-off clothing. The shop had been started by League volunteers, and the proceeds from sales were donated to charity. College students were the major purchasers of these goods, with the occasional young socialite needing a fabulous gown for a special occasion. The Ladies League hired Blanche as the manager, the shop's only paid employee. She managed it successfully for 5 years, learning how to run a business and making connections with the patrons. Blanche got to know them well, along with the history of each dress and gown brought in—what was in style, what made them select that gown, how frequently it was worn, and the like.

She began to fantasize and then to think more actively about setting up her own shop, which would carry special-occasion attire for women. She knew that she had the skills and the connections to make a go of it. She shared this idea with some of her most valued patrons, and they encouraged Blanche to go ahead. Blanche became more passionate about this and opened her shop, named Blanche's; it became the love of her life. She was the star and everyone around her sought her advice about clothing, certainly, but also about entertainment ideas, people, places, and things. Her photo often appeared in the Lifestyle or Society section of the newspaper. The name *Blanche* became synonymous with haute couture and social standing. She was gifted at finding just the right gown to suit the occasion and the wearer. Her patrons used her as their therapist, coach, and confidant. They eagerly awaited her return from the New York and Paris shows semiannually. And they adored her.

Blanche had remarkable energy and retained youthful vigor until her early 70s. Then she started to feel weak and fatigued. At first she attributed this to aging, but in time sought medical attention as she was having increasing difficulty walking. On several occasions she felt that her legs would buckle under her.

After an extensive medical workup by the very best doctors, Blanche was diagnosed with a disease causing multiple spinal tumors. Initially, these were addressed surgically, but inexorably progressive and irreversible cord damage occurred, with corresponding motor impairment. Ultimately, Blanche came to need extensive skilled care and was admitted to the SNF as a permanent resident.

Initially, she was charming and pleasant. Before long, however, she began to be snippy to the aides as they cared for her. She would lean on her call button repeatedly, and chastise the person who responded for being too slow, and for making her wait. If the person explained that he or she was tending to another resident, Blanche would become furious.

She remained fastidious about her nail care, demanding that the manicurist who came to the facility take care of her first and only use a special polish. On one occasion when the manicurist had run out of this particular polish, Blanche flew into a rage, verbally assaulting and terrifying her.

She was equally imperious with the dietary staff. Nothing they served was acceptable. Although the staff made efforts to meet her demands, the SNF food could not measure up to Blanche's discriminating palate.

Blanche's personality disorder had been kept under wraps for most of her life due to many favorable circumstances. However, within the context of the SNF, and without the checks and balances of her gratifying career, her hostile edge became dominant and her charming side had all but disappeared. She constantly berated the aides, admonishing them for their ineptitude and ignorance, being fiercely demeaning. One after another of the aides requested not to be assigned her care, and some flatly refused the assignment.

The initial phase of the consultation included meetings with Blanche to learn her story and to hear her side of the conflict. She was pleased by the consultant's attention. The fact that the staff was so troubled by her situation that they called in a consultant was consistent with her belief that she was a special resident. She expressed a keen, and accurate, awareness that the staff was avoiding her and that she was receiving less actual care than she had received earlier. Her desire for more care and her belief that she was entitled to it allowed the consultant to engage Blanche in a cooperative effort to revive and revise the special care she deserved. She was also able to endorse the fact that interacting with others was very difficult for her. "Take, take, take. I can barely move, so what can I give?"

The challenges of the consultation included how to reduce the hostility felt by the staff so they would be open to a renewed treatment contract with Blanche. To that end, the consultant told them her story, and how she came to be the person she was. They were led to an understanding of just how high she believed she was and what this fall felt like to her. Her imperious behavior was reframed as her way of reestablishing the hierarchy with which she felt most familiar. If Blanche couldn't raise the pedestal, then she would lower the floor.

Another challenge was how to enable the staff to reflect Blanche's specialness so that she would not feel the need to debase them. They were asked what they could authentically admire about Blanche, and they were able to identify her lovely fingernails, certain of her possessions, and her exciting social experiences. It was requested that Blanche ask her family to bring in her publicity scrapbooks of her career, including photos of her at many glamorous events. The staff were encouraged to look through these before beginning a care procedure and during it to talk with Blanche about one of these wonderful occasions. This would allow Blanche to feel that she was giving and not just taking during their necessary interactions.

In long-term care facilities, photographs of the residents representing their preaged, preinfirm life often are affixed to the doors of their rooms. This practice has several purposes, not least among them being that they remind all who enter that the residents, in their current condition, were at another time in a very different condition and a different place in life.

In addition to a photograph of Blanche in a beautiful gown, looking elegant and most special, a large business card was on her door:

> Blanche E.,
> Fashion Consultant
> Social Events Planner
> "Please Allow Me to Help You While You Help Me"

Blanche would always need much admiration from others, but her grandiosity and lack of interest in the phenomenology often denied her the very attention and mirroring of her specialness that she desperately sought.

The results of this intervention were quite remarkable. The staff, at first cautious and skeptical, but willing to try again, responded to the consultant's request to select a page from the scrapbook and ask Blanche about something in the picture while carrying out the care procedure. Blanche was happy to reminisce, and she offered colorful stories, often in dramatic detail, for at least as long as the procedure lasted. Questions and comments from the staff member followed quite naturally and each became engaged with the other in a real way. Blanche felt validated that her experiences and talents continued to have value. When her caregivers asked her advice about something in their own life, she was able to make appropriate suggestions. In time, Blanche became one of the staff's favorite residents, assuming the special status she had always believed befitted her.

There was a nice secondary gain to this as well. Blanche's family members visited more often and stayed longer during visits. Her narcissistic needs now gratified, her charming self was allowed to reemerge.

The Fearful or Anxious (Cluster C) Personality Disorders and Aging

Cluster C Personality Disorders: Avoidant, Dependent, and Obsessive-Compulsive

4

Chapter

The similarities of the three personality disorders in Cluster C include underlying pervasive nervousness, anxiety, or fearfulness. Compared with the erratic and impulsive personality disorders in Cluster B with their characteristic interpersonal chaos, the Cluster C personality disorders often present with debilitating indecision, social inhibition, and avoidance. Based on the anxious nature of these personality disorders, it should not be surprising that when sufferers seek psychotherapy, they often do so to deal with their feelings of fear and apprehension. Like the personality disorders discussed in the preceding chapters, individuals with Cluster C personality disorders typically have little sense that their personality is maladaptive or part of the problem. Notably, there has been less systematic research conducted on the personality disorders in Cluster C compared with those in Cluster A (Schizotypal Personality Disorder in particular) and Cluster B (Antisocial and Borderline Personality Disorders in particular; Paris, 2005), and even less research targeting Cluster C personality disorders and older populations. An important developmental finding is that the onset of the anxiety-based

(Cluster C) personality disorders may be seen very early in life. Paris (1998) documented that unusually shy infants are at risk for anxiety disorders (on Axis 1) and Cluster C personality disorders as adults. The *DSM-IV-TR* diagnostic criteria for the three Cluster C disorders are provided in the following subsections.

Avoidant Personality Disorder

Clinical Description

This disorder manifests itself as a pervasive pattern of social inhibition or intense shyness, coupled with a longing for relationships. People with Avoidant Personality Disorder are extremely sensitive about how others perceive them, and they are especially preoccupied with and afraid of social criticism or rejection. As a consequence, they typically avoid entering into social situations in which they might be scrutinized or rejected. Cognitively, they tend to exaggerate the risks associated with new activities and people, and they are also prone to interpret comments from others as critical—confirming and justifying their fears. In essence, the avoidant type rejects others first to avoid being rejected by them. As a consequence, they are often isolated and lonely.

When they are in relationships with others (e.g., close relatives), people with Avoidant Personality Disorder have strong fears of being ridiculed and therefore are highly controlled, reserved, and restrained. They often come across as self-effacing, diffident, and uncertain. Their social anxiety is frequently palpable and detected by others. Their shyness is fueled by powerful feelings of inadequacy and low self-esteem. They see themselves as agonizingly socially inept, incompetent, inferior, and unappealing to others, who surely will reject them if given the opportunity. They further believe that they cannot cope with the anxiety associated with social relationships, choosing to avoid them instead. Prone to embarrassment, shame, and feeling foolish, they steer clear of social opportunities.

Because the avoidant type is extremely detached and socially isolated, this disorder can sometimes be confused with the schizoid type (in Cluster A), which shares many of these same behaviors. However, there is an important distinction between the two personality disorders. Whereas schizoid individuals prefer interpersonal distance and are comfortable with isolation, avoidant individuals desperately want to be connected to others, but their intense social anxiety and shyness prevents this. Avoidant Personality Disorder is closely related to social phobia (also called social anxiety disorder), coded on Axis I. An example of social phobia is a person who is fearful of speaking in public or of eating in front of other people, fueled by fears that he or she will do something embarrassing. In fact, many people with social phobia also meet the diagnosis for Avoidant Personality Disorder, although the main distinction is that the shyness and social anxiety are more pervasive and enduring in the personality disorder than in social phobia. Table 4.1 lists the *DSM-IV-TR* diagnostic criteria for Avoidant Personality Disorder.

Table 4.1   *DSM-IV-TR* **Diagnostic Criteria for Avoidant Personality Disorder (Code: 301.82)**

A pervasive pattern of social inhibition, feelings of inadequacy, and hypersensitivity to negative evaluation, beginning by early adulthood and present in a variety of contexts, as indicated by four (or more) of the following:

(1) avoids occupational activities that involve significant interpersonal contact, because of fears of criticism, disapproval, or rejection

(2) is unwilling to get involved with people unless certain of being liked

(3) shows restraint within intimate relationships because of the fear of being shamed or ridiculed

(4) is preoccupied with being criticized or rejected in social situations

(5) is inhibited in new interpersonal situations because of feelings of inadequacy

(6) views self as socially inept, personally unappealing, or inferior to others

(7) is unusually reluctant to take personal risks or to engage in any new activities because they may prove embarrassing

Source: From *Diagnostic and Statistical Manual of Mental Disorders*, fourth edition, text revision, American Psychiatric Association, 2000, Washington, DC: Author. Copyright 2000 by American Psychiatric Association. Reprinted with permission.

Potential Age-Bias of Criteria

Several criteria for Avoidant Personality Disorder seem to fit poorly for older adults. Probably the most inappropriate is Criterion 1 (avoids occupational activities that involve significant interpersonal contact, because of fears of criticism, disapproval, or rejection) because the vast majority of older adults are no longer in the workforce and therefore detection of their avoidance in this area makes little sense. We do not see a reason why this criterion focuses explicitly on the avoidance of occupational activities, rather than on the avoidance of any type of activity due to social fears, which more accurately describes the avoidant type. An argument can also be made that Criterion 4 (is preoccupied with being criticized or rejected in social situations) may not necessarily reflect a personality defect but may be a reasonable reaction for those in later life who experience increased social rejection due to negative stereotypes about aging and the rampant ageism in society.

Furthermore, Criterion 5 (is inhibited in new interpersonal situations because of feelings of inadequacy) may be problematical for some older adults, especially when widows and widowers reenter the dating world after being "out of the scene" for many years. Feeling self-conscious and inhibited in this context is reasonable and should not be viewed as a core personality deficit. Finally, Criterion 7 (is unusually reluctant to take personal risks or to engage in any new activities because they may prove embarrassing) may not apply well in the later-life context, especially when physical problems experienced by some older people (e.g., incontinence, hearing loss, requiring oxygen, wearing a colostomy bag) may realistically be sources of potential embarrassment. In these cases, hesitance to engage in new activities may be reasonable until the person has had a chance to improve physically or to adjust psychologically to the infirmity if it cannot be treated medically.

Theorized Pattern in Later Life and Possible Impact of Aging

Some degree of social anxiety is experienced by most people. During adolescence, social discomfort is typical, although it tends to diminish as people mature and become more comfortable with themselves. It is particularly sad when intense social inhibition persists into later life because it seems as if the intensely shy older person has missed out on the normal developmental pathway to social poise and confidence experienced by many of his or her peers. It is also sad to see older adults so lonely and disconnected, primarily due to their own internal struggles, especially at a phase in life when social networks typically are smaller but more selective and meaningful than they are earlier in life (Lang & Carstensen, 1994). A distinction to be made here is among older adults who are isolated by adverse circumstances in later life but who have not had a lifelong pattern of social inhibition, older adults who are alone by choice and able to enjoy their solitude, and older adults who are isolated but desperately lonely, too shy to seek warmth and comfort from others. Clinicians should assess whether the isolation is due to adventitious circumstances (e.g., losses, illness), choice, or lifelong traits of shyness, timidity, and inhibition (the latter being indicative of personality pathology).

Older adults with Avoidant Personality Disorder are particularly vulnerable to the social losses that are commonly a part of later life (e.g., death of marital partners, friends, and peers; migration of children), because their networks are generally constricted. Although avoidant individuals may have been involved in relationships with a small number of friends or family members earlier in life, they have great trouble replacing relationships that they have lost. Because they are hesitant to try to meet new people or engage in new activities unless they are "guaranteed" of being liked, they may become an annoyance to social directors of diverse communal living settings. Avoidant individuals often come to later life lonely, anxious, and frightened, and they can easily become more alone and frightened as their limited networks inevitably shrink.

Another pattern is that of older adults with this disorder who do not apply for or accept needed social or supportive services due to their fears of being evaluated and found wanting. One of our patients, a 67-year-old diabetic woman, refused a physical rehabilitation strategy of swimming in a pool because she was afraid of having to interact with the other swimmers and fearful of being rejected. When individuals with this disorder present for psychotherapy, a potential complication is that they easily become overly dependent on the clinician and too eager to please the clinician. Interventions that bolster social skills and assertiveness can help patients deepen relationships outside the safety of the therapy relationship and reduce their social isolation.

The Case of Sara: Avoidant Personality Disorder

Sara J. is a 78-year-old woman who has been living independently in a senior housing complex for the past 5 years. She has been a nearly invisible resident, but has recently come to the attention of the management. It is felt that she now needs to move into the assisted living area as she has rapidly progressing macular degeneration resulting in near blindness and is in need of assistance with daily activities. Sara has not been able to handle the prospect of the transfer well. She has become extraordinarily anxious and has had to be transported to the Emergency Room of a local hospital several times with complaints of dizziness and shortness of breath. On each admission, she was evaluated thoroughly by the hospital staff, who determined that anxiety and panic were at the root of her somatic distress. They gave her a prescription for an anxiolytic and she was returned to her apartment. The manager spoke with Sara and convinced her that talking to a counselor would be helpful and that she would benefit from the support around her need to move and adjustment to her failing vision. Embarrassed after this most recent trip to the ER, Sara consented and allowed the manager to arrange an appointment with a mental health clinician.

For Sara, any move was frightening. She had never moved far from the town where she had been raised. She was always comfortable with things staying the same, and very uncomfortable with change. Sara was the only child of parents who had her late in life after having given up hope of having children. Sara's mother had three prior pregnancies resulting in two miscarriages and the birth of a stillborn boy 6 years before Sara was born. After this last tragic loss, the parents stopped trying to conceive, but along came an unexpected and uncomplicated pregnancy. Sara was of average size, healthy, and achieved normal developmental milestones. Her mother, however, was terribly frightened that something bad would befall her only child and dedicated herself to protecting Sara from anything, or anyone, that could possibly cause her daughter harm. "Please be careful. You might hurt yourself. Are you sure you're all right?" were always in the verbal background of Sara's childhood. It was more than just the words. Sara's mother was palpably anxious about virtually everything. She was always doing battle with hidden germs and hidden enemies that could threaten her child's life. When Sara ventured outdoors to play with a neighborhood child, her mother would call her in after a brief period: "Sara. Come in now. You've had enough germs for the day." Other children were never invited into the house. So Sara became a very shy, timid, and super-cautious little girl, raised as a companion to her equally shy, timid, and anxiety-ridden mother.

Sara's relationship with her father was different. He was a physician in the town, respected by his patients, serving them tirelessly, usually at the price of being unavailable to his family. He had never recovered from the loss of his baby boy. He had dreamed of a son to follow him into medicine and some day to take over his practice. Sara, the timid little soul, was far from the son of his dreams. Besides she was her mother's mirror image and ally; there was little room for him in their lives. He felt angry, and Sara, meek, self-effacing, and socially awkward, became the magnet for his sarcasm and caustic comments. As she started developing physically in adolescence, he would delight in teasing her to the point of humiliation; then she would run from the room in tears.

During adolescence, Sara became even more shy. This coupled with the expectable awkwardness of teenage years, made Sara spend considerable time thinking about how to avoid interaction with others. She knew that anyone would quickly discern that she was different and ineffective and would ridicule her. The best she could hope for was to try to be invisible, except with her mother and aunties, who were a lot like her and intuitively understood how she felt.

But Sara also spent considerable time longing to be like the other girls in school; to have their confidence, to know how to act and what to say. She developed one friend, Nancy, but Nancy had other friends, too, and asked Sara that although they were good friends to please not hang on her all the time. On the days when

Nancy was with other girls after school, Sara would walk home alone. She knew a special way home that took a little longer, but none of the other kids took that route, so she wouldn't have to see them or speak to them. When Nancy developed crushes on boys, Sara was finally, totally, out of her league, and their friendship silently ended. If she couldn't talk to girls, she surely could not talk to boys. All she knew about men, and therefore boys, was that they could tease, reduce her to hideous blushing and tears, and cause unbearable embarrassment.

After high school, Sara declined the opportunity to go away to college. Rather, she chose to take an entry-level job in the accounting division of a company in town and to take business courses at night at the community college. She completed a degree after 8 years and was promoted in her job. All this time, she lived at home with her parents. What little social life she had was around extended family, and even there she would decline the invitation if the event was to be too large or bustling, or at the last moment develop some somatic ailment that kept her at home. She did love the movies, however, and would see every film that came to town. It was through the movies that Sara developed a rich inner fantasy life in which she was socially adept, charming, graceful, and above all could never be hurt by anyone.

When her parents died, she remained in the house, and her life changed very little. She did miss talking with her mother, one of the few people with whom she had ever felt comfortable. She never recalled blushing or needing to flee from her mother. She missed her father, too, a little. He had become softer in his old age, and she found finally that she could talk with him. He had stopped being angry that she was who she was and not who she wasn't.

Sara's life was overall quiet and peaceful. By avoiding all but the most superficial and necessary contacts with others, she was able to keep her anxiety under control. In time she supplemented the movies with television dramas to feed her fantasies. She became very attached to characters in the shows and mourned their loss when a series would end. They had become her family, friends, and lovers. They accepted her uncritically.

There came the time when the old house needed extensive, costly repairs, and Sara decided to sell it, applying for an apartment in the nearby senior housing complex that offered both independent and assisted living units. When her name rose to the top of the list for an independent apartment, she became overwhelmed by the prospect of moving, and turned it down. Her name was subsequently placed at the bottom of the list, but she was told that the next offer would need to be accepted. Two years later, she was again called and told that a unit had become available. This time Sara accepted the offer.

A cousin helped her with the move, which was less painful than she had anticipated. Her new apartment was clean and quiet, and mercifully, no welcoming committee greeted her. She was able to move, settle in, and become comfortably invisible. The weekly activities calendar went unread. She smiled and said hello to residents she saw in the hallway. Otherwise, she maintained her solitary life much as it had been before. She continued to drive to the shops and services she was familiar with, as necessary, until her eyesight began to deteriorate. She consulted a specialist, but the news was not good. He predicted a rapid visual decline and advised Sara to plan to move into the assisted living and also to work with a specialist in adaptive equipment for the visually handicapped. Sara arranged for this woman to visit her in her home, but felt that the specialist was very critical of her and maybe thought she was exaggerating the degree of her impairment. It took Sara an hour to stop trembling after the woman left, and she did not arrange for another visit.

Sara was lost without her car. She was not willing to join other residents in the shopping van, a semiweekly excursion that was both practical and social. She muddled through as best she could by calling and having things delivered until even using the telephone became a challenge. There were times when she had little to eat in her refrigerator. She tried hard to keep bad thoughts from her mind, but her heart would race and sometimes she felt like she could not breathe. When this happened, she called 911.

The first step in the treatment plan was the environmental engineering phase that involved Sara's moving from her apartment into an assisted living unit. She trusted the housing manager and her cousin, so these would be the two people to ease the transition and shepherd Sara through the move. Once she was settled in, the manager arranged to introduce Sara to one resident who would be her tablemate in the dining room. This resident had been handpicked for the role. Her name was Mona and she was quiet, centered, and accepting. Mona was happy to have been chosen to help with the new, shy resident. The manager also facilitated an introduction between

Sara and her primary home health aide. The third critical introduction was to the counselor who was available to meet with Sara in her apartment.

Sara can clearly be diagnosed with Avoidant Personality Disorder (APD), meeting most of the diagnostic criteria. As far back as she can remember, she has suffered from feeling inadequate and always at risk of being negatively evaluated by others. She has assiduously avoided all but the most necessary, or superficial, interpersonal relationships beyond her immediate family. To others, Sara has appeared shy and quiet; frequently she went unnoticed. Sara would carefully avoid new situations whenever possible. She was risk aversive, less because of the inherent danger of an experience, more so because of the danger of being criticized by others. She could not bear being scrutinized and found wanting.

When she was young, she actively longed for a pure, uncritical relationship, but the unmet longing dissipated with the years. She came to repress such thoughts because they increased her anxiety. It was far safer to project her yearning onto cinema characters, weaving these into an elaborate fantasy life. This parallel life, however, was highly dependent on her vision. When this began to fail, Sara was losing not only her ability to function independently, but also her most intimate relationships.

Three overarching goals were established for Sara's therapy. The first was the most external and therefore the least likely to meet resistance from Sara. This included the concrete steps to support Sara's transition into assisted living, and make it her new home. The second would be to create and support a minimal number of important relationships in her new setting; initially the manager, her aide, and Mona. Her past relationship with her film family would need to be validated and accepted honestly and uncritically. Sara would need to trust that the therapist would understand and respect her fantasy life. It had served Sara well over many years, and it was imperative that the therapist would acknowledge how difficult it must be to give that up and risk new relationships with people in an unscripted universe.

Her treatment plan would initially offer immediate symptomatic relief for her anxiety. A psychopharmacologist would likely prescribe an SSRI as a first-line medication, one with an antianxiety property. More traditional antianxiety medications, notably the benzodiazepines, are not well suited to older adults, especially as a long-term treatment. Relaxation training would also helpful for anxiety management.

Cognitive-behavioral therapy would be a most appropriate treatment. This would incorporate social skills training, a behavioral hierarchy, and cognitive restructuring. The social skills training component would redress a highly impoverished history of social interactions, consistent with APD. The training exercises would be designed to be specific to Sara's current social needs (e.g., assertiveness training with aides and other residents). A direct focus on necessary but anxiety-provoking situations would be most effective. Change occurs when need surpasses resistance and where success is naturally reinforced.

Cognitive therapy would enable Sara to revisit significant past experiences where she has misinterpreted responses as being critical or has overvalued their meaning. Sara's dominant cognitive distortions would be gently identified and addressed. She would be taught to check out meaning and entertain alternative meanings. This could be achieved organically within the therapy, using the therapy as a microcosm of the outside world, with the essential caveat that the therapeutic encounter must be couched in absolute safety and trust, necessary for the achievement of the alliance. Even so, Sara can be expected to test the therapist, and to be hypervigilant around any perceived slight or critical judgment. These instances of misperception and excessive sensitivity can be used to deepen and advance the therapy and the alliance. However, if not recognized and addressed, they could also damage the therapeutic relationship, possibly leading Sara to reject the therapist before being rejected herself. The ultimate goal is to enable Sara to trust a few people enough to reduce the conflict between her need for the mutual interdependence her condition requires and her need to avoid the attention of others.

Dependent Personality Disorder

Clinical Description

Individuals with this disorder have an excessive need to be taken care of by others. As such, they are characteristically submissive, clinging, and needy, ever fearful of being alone. They are reluctant to make even minor decisions, relinquishing this responsibility to others or only doing so after receiving excessive advice and reassurance. Chronically feeling inadequate, dependent individuals desperately need others to assume responsibility for them. They lack confidence in their abilities and have difficulty initiating tasks or doing things independently. Although often characterized as passive and indecisive, people with this disorder are not without their own opinions or beliefs, but if challenged, they will quickly retreat to prevent the loss of support or approval.

Individuals with Dependent Personality Disorder can be excessively self-sacrificing, willing to take on onerous or demeaning tasks as a way to secure the affection of others. In many cases, they are taken advantage of by others, yet they tolerate mistreatment and often remain in unhealthy or abusive relationships because their fear of being alone overrides their desire to be treated decently. They are also likely to be unassertive and unwilling to make demands on others, seeing themselves as not worthy of expressing themselves and also fearing disapproval. Their predominant self-perception is that of being helpless and unable to negotiate life successfully without assistance. As a result, people with this disorder typically are preoccupied with maintaining relationships and experience a constant overwhelming fear of being abandoned or cast off to fend for themselves.

When important relationships end, dependent individuals will go to great lengths to secure another supportive relationship as quickly as possible. Their fear of being alone outweighs their fear of rejection. (This ability to seek out new relationships at all costs contrasts starkly with the avoidant type who goes to great lengths not to seek out relationships.) Finally, the dependent individual tends to consider other people as being more important and competent than he or she is, responding by appeasing others and acting submissively. Table 4.2 lists the *DSM-IV-TR* diagnostic criteria for Dependent Personality Disorder.

Potential Age-Bias of Criteria

Two criteria for Dependent Personality Disorder may be problematical in the later-life context, especially where a dementing

Table 4.2　*DSM-IV-TR* **Diagnostic Criteria for Dependent Personality Disorder (Code: 301.6)**

A pervasive and excessive need to be taken care of that leads to submissive and clinging behavior and fears of separation, beginning by early adulthood and present in a variety of contexts, as indicated by five (or more) of the following:

(1) has difficulty making everyday decisions without an excessive amount of advice and reassurance from others

(2) needs others to assume responsibility for most major area of his or her life

(3) has difficulty expressing disagreement with others because of fear of loss of support or approval. Note: Do not include realistic fears of retribution

(4) has difficulty initiating projects or doing things on his or her own (because of lack of self-confidence in judgment or abilities rather than a lack of motivation or energy)

(5) goes to excessive lengths to obtain nurturance and support from others, to the point of volunteering to do things that are unpleasant

(6) feels uncomfortable or helpless when alone because of exaggerated fears of being unable to care for himself or herself

(7) urgently seeks another relationship as a source of care and support when a close relationship ends

(8) is unrealistically preoccupied with fears of being left to take care of himself or herself

Source: From *Diagnostic and Statistical Manual of Mental Disorders,* fourth edition, text revision, American Psychiatric Association, 2000, Washington, DC: Author. Copyright 2000 by American Psychiatric Association. Reprinted with permission.

illness is present. Older persons with cognitive impairment may show deficits in their abilities to make reasonable decisions for themselves, display previously held good judgment, and initiate constructive behaviors (lack of initiation is a classic sign of frontal lobe impairment). In these cases, it would be incorrect to conclude that the person has met the threshold for Criterion 1 (has difficulty making everyday decisions without an excessive amount of advice and reassurance from others) and Criterion 4 (has difficulty initiating projects or doing things on his or her own [because of lack of self-confidence in judgment or abilities rather than a lack of motivation or energy]), especially if these behaviors are not lifelong traits or can be accounted for by organic changes in the brain.

Criterion 6 (feels uncomfortable or helpless when alone because of exaggerated fears of being unable to care for himself or herself) and Criterion 8 (is unrealistically preoccupied with fears of being left to take care of himself or herself) may not apply well in situations where the older person is extremely frail or disabled and has significant anxieties about being left alone and not receiving adequate care and support from others. At issue here is how reasonable the person's fears and concerns are. If the fears about having to care for oneself are not exaggerated or unrealistic, then it would be incorrect to see the person as exhibiting traits of Dependent Personality Disorder. If the fears are excessive and disproportionate (even in physically frail older adults), then dependency may be a core issue for the person.

Theorized Pattern in Later Life and Possible Impact of Aging

The most onerous age-related stressor among individuals with dependent personality is widowhood. Severe problems are likely to arise for the dependent older person whose spouse dies, leaving the person in the threatening (and unfamiliar) position of having to depend on him- or herself. After such a loss, dependent older adults commonly appear helpless, unable to perform the most mundane functions after decades of relying excessively on their partners. Feeling lost and vulnerable, these older adults often turn to their adult children to fill the void left by the deceased spouse on whom they depended. In many cases, their excessive neediness quickly becomes burdensome and arduous, frequently leading to their children feeling overwhelmed and annoyed.

A dramatic example of this pattern was observed in one of our patients, a 74-year-old woman, whose husband had died several months before the consultation. One of the patient's daughters reported that the patient was unable to change out of her pajamas in the morning because her husband was no longer there to tell her which outfit to wear. On taking the patient grocery shopping, the daughter discovered that she was unable to make even basic decisions (e.g., which cereal to buy). Although her name had been on the checkbook for many years, it also became apparent that the patient did not know how to write a check, and a stack of unpaid bills accumulated in her house. The children in this family had been aware that for many years their father had taken care of their mother, but they did not realize the degree of her dependency until after he died.

Older persons with Dependent Personality Disorder are also likely to actively seek out and overly rely on other supportive individuals and services, easily becoming burdensome. Facing retirement, the older adult with Dependent Personality Disorder may welcome the occurrence and the concomitant freedom from those responsibilities. In contrast to the other personality disorders we have already discussed, increased dependency is not particularly challenging for the aging dependent type. In fact, quite the contrary, the dependent type may enjoy such opportunities for greater dependence in later life, relishing increased opportunities to receive the care and nurturance of others. A key distinction to make is between older adults who are dependent on others due to unfortunate life circumstances (e.g., illness) and those whose dependence is excessive to the current situation.

The Case of Toby: Dependent Personality Disorder

Toby L.'s husband called the psychologist to schedule an appointment. "I don't know if you want to see us together or just my wife. She's driving me absolutely crazy. I love her, but I'm really at the end of my rope here. She's crying in the next room even while I'm calling you." An appointment was set for the couple to come in. The clinician intended to meet with them together to identify if this would become a couples therapy case or an individual case, and, if so, who would be the identified patient.

Mel and Toby L., a couple in their late 70s, appeared early for their appointment, both rising as one to greet the therapist when she met them in the waiting area. She noted that on entering the office, Mr. L. sat on the sofa first, and then his wife sat beside him. She was smiling a sad smile and holding his hand. Mr. L. looked weary and irritated. He was not smiling.

Mr. L. answered the therapist's questions for the couple and was the narrator of their story. When the therapist pointedly directed a question to Mrs. L., she would look at her husband for permission to talk. Her brief comments were followed by a glance toward him seeking his approval. Typically, he would clarify or offer some revision of what his wife had just said.

The couple had been married for over 50 years and had raised two daughters. Both of their daughters were married and lived not too far away. Toby and Mel were devoted to their three school-age grandchildren. Their daughters were in good marriages and generally doing well. At this time, the extended family did not appear to contribute to the couple's distress. However, the older daughter had been increasingly setting limits on her mother's demands and intrusions into her own privacy. Toby not only would insist on knowing how to reach her daughter in an emergency when she made a business trip, but also would call her daughter on her cell phone to make sure the plane landed safely each time she left and returned from a trip. Toby carried around with her a calendar of when each child (and grandchild) would be away, where they were staying, and how they could be reached. The daughter refused to comply when her mother started requesting the name of the carrier and the flight number stating, "I want to listen to the news on your travel days."

What led to Mel's call of distress was that his wife began to insist that he take her grocery shopping and drive her to and from the hairdresser's. The absolute red flag was when Toby began to insist that Mel accompany her on lunch dates with her women friends. Toby would proclaim, "I need you to keep up the conversation. I just can't do it alone. I'm not up to it, and you're so good at chitchat."

When asked if there were any other events or behaviors he experienced as particularly disturbing, Mel responded that Toby's constant illnesses and complaints led to so many doctor visits that there was little time for anything else, especially because Toby's energy level was low. "If you look at our calendar, there's not a day when we don't have some doctor or lab appointment, or physical therapy appointment, and almost all of them are for her. Toby carries a calendar for all those appointments, too. And a notebook. You have no idea how many different doctors she sees."

At that point, Toby hesitantly spoke up: "I see them because I'm sick and can't take most medicines so they don't know what to do with me. Most of them start out being nice, but I guess I discourage them, and I've got to have someone there to call, and they have to get back to me, too." The therapist could hear a note of panic creeping into Toby's voice.

"And another thing that really gets to me," Mel went on, "I just don't understand it. Toby was a professional, a teacher's teacher, and she wasn't clinging to anyone's coattails, as far as I know. I don't know what is happening here, but it's not good for her, and it's not good for me." As his anger became apparent, Toby began quietly to weep.

Toby L. was born and raised in a small midwestern town into one of very few Jewish families. Her father owned a store in the center of town selling blue jeans and work gear. He was a quiet but friendly man devoted to his customers, who in turn, were devoted to him. Business was steady and good. Toby had one brother, 4 years her senior, who was raised and primed to take over the store someday. The family was close and tight, perhaps as protection against the outside, feeling somewhat different from their neighbors. Toby adored her brother. He grew to be tall and good-looking, was a popular fellow and good at sports. With her father working in the store long hours and her mother running the house and functioning as the store's bookkeeper, Toby and her brother spent much time together. He effectively was an auxiliary parent to her, and shepherded Toby through many of the trials of growing up.

Toby was always a frail child, prone to catching everything, and needing much rest. She was not especially pretty and not at all athletic. She was, however, highly intelligent, and much of the attention she received at home and at school rewarded this. She was the smart one but also the fragile one.

When Toby's brother graduated from high school, World War II was being waged. He enlisted in the U.S. Army, which was the patriotic thing to do, with the intention of returning home after the war to work with his father in the store. He would probably marry his high-school sweetheart and raise a family in that same town. However, he never returned from the war. He was killed in action. Toby's mother became a Gold Star Mother, devoted herself to his memory, and idealized his role as a soldier. Toby's father died 6 months after his son was killed. And his father, Toby's beloved Papa, died soon after. Within 1 year, Toby had lost her grandfather, father, and brother, who were collectively her anchor, support, and strength. She was 19 years old and in college that year. She would never return to the family home, and she would never again trust that those she depended on would stay safe and return if they went away.

Toby completed college and went directly on to graduate school to earn an advanced degree in education, specializing in curriculum development. At the university, she met a nice fellow student who was charmed by her intelligence, much superior to his own, in combination with a wispy physical presentation. A big guy with a big heart, he quickly fell in love with Toby and took her under his wing. He would drop her off at school each morning and pick her up at the end of the day. In time she learned to drive, albeit cautiously. They married, and after her first daughter was born, Toby gave up work to devote herself to her husband and their little family. Only when both girls were through school did Toby return to work, joining the faculty of a nearby teacher's college.

Toby's life had two tracks, home and work. At work, she was well respected by her colleagues as well as her students. Somewhat dour and humorless, she was not a beloved teacher, but rather a respected one, being approachable, conscientious, and consistent.

At home, she was competent but always doubting this. She would watch how others did things. She would ask for directions and assistance just to reassure herself that what she was doing was right. She would solicit her husband's advice about most everything, but ultimately came to resent his self-confidence, which she equated with competence, comparatively diminishing her own. When her resentment came to consciousness, at times she would fantasize about divorcing Mel, or that he would die and she could be on her own. Then she would feel very anxious and nearly panic because she knew deep down that she could not make it on her own. She believed that without his help and guidance, she really couldn't get by in the world.

Around this time, in her late 40s, Toby developed a strange collection of symptoms. She became terribly fatigued, lost her appetite and subsequently significant weight, and often felt sweaty and tremulous. She could barely manage to go to work. When she came home, she went to bed. Her husband took over the household chores to allow his wife to rest. She went from one doctor to another, but none could determine the cause of her illness. Many medications were prescribed. Toby tried them all, to no avail. She could not tolerate their side effects and frequently stopped taking the medication after only one or two doses. There was one pill she could tolerate, however, and she came to depend on it. That was a benzodiazepine, which she took before bed to help her sleep, and sometimes a half during the day if she felt especially shaky. This pattern continued over the years. Toby never increased the dosage, but she was never willing to discontinue the drug. A further development during this period was her increased awareness of her husband's presence and accessibility, especially when she felt ill or in distress. Always concerned about where he was going and how long he would be gone, she now experienced a cycle of great apprehension followed by relief when he returned, accompanied by symptoms of autonomic nervous system arousal and recovery.

Toby meets the criteria for a diagnosis of Dependent Personality Disorder. She is submissive, clingy, and profoundly fearful of separation from those on whom she depends. The facts of autonomy and functional independence in an isolated life sphere do not challenge her internalized identity as a passive and timid soul who cannot function without the help of others. Typically, there is a person or two who is internalized as the dependent person's leader. If the leader is lost, the individual with a dependent personality must find a replacement. Toby's brother, father, and grandfather came to be replaced by Mel, whom she relied on for decision making, advice, and reassurance. He served as her protector and guide. She always would need someone on whom to depend, and she would need constant reassurance that this person would be accessible and available. We heard echoes of that when Toby reported that, no matter whether the doctors could help her, she absolutely needed to know that they were there for her.

Frequently, the genesis of this personality disorder includes some life event that triggered a fear of loss or abandonment by the person on whom the child or young adult depended, as happened dramatically in Toby's life. Having been excessively or seriously ill during childhood also adds to the probability that this personality disorder will develop, especially when the label of being a fragile child is applied and independence is discouraged. The message such children get from the family is one of inability to care for themselves and trust that someone will always be there to guide them and care for them. The dominant ego defenses include idealization (of the protector/leader) and reaction formation (to avoid conflict and anxiety emanating from a fear of abandonment).

Comorbid anxiety disorders are often present in individuals with Dependent Personality Disorder as they are inherently anxious and fearful. Their internalized anger, with feelings of resentment and profound inadequacy, puts them into great conflict. They cannot risk confrontation and alienation from those on whom they depend and induce in themselves great suffering when even contemplating this. Their help-seeking and reassurance-seeking behavior can be annoying, but to their protector, this behavior, at least originally, often is gratifying. It is frequently the case, as with Mel and Toby, that what began as a match made in heaven only shifted to living hell when there was a significant change in the system. In this instance, the change was inherent in the aging process. Mel developed a few age-related health problems that were minor, but nonetheless were terrifying intimations of mortality to Toby. Toby also was aging, and was not able to tolerate the usual age-related aches and pains. In addition to an Axis II diagnosis of DPD, she also meets the criteria for an Axis I diagnosis of Undifferentiated Somatoform Disorder. She presents with complaints of fatigue, gastrointestinal disturbances, loss of appetite, and multiple aches and pains that have persisted for years, cause significant distress, and impair her daily functioning. This also increases her clinging and reassurance-seeking behavior, along with her desperate need to be able to contact and access those on whom she depends.

A treatment plan was developed to include four aspects: pharmacological, individual, couple, and group therapies. The pharmacology aspect would suggest a selective serotonin reuptake inhibitor (SSRI) as a first-line medication to reduce the anxiety and treat a probable underlying dysthymia. It would be explained to Toby that this medication was in a different class of drugs from those she had tried before and that it was very well tolerated. Because of her special sensitivity to medications and intolerance of any somatic change, the medication would be introduced and raised to treatment level very slowly, and she would have frequent scheduled contact with the pharmacologist to report her sensations and receive support and encouragement to remain on the medication long enough to give it a chance. As trust in the pharmacologist developed, Toby would be gradually weaned off the benzodiazepine. The SSRI also works on anxiety symptoms, is not addicting, and does not have the side effects of benzodiazepines, which are especially dangerous for older adults.

The individual therapy would be a combination of cognitive, behavioral, and supportive psychotherapies, overall a pragmatic approach. The therapeutic alliance would need to engage Toby's trust and also allow and tolerate the initial transfer of dependency. It also would need to provide a context that could reduce her anxious dependency without denying her the secondary gains of this personality disorder, including the protection and attention of her husband. This will be a real challenge, and the clinician can expect to be tested for accessibility. The main goal would be to reduce the dependency/clinging behaviors, but not to eliminate them. A secondary goal would be to link the secondary gains of the unwanted behaviors to the new (less dependent) behaviors. For example, she could be coached to share with her husband her successes, rather than her ineptitudes and deficiencies, and gain his attention and support in that way. She could join her husband on an errand or an outing and offer to drive him. Toby would also be led to understand how she has come to respond with anxiety to the anticipation or fear of aloneness. She would be encouraged to identify the thoughts that lead to the anxiety, her dependency worries, and how many of her dependent behaviors are attempts to reduce this anxiety. Might there be other ways to achieve that? Stress reduction and relaxation training techniques could be introduced at this point.

The couple therapy should be interspersed with the individual therapy, to direct and support positive changes. Their strengths as a couple would be validated and valued. Toby would need to be reassured that should she become less dependent (or more independent), she would not risk her husband's disapproval and thereby increase her fear of his abandonment (equated with less attention and less protection). As she is so concerned about his health and well-being (to ensure his availability), she could be encouraged to understand that allowing him greater breathing room is better for him and therefore for her. For his part, Mel could be coached how best to support his wife's reduced expressions of dependency and reinforce her (relatively) independent behaviors through his greater recognition, attention, and positive regard.

In time, Toby could be transitioned to group therapy. Again, the goal would be to engage and support her independence while accepting the help that becomes necessary as one ages. An older woman's empowerment group would be a good choice at this point. A caution certainly would be the effect that ensuing change would have on the couple. It is therefore important that the couple's therapy continue, at least intermittently, to monitor their adaptation to changes that occur.

Obsessive-Compulsive Personality Disorder

Clinical Description

This disorder is characterized by a preoccupation with rules, details, organization, orderliness, and internal and external control. People with Obsessive-Compulsive Personality Disorder are highly perfectionistic, and they apply their overly strict standards to their own behavior and that of others. This preoccupation with details, lists, schedules, routines, organization, and perfectionism is so engrossing that the major point of the activity or project often becomes obscured, "lost in the details." They are paragons of rigidity, inflexibility, scrupulosity, and inefficiency. They tend to be stubborn, rigid, serious, exacting, interpersonally formal, overly conscientious, and moral. Their pervasively rigid, moralistic, and uncompromising style negatively impacts their interpersonal relationships.

Often described by others as *workaholics,* people with this disorder forgo pleasurable activities and friendships for the sake of productivity. Ironically, their productivity often suffers because the point of many activities is lost among the rules, regulations, lists, and schedules to which they scrupulously and conscientiously adhere. Delegation of responsibility or work to others is unheard of, usually for fear that the task will not be completed their way (the right way). Individuals with this disorder are controlled and controlling. They are emotionally constricted and have trouble expressing affection. They prefer an intellectualized and logical approach to life and relationships, devoid of spontaneity, creativity, and joy. They demand that others submit to their wishes and have a hard time considering alternative points of view. They frequently hoard their money, possessions, and feelings and are stingy in their spending on themselves. They are also unable to get rid of worthless objects. A vivid metaphor for this type of pathology is that sufferers "do not see the forest for the trees." Often, their preoccupation with the details, rules, and regulations leaves them unable to perceive the broader context, forever failing to appreciate the "big picture."

A distinction should be made between this personality disorder and Obsessive-Compulsive Disorder (OCD), which is an anxiety disorder coded on Axis 1. Individuals with Obsessive-Compulsive Personality Disorder typically do not have true obsessions (intrusive thoughts that flood the person's mind) or compulsions (behaviors that the person feels compelled to perform, usually to counter their obsessional thoughts) that define OCD. Moreover, those with the personality disorder are not typically anxiety ridden, although they are scrupulous, punctilious, assiduous, and meticulous.

Obsessive-Compulsive Personality Disorder is a particularly good illustration of the dimensional nature of personality traits and the distinction between "style" and "disorder" (discussed in detail in Chapter 11). In many contexts, some obsessive-compulsive behavior is highly adaptive. The traits of being organized, setting high standards for performance, being punctual, and committed to work are highly valued in professional life. A question we have posed to students during training is "Who would not want their neurosurgeon to be exacting and perfectionistic during their surgery, making sure everything is completed perfectly?" As obsessive-compulsive traits become more pronounced, pervasive, and central, however, performance and productivity begin to suffer because the person's rigidity and perfectionism become paralyzing. Like many of the personality disorders, a little bit of some of the traits can be adaptive. Once the traits move to the extreme end of the continuum, they result in dysfunction and impairment, conceptualized as a shift from style to disorder. Table 4.3 shows the *DSM-IV-TR* diagnostic criteria for Obsessive-Compulsive Personality Disorder.

Potential Age-Bias of Criteria

Compared with the other personality disorders, Obsessive-Compulsive Personality Disorder seems to have the least

*Table 4.3   DSM-IV-TR **Diagnostic Criteria for Obsessive-Compulsive Personality Disorder (Code: 301.4)***

A pervasive pattern of preoccupation with orderliness, perfectionism, and mental and interpersonal control, at the expense of flexibility, openness, and efficiency, beginning by early adulthood and present in a variety of contexts, as indicated by four (or more) of the following:

(1) is preoccupied with details, rules, lists, order, organization, or schedules to the extent that the major point of the activity is lost

(2) shows perfectionism that interferes with task completion (e.g., is unable to complete a project because his or her own overly strict standards are not met)

(3) is excessively devoted to work and productivity to the exclusion of leisure activities and friendships (not accounted for by obvious economic necessity)

(4) is overconscientious, scrupulous, and inflexible about matters of morality, ethics, or values (not accounted for by cultural or religious identification)

(5) is unable to discard worn-out or worthless objects even when they have no sentimental value

(6) is reluctant to delegate tasks or to work with others unless they submit to exactly his or her way of doing things

(7) adopts a miserly spending style toward both self and others; money is viewed as something to be hoarded for future catastrophes

(8) shows rigidity and stubbornness

Source: From *Diagnostic and Statistical Manual of Mental Disorders,* fourth edition, text revision, American Psychiatric Association, 2000, Washington, DC: Author. Copyright 2000 by American Psychiatric Association. Reprinted with permission.

deficiency in terms of criteria likely to be problematical in their application and relevance to individuals in later life. On the surface, Criterion 3 (is excessively devoted to work and productivity to the exclusion of leisure activities and friendships) may not be appropriate in the late-life context because older adults have lower formal employment rates than younger and middle-aged adults. In defense of this criterion, however, the terms *work* and *productivity* do not necessarily imply being in a paid position, so sharp criticism of this criterion may not be justified.

A more reasonable critique, however, may be directed at Criterion 7 (adopts a miserly spending style toward both self and others; money is viewed as something to be hoarded for future catastrophes). This criterion may be problematical among some older adults, given that financial pressures are common among older people (with poverty being especially common among older women and minorities) and therefore, having to be cautious with savings makes good sense. Another mitigating circumstance about the present cohort of older adults is that many current 80- and 90-year-olds were children of the Great Depression in the 1930s, and many were indelibly marked with concerns over food and possessions, supporting a cohort effect for this criterion. To the extent that an older person's concern about finances and thrifty spending habits are reasonable and contextually valid, it would be less likely to be a sign of an obsessive-compulsive personality. Lifelong stinginess, especially when money has not been in short supply, is more indicative of this type of personality pathology.

Theorized Pattern in Later Life and Possible Impact of Aging

Older people are often stereotyped as being rigid, which is a hallmark feature of Obsessive-Compulsive Personality Disorder. Indeed, popular but pejorative characterizations of aging are that older people typically become set in their ways and have "hardening of the attitudes." In contrast, there is little evidence that older adults become more rigid in personality as a function of normal aging. Where increased rigidity is observed, it is usually an understandable reaction to physical or emotional threats or crises. A related point is that older people, in general, are not any more resistant to change than younger people, despite the popularity of this myth. In fact, the ability to adapt depends more on lifelong traits of either flexibility or inflexibility than on anything inherent in later life (Butler et al., 1998). These caveats having been said, old age may be a particularly challenging phase of life for older adults with Obsessive-Compulsive Personality Disorder.

Increased dependency on others is likely to be an especially difficult stressor for obsessive-compulsive older adults. Their lifelong pattern of doing things their own way makes them resistant to change and unable to tolerate needing help from others. Believing there is only one way to accomplish tasks, they have a great deal of difficulty in being flexible with lost or reduced physical and cognitive functions. One of our patients, a physically ill 80-year-old man recently admitted to a skilled nursing facility, bemoaned that he could no longer enact his lifelong motto, "My way or the highway," when dealing with his doctors, physical therapists, and the nursing home staff. Older adults with Obsessive-Compulsive Personality Disorder may resent or be offended when offered help, which they interpret as a statement that they are not in complete control. When receiving help becomes inevitable, obsessive-compulsive older adults may react with catastrophic depression.

Another potential stressor is retirement. Older individuals with Obsessive-Compulsive Personality Disorder are likely to cope poorly with retirement, especially where they have had occupational success and have come to define their identity largely through their work role and accompanying prestige and status. Although they are resistant to and uncomfortable with change, retirement brings about a host of new routines that they must painstakingly develop. This often leads obsessive-compulsive older adults to experience a great deal of distress. It is hard for them to enjoy the fruits of their labors and relax. To do so would be perceived as a waste of time.

Another pattern is that the problem of hoarding useless items often becomes more evident in later life. One of our older patients with Obsessive-Compulsive Personality Disorder habitually collected newspapers and magazines, unable to discard them even after having read them. Over many years, the stacks became so large that it became nearly impossible to move from room to room except for a small path that he kept clear. Furthermore, his basement was overflowing with old papers, and his garage was mostly filled with useless, broken appliances (e.g., toasters, blenders, microwave ovens) that he refused to discard even after buying new ones. His thought process, seen by him as reasonable, was "You never know when you might need them." There are other, organic, reasons contributing to hoarding (such as dementia), and these possibilities should be considered as well.

A further problem facing older adults with Obsessive-Compulsive Personality Disorder is that they typically do not have adequate social support networks in place. A lifetime of devotion to work and productivity, rather than to the development of relationships and interests, coupled with emotional coldness and distance, typically leaves these individuals without many supportive relationships. Depression is a common emotional reaction when aging obsessive-compulsive types realize that their lifelong devotion to order and schedules has prevented them from achieving connections and meaningful relationships, even with family members. Because they lack appropriate supports, all the vicissitudes of aging are likely to be compounded in their impact.

We conclude this section by briefly noting a potentially adaptive function of the obsessive-compulsive personality style that we have seen in a few cases. Older adults who conscientiously take care of themselves, stick to an active daily regimen, and keep busy with many details may derive some benefit. One of our elderly patients (with obsessive-compulsive personality features) scrupulously adhered to an exercise routine (bike riding and weight lifting) that kept him in terrific physical shape for much of his life. He experienced difficulties, however, when fatigue caused by cancer and his chemotherapy prevented him from exercising as much as he had previously.

The Case of Louis: Obsessive-Compulsive Personality Disorder

Louis M. was referred to the psychologist by his internist who had cared for Louis and his wife for many years. The physician lived in the same town and knew Louis not only as a patient but also as an active resident of the community. Louis's name was frequently cited in the town's weekly newspaper. He was outspoken, relied on well-documented facts, and had served over the years as a town selectman and chairman of the town's project development committee.

His civic activities were in addition to his vocation as an attorney specializing in tax law. He was a partner in a prestigious law practice in the city, his being the only ethnic name on the roster, a distinction of which he was proud.

Louis was born the second of two sons to immigrant parents who lived in the Italian district in a large metropolitan area. His father, Luigi, worked as a gardener for the diocese, putting in long hours in backbreaking work. Although he enjoyed working with his hands in the soil, Luigi desperately wanted his sons not to follow him in his line of work, but to get an education and make something of themselves. To this end, he and his wife were extremely frugal, saving their money only to spend on their sons. Louis's mother was a pious, devout, and fearful woman. She harbored a great, quiet anger, her life governed by duty and sin. She raised her sons to be clean of body, heart, and mind, and to repent and pray away any transgressions. The brothers, both handsome and intelligent boys, grew to be fiercely competitive, jockeying for position within the family, seeing who could be the best behaved in their parents' eyes. When one or the other did something bad, the other brother would make certain to let their mother and father know about it. The transgression would then be met with a punishment. Most often, while they were young, this meant Luigi removing his belt and meting out a few whips across the erring boy's back and buttocks to make sure that the wrongdoing was never repeated, and to get the devil out of the boy's soul.

Louis learned early that cleanliness was next to godliness and that godliness was the most valued virtue. He learned to be exceptionally neat and to live his life according to the rules. When there was no rule to fit an occasion, Louis would create one, until there were many rules he needed to follow. If he did not follow them, he would feel uncomfortable, worried, and frightened. Louis did not like change. He liked things just the way they were, to remain in order, and to be predictable. As a little boy, he learned to polish his shoes and would line them up along the closet floor with the toes evenly aligned. His brother would torment him by disturbing the order or alignment of the shoes. Although their parents would not indulge fussiness in their children's eating behavior ("Eat what you're served and be grateful for it"), Louis would insist that the different foods on his plate be kept separate and not touching. At school, his desk always received the teacher's compliments for tidiness. Louis was held up as a model for the other students, who paid him back by taunting him on the playground. In his desk, as with his closet and dinner plate, all the items were kept separate and perfectly aligned. The homework he turned in was impeccably neat. If there was one crossed-out word, one erasure, Louis would do it over again until he achieved a final, perfect product.

Louis's propensity toward perfection, strong work ethic, and dedicated avoidance of sin led others to describe him as being somewhat dour, with a peculiar intensity. They also recognized that these same characteristics would likely ensure his success in life and would carry him far.

After high school, Louis earned a full academic scholarship to a Catholic university out of state, which afforded him a fine education as well as permission to leave his parents without committing the sin of going against their wishes. He made a few friends at college, but mostly he concentrated on his studies with an eye toward law school. Earning a near-perfect grade point average, Louis went directly on to law school following graduation. He was able to avoid military service due to mild scoliosis, a condition that did not limit his activities but that earned him a rejection from the military.

He completed law school at age 24, and moved back to the city where his parents lived, sharing an apartment with another fellow also just beginning a law career. Louis assumed a position as a law clerk with an old and honorable firm specializing in tax law. Although now living on his own, he continued to have dinner with his parents at least once a week. When he was 27, his clerkship completed, and his law career effectively launched, Louis proposed marriage to Marie, the young woman he had been courting over the previous year. Marie, 4 years Louis's junior, was a beauty, with thick, flaxen hair and the bluest of blue eyes. Trained as a legal secretary, she worked for the law firm next door to Louis's office. She saw him daily, and while deferential to attorneys, she one day got the courage to ask Louis if he would like to join her for a short walk after lunch. Flattered, he agreed, and so their relationship was launched, culminating in marriage the following year. It was not a highly romantic relationship, as Louis was stilted in expressing anything that suggested weakness or a lack of control, and he kept his emotions tightly wrapped. But Marie was an expressive, warm young woman who idealized Louis and believed that his ever-present cool head was a hallmark of great intelligence and maturity.

Two major changes in Louis's life contributed to the expression of psychopathology and increased distress. One was his retirement from the law practice, and the other was the development of hypertension and cardiovascular disease leading to his discontinuing community activities. Together, these effectively created a double retirement. Subsequently, Louis manifested several problematic behaviors. He developed sleep difficulties and began to grossly overeat, gaining considerable weight, which added to his medical morbidity. Now at home for most of the day, he became watchful of Marie and sharply critical of her every move, lashing out at her for not doing things the right way or for being sloppy. On one occasion, he swept the contents of a kitchen cabinet onto the floor in a pique of anger after discovering that Marie had not securely replaced the cap on a peanut butter jar. Typically, Louis's temper outbursts were followed by his verbal self-flagellation and compulsive overeating. "I am so bad. You should have never married me. I'm a horrible, bad person, Look at me: A sick, fat old man. I don't know why you don't hate me."

Individuals with Obsessive-Compulsive Personality Disorder (OCPD) structure their lives around a triad of orderliness, perfection, and control, which is expressed both internally and interpersonally. Dedication to this triad limits their flexibility, efficiency, and ability to compromise or to change course, even when indicated. Their characteristic overattention to detail means sacrificing regard for the big picture. They often lose sight of the purpose of an activity or project, instead getting bogged down in the details of its organization and plans.

Their strict reliance on rules is frequently imposed on others. They can therefore be very difficult people to please, to work for, and to live with. In Louis's case, he was fortunate to have had a long-term secretary/office manager at work who shared many of his OC traits. In addition, she was socially adept and able to run interference for him with clients who were at risk of annoying Louis and thereby causing an inappropriate show of temper. Things were very different at home, however, with a wife who was a big-picture person, governed more by intuition and empathy than by rules and intellectualization.

As exemplified by Louis, individuals with OCPD often experience marked distress when they cannot gratify their perfectionist tendencies and need to embrace excellence as the exclusive standard. Those with OCPD are typically devoted to work, often are regarded as workaholics, and are intense and overly conscientious about whatever task they undertake. It is easy to see how this devotion to productivity and fastidious attention to detail can take the pleasure out of even a pleasurable activity.

The essence of OCPD, a need to maintain control, is accompanied by several erroneous beliefs that support the disorder. These beliefs include that perfection is attainable, that negative events can be avoided if rules are followed, and that the head must govern the heart. While often attracted to their opposite, a personality with a more histrionic style, they tend to become intolerant of those who allow emotions to reign over clear thought. They consider such individuals to be out of control and thus in need of being controlled. They are often perceived by others as being stilted, especially in the affective domain, which is inherently unfettered by rules. Often respected by others because they are honest as the day is long and perfectly fair, they rely on morals as codified rules, which are immutable and unbendable.

Being profoundly rule-governed, when those with OCPD cannot apply a rule, they tend to become overwhelmed by anxiety and, cognitively, by doubt and uncertainty. It can be difficult for them to make a decision, as they are prone to anguish over the pros and cons attending any choice, becoming immobilized by indecision as no decision is considered perfect or without risk. These same traits and tendencies, however, enable many with OCPD to be high achievers. Consistent with the prototypical Type A personality, they can be hostile, competitive, and time urgent, but ultimately the master of the universe.

Following several transient ischemic attacks portending an actual stroke, Louis did indeed suffer a cerebrovascular accident (CVA), which was mild but nonetheless resulted in a hospitalization of several days' duration. During this time, his physician was able to reach Louis and explain that his life—both its quantity and quality—was in jeopardy if he did not make some changes. Louis willingly participated in the hospital's cardiac rehabilitation program, which included exercise, nutrition, and stress management components. He declined the opportunity to join a support group with other patients, but did accept his physician's referral to meet privately with a psychologist.

It is important to understand that people with OCPD are likely to resist accepting psychological treatment, as they consider that this places them in a one-down position relative to the therapist. This, then, harkens a loss of control, which they fear at their core. An advisable approach to establishing a therapeutic alliance is to join the patient at the level of the head, rather than the heart, and to reinforce the concept of the treatment as a collaborative venture, always under the patient's control.

After Louis's individual psychotherapy got underway, and the alliance was well established, couples therapy was suggested to Louis and Marie. The goals for this were threefold: improve their communication and positive connection; reduce the expressions of Louis's displaced anger and need to control; and enable each spouse to come to know, and relate to, the other *as they are now.*

The individual treatment plan incorporated four types of therapy: Pharmacological, Cognitive-Behavioral, Psychodynamic, and Supportive. For Louis, the first order of (therapeutic) business was to treat an underlying depression. This was presented to him in terms of a biological deregulation requiring chemical correction, especially because he would otherwise regard depression as a moral weakness. He was started on a course of SSRIs and had a favorable response. The medication helped him by decreasing his worries, obsessive ruminations, and compulsive eating. The same medication has anxiolytic properties as well as serving as an antidepressant. Although Louis said he did not feel any different on the medication, his wife reported that he was distinctly less irritable and less likely to explode. Over time, she also reported that he was much less likely to walk around saying nasty things about himself. About this, Louis almost concurred, allowing that maybe it was true.

Cognitive-behavioral therapy addressed his worries and anxiety through identifying and testing Louis's underlying maladaptive core beliefs. These included his excessive sense of responsibility, his belief that there is only one way of doing something, that truth is objective, and that less than perfect control is equated with chaos.

Biofeedback was also added to his treatment plan. Louis did very well with this stress reduction technique, especially well suited to his OC tendencies.

The psychodynamic modality worked on uncovering historically significant material and on linking and labeling Louis's history of experience with emotions.

The greatest focus was on the material that most strongly informed the development of Louis's dysfunctional core beliefs. These included the emotional neglect by his parents, singularly focused on earning a living and bringing up the boys right; the psychological torment by his brother when their sibling rivalry turned sadistic; the instilled fear of a punitive God; and the danger inherent in normal human weakness.

With OCPD, the most common defense mechanisms are isolation of affect (doing), undoing, and reaction formation. For Louis, isolation of affect was dominant. It was evident when he spoke of his father whipping him "for my own good" when he was a child seen as transgressing a rule. Louis recounted these episodes without memory of the way they made him feel (terrified, ashamed, etc.). The role of the therapist then is to become (model) the voice of affect and to encourage the connection between the feeling and experience. Once the more distal linkages are made, Louis is encouraged to make these connections with current experiences. For example, when his wife makes plans for them to dine out with friends, for him to recognize that he feels anxious because he believes he will lose control and eat unhealthily or excessively. The next step is to work to identify actions he can take to avoid this behavior and thus prevent the anxiety from escalating.

Supportive psychotherapy included reinforcing Louis's compliance with his nutritional and exercise regimens, including a psychoeducational component addressing the connection between mind and body (and between feelings and behaviors).

In psychotherapy with those with OCPD, the transference is often reflected through ways the patient attempts to secure control in the relationship. This can be expressed directly though his challenging the therapist or opposing interpretations or assignments. Even gentle inquiry can be misperceived as the therapist's attempt to achieve control. It can also be expressed in more veiled ways, such as through setting and changing appointments, requiring the therapist to accommodate the patient.

The countertransference in working with those with personality disorders in general is likely to be powerful. With the individual with OCPD, boredom is frequently experienced, as the patient is typically humorless and wedded to the cognitive. His presentations lack playfulness, spontaneity, and the affective coloration that so enriches and enlivens a therapy. This paucity of emotional tone can, over time, lead to feelings of impatience for the patient to finally "get it," and a temptation to advance the therapy too hard, too soon.

The most central belief contributing to the OCPD pathology is that of order and perfection as being obtainable if only the rules are followed. They strive mightily to reach the Holy Grail of Perfection. They overvalue themselves while undervaluing others, as few others are seen as maintaining their level of anticipation of contingencies and attention to detail. Above all, they value achievement and productivity and leave little time for relaxing and letting down their guard. Although often highly intelligent, they lack psychological-mindedness and insight; they cannot entertain the point of view of others, where this differs from their own. Their way is the right way. Their truth is the only truth.

Having an OCPD is time consuming, labor intensive, and not much fun. Although hard to live with or work for, these individuals are always hardest on themselves. They are most fearful of loss of control and of the threat of needing to be dependent. It is easy then to understand how this personality disorder can be especially challenged and threatened by the vicissitudes of old age. Louis functioned well during his industrious, workaholic years. He became distressed and symptomatic when he lost the foci for his dominant personality traits on retirement from work and development of health problems that limited his activities.

Other Personality Disorders and Aging: Sadistic, Self-Defeating, Depressive, Passive-Aggressive, and Inadequate

5

Chapter

In Chapters 2, 3, and 4, we examined the 10 standard personality disorders in the *DSM-IV-TR*. In this chapter, we discuss several other patterns of personality disorder pathology that were described in previous versions of the *DSM*. As in the earlier chapters, we provide a clinical description, discuss possible problems with the diagnostic criteria for older people, and describe how the disorders might be manifested in later life. It would be a mistake to conclude that these disorders are not as important or relevant simply because they are not part of the official classification system. In fact, most of the disorders we describe in this chapter have a long and rich clinical tradition, and patients with these patterns do present for help in clinical practice. The debates about official classification usually center around whether these other personality disorders are discrete diagnostic entities (not variations of the standard personality disorders) and disagreements about how to define and operationalize the criteria for these personality disorders.

Whereas the *DSM-III* contained elaborate appendixes, none were devoted to additional or speculative personality disorders. In 1987, the publication of *DSM-III-R* began a new tradition—the use of the appendixes to introduce new or speculative syndromes and personality disorders for study and perhaps validation. *DSM-III-R*'s Appendix A: *Proposed Diagnostic Categories Needing Further Study* included two (the Sadistic Personality Disorder and Self-Defeating Personality Disorder). *DSM-IV* and *DSM-IV-TR* continued this tradition in Appendix B: *Criteria Sets and Axes Provided for Further Study* in which two personality disorders were added (one new [Depressive Personality Disorder] and one [Passive-Aggressive Personality Disorder] that was previously listed on Axis II in *DSM-III-R*). In the current manual, both Sadistic Personality Disorder and Self-Defeating Personality Disorder were dropped from the appendix. The diagnostic criteria for the four personality disorders discussed in this chapter are provided separately in the following sections.

Personality Disorders in DSM-III-R Appendix A and in DSM-IV-TR Appendix B

In this section, the Sadistic and Self-Defeating Personality Disorders from *DSM-III-R* Appendix A and the Depressive and Passive-Aggressive Personality Disorders from *DSM-IV-TR* Appendix B are discussed with emphasis on their prominent features, potential inadequacy of the diagnostic criteria for geriatric variants of the disorders, and impact of aging on their expressions.

Sadistic Personality Disorder: *DSM-III-R* Appendix A

Clinical Description

People with Sadistic Personality Disorder are pervasively cruel, demeaning, and verbally and physically aggressive in most of their relationships. The sadistic behavior is typically more evident when the sadistic individual is in a position of power, as in the role of a father, mother, or uncle, or in occupational settings as a boss or in any position where there are subordinates. In contrast, individuals with Sadistic Personality Disorder often manage to contain their behavior when they are in subordinate positions, at least toward the person in the position of power over them. Sadistic individuals take pleasure in the suffering of others, including animals. Like the antisocial personality, lying is frequent, but the sadistic personality lies with the intent of inflicting pain on others and not merely to achieve some other goal. Although the *DSM-III-R* indicated that the pattern must be evident by adulthood, numerous studies have found the onset of sadistic behavior as early as childhood.

Individuals with Sadistic Personality Disorder often use physical violence and cruelty to establish their dominance and complete control in a relationship. An excellent example of such a person was Martin Burney (played by Patrick Bergin) in the 1991 movie, *Sleeping with the Enemy*. Laura Burney (played by Julia Roberts) looks to be a happily and wonderfully married woman. However, we discover that Martin is a highly threatening, abusive, and brutally controlling husband. Laura comes to live in constant fear of his pervasively tyrannical behavior.

The sadistic person's threatening behavior will often escalate to interpersonal violence if he or she thinks that the person being subordinated is resisting control or is no longer intimidated. It is thought that there may be nonviolent forms of Sadistic Personality Disorder, that is, those individuals may not resort to physical violence in relationships although they may still be psychologically abusive, and they still may harbor deep fascinations for weapons of violence, torture, and literature and media with such themes (Millon & Davis, 2000). Notably, a diagnosis is not typically given if the sadistic behavior has been directed toward only a single individual, like a spouse, nor should it be given if the behavior is exhibited solely for purposes of sexual arousal (a diagnosis of Sexual Sadism should be given in such cases although it is highly debatable whether a comorbid diagnosis of Sadistic Personality Disorder should not also be given).

Millon and Davis (2000) have proposed four types of Sadistic Personality Disorder: explosive, spineless, enforcing, and tyrannical. Explosive sadistics react suddenly with verbal abuse and violence. It appears as if they reach a threshold of tolerance, and then respond rapidly and violently against what they consider "safe" targets, that is, ones that cannot retaliate. Millon and

Davis hypothesize that explosive sadistic types are hypersensitive to any hint of betrayal by those with whom they have relationships, and they explode with rage when their feelings of humiliation reach intolerable levels. In this regard, they may also have features of borderline personality disorder.

In contrast, spineless sadistics have predominately avoidant personality disorder features. These individuals are essentially highly insecure, and they have a "strike first" attitude to counter their insecurities and feelings of powerlessness. Millon and Davis (2000) propose that people who join hate groups often have the spineless type of Sadistic Personality Disorder. They also hypothesize that spineless types take out their aggression and hostility on especially defenseless or helpless targets.

According to Millon and Davis (2000), the enforcing Sadistic Personality Disorder type has obsessive-compulsive personality disorder features. They sublimate their hostility by enforcing rules, often in a demanding and authoritarian manner, that allows no dissent or even rational objection. They may see themselves as defenders of justice and correctness, but it often is a mask to hide their basically cruel and hostile nature. They may be typified by the "hanging" judge and the "mean" cop. A milder version of this type was seen by one of us in therapy. This patient reported "compliance problems" with his spouse, and for an example said his wife resisted his demands that she face all cans and boxes in the pantry with the labels outward. He said he was trying to get her to understand that her labeling problem was only a symptom of her general inability to become a good wife. He went to great lengths in therapy to justify his demands on his spouse. Ironically, he sought therapy not for himself but to help him manage his wife better.

Tyrannical sadistic types have depressive and paranoid personality disorder features. Millon and Davis (2000) propose that they are perhaps the most frightening and pathological of all four types. Tyrannical types are cruel and absolutely inhumane. They often instigate and carry out the most verbally and physically abusive sadistic acts on other people and animals, and they will also direct others to carry out these horrible acts. There have been numerous world dictators who have exhibited these traits, such as Joseph Stalin, Adolf Hitler, and more recently Pol Pot and the Khmer Rouge movement.

Like most other personality disorders, persons with Sadistic Personality Disorder typically do not see any problems with their behavior (and, in fact, usually see the positive outcomes of getting what they want). As consequence, treatment is particularly difficult with this personality disorder. The longer one has exhibited these behaviors and the longer symptoms have gone uncorrected, the more difficult therapy becomes. Table 5.1 lists the diagnostic criteria for Sadistic Personality Disorder.

Table 5.1 **Diagnostic Criteria for Sadistic Personality Disorder (*DSM-III-R*, Appendix A)**

A. A pervasive pattern of cruel, demeaning, and aggressive behavior, beginning by early adulthood, as indicated by the repeated occurrence of at least four of the following:
   (1) has used physical cruelty or violence for the purpose of establishing dominance in a relationship (not merely to achieve some noninterpersonal goal, such as striking someone in order to rob him or her)
   (2) humiliates or demeans people in the presence of others
   (3) has treated or disciplined someone under his or her control unusually harshly, e.g., a child, student, prisoner, or patient
   (4) is amused by, or takes pleasure in, the psychological or physical suffering of others (including animals)
   (5) has lied for the purpose of harming or inflicting pain on others (not merely to achieve some other goal)
   (6) gets other people to do what he or she wants by frightening them (through intimidation or even terror)
   (7) restricts the autonomy of people with whom he or she has a close relationship, e.g., will not let spouse leave the house unaccompanied or permit teen-age daughter to attend social functions
   (8) is fascinated by violence, weapons, martial arts, injury, or torture
B. The behavior in A has not been directed toward only one person (e.g., spouse, one child) and has not been solely for the purpose of sexual arousal (as in Sexual Sadism).

Source: From *Diagnostic and Statistical Manual of Mental Disorders,* third edition, revised, American Psychiatric Association, 1987, Washington, DC: Author. Copyright 1987 by American Psychiatric Association. Reprinted with permission.

Potential Age-Bias of Criteria
Criterion A1 (has used physical cruelty or violence for the purpose of establishing dominance in a relationship) is likely problematic due to decreased physical strength and stamina associated with normal aging. However, emotional cruelty seems to know no age limits, so this particular symptom may be acted out in proxy fashion especially among frail sadistics. Additionally, a common pattern with aging is to have fewer social relationships. Along with reduced interpersonal contacts due to retirement, these contextual factors may restrict the sample of safe or helpless targets for aging sadistic individuals. The sadistic criteria that involve dominance relationships (parent-child, boss-worker) may indeed be no longer applicable throughout the life span.

Theorized Pattern in Later Life and Possible Impact of Aging
In our experience, it is likely that most Sadistic Personality Disorder traits persist as people age. Indeed, pathologically mean people do not become nice simply as a function of age. Whereas the sadistic criteria that involve physical domination may be somewhat less appropriate for older persons, the general sadistic demeanor and pattern of cruelty often persists throughout the life span. Thus, aging may restrict some physical expressions and symptoms of the Sadistic Personality Disorder, yet the overall cruel and demeaning behaviors remain. Age by itself, however, does not preclude physically sadistic acts. One of us consulted on a case where the husband, in his late 70s, was continuing to rape his wife, who was helpless with dementia and profoundly frail, until she ended up in the hospital.

We have also seen some cases in which the sadistic behaviors seem to exacerbate as the older person's phenomenal and real world shrinks, for example, to those who provide physical assistance, that is, nursing staff and caretakers and other residents. When the aging individual with Sadistic Personality Disorder moves to a congregate living or long-term care facility, the targets for their abuse increase. Their old predilections for humiliating and demeaning people in front of others may persist, as well as their well-practiced penchants for taking pleasure in the suffering and misery of those around them. They make take secret delight in obstructing the work of their caretakers, medical professionals, mental health professionals, and their own family members. They may similarly take pleasure in the misfortunes and deteriorations in the health of fellow residents.

Self-Defeating Personality Disorder: *DSM-III-R* Appendix A

Clinical Description

The basic pattern of the Self-Defeating Personality Disorder involves behaviors that undermine the person's ability to be successful, happy, and healthy in a wide variety of contexts. Self-defeating people are habitually attracted to people who invariably disappoint them, hurt them, or make them suffer. They typically reject or avoid pleasurable experiences. They typically fail to accomplish tasks that are critical to their own success (despite the ability to be successful at such tasks) such as educational goals and objectives in occupational settings. They also resist and render useless efforts by others to help them be successful, and they tend to invoke angry or rejecting responses from others, yet later report that they feel demoralized, hurt, and disappointed by how others have responded. They usually rationalize their self-defeating behavior, and they may argue vehemently with their therapists about the justification for their actions. One of our patients in her 6th year of a 2-year master's program, argued vociferously that finishing her program symbolically represented death (in part because she was a diabetic). She clung to her rationalization despite pleas from her therapist and family and despite evidence from standardized tests (she scored in the 95th percentile on the Graduate Record Examination) that she had the ability to complete her degree program. Ironically, she also devoted her time to a research professor who was not supervising her thesis and who did not pay her. The latter behavior also met an official criterion of the Self-Defeating Personality Disorder diagnosis: engages in excessive self-sacrifice, not solicited by the recipient of the sacrifice.

One of us also performed an intake on a 58-year-old woman about to undergo gastric surgery. As she recalled her husbands from her first three marriages, all of whom she reported as abusive alcoholics, she blithely exclaimed, "it seems like there's a pattern here." When asked about her current husband, she dismissively said, "Oh, he's an alcoholic." Despite the possibility that her definition of alcoholism may have been overly broad, the possibility that she has been chronically attracted to abusive men or people harmful to her was likely. In therapy, such patients may readily comply with initial requests of the therapists and also may initially make insightful comments about their past behaviors. However, with time, the therapists usually come to realize the difficulties that self-defeating persons make for themselves and the myriad ways they manage to disrupt and prevent real therapeutic success.

After the apparent establishment of solid and trusting rapport with their therapist, self-defeating personality disordered patients may start to make special demands and then react with noticeable anger and disappointment when their unrealistic requests are not met. In therapy, these patients may also engage in a "yes, but" game, as they come up with reasons for maintaining unhealthy behaviors. The therapist's attempt to subtly suggest more assertive and successful modes of behaving are often met with sometimes subtle and sometimes blatant refusal. These interactions often mirror their social and family interactions as well, where offers of assistance are also met with rejection, despite clear needs for the help and assistance. Not surprisingly, people with Self-Defeating Personality Disorder very often do not comply or agree with treatment plans but are adept at sabotaging them to confirm that "nothing helps." Table 5.2 lists the *DSM-IV-TR* diagnostic criteria for Self-Defeating Personality Disorder.

Potential Age-Bias of Criteria
Some of the possibilities for meeting Self-Defeating Personality Disorder criteria may be curtailed with the aging process, such as there may be fewer opportunities to undermine occupational and educational goals. These situations, where the older person may

Table 5.2   **Diagnostic Criteria for Self-Defeating Personality Disorder (*DSM-III-R*, Appendix A)**

A. A pervasive pattern of self-defeating behavior, beginning by early adulthood and present in a variety of contexts. The person may often avoid or undermine pleasurable experiences, be drawn to situations or relationships in which he or she will suffer, and prevent others from helping him or her, as indicated by at least five of the following:

  (1) chooses people and situations that lead to disappointment, failure, or mistreatment even when better options are clearly available

  (2) rejects or renders ineffective the attempts of others to help him or her

  (3) following positive personal events (e.g., new achievement), responds with depression, guilty, or a behavior that produces pain (e.g., an accident)

  (4) incites angry or rejecting responses from others and then feels hurt, defeated, or humiliated (e.g., makes fun of spouse in public, provoking an angry retort, then feels devastated)

  (5) rejects opportunities for pleasure, or is reluctant to acknowledge enjoying himself or herself (despite having adequate social skills and the capacity for pleasure)

  (6) fails to accomplish tasks crucial to his or her personal objectives despite demonstrated ability to do so, e.g., helps fellow students write papers, but is unable to write his or her own

  (7) is uninterested in or rejects people who consistently treat him or her well, e.g., is unattracted to caring sexual partners

  (8) engages in excessive self-sacrifice that is unsolicited by the intended recipients of the sacrifice

B. The behaviors in A do not occur exclusively in response to, or in anticipation of, being physically, sexually, or psychologically abused.

C. The behaviors in A do not occur only when the person is depressed

Source: From *Diagnostic and Statistical Manual of Mental Disorders,* third edition, revised, American Psychiatric Association, 1987, Washington, DC: Author. Copyright 1987 by American Psychiatric Association. Reprinted with permission.

have been clever at disrupting or failing when younger, no longer seem as relevant. Although most of the other symptoms of the disorder arguably would not seem to be impacted much by aging, the manifestations of the disorder can be affected by aging.

Theorized Pattern in Later Life and Possible Impact of Aging
One pattern we have observed is that older people with Self-Defeating Personality Disorder create inappropriate excuses as

they age such as "I'm far too old for that" when they are not, and "I could never do that at my age," while many people are successful at their age in such endeavors. Older persons who have long had Self-Defeating Personality Disorder features have the opportunity to exhibit these traits as they age, especially as their actual needs for physical or instrumental assistance increase. One of our patients, who broke her hip at 85 years old, insisted that she could return to her home without any outside help, yet complained vehemently to her adult children that she was being neglected. Her adult children reported her consistent efforts at thwarting their good intentions: They offered to pay for maid service—her reply, "they'll steal from me"; they wanted to provide food service—"they all have lousy food"; they tried to set up therapy—"they just want your money." Whereas being successful at deflecting help may be a lifelong trait, opportunities to render help ineffective often present with greater frequency in later life, and as such, these traits may become more obvious.

Although opportunities to choose people and situations that may be unhealthy or unsuccessful may diminish somewhat as people age (due to lowered social opportunities), the limited available opportunities are typically met with chronic and well practiced self-defeating behaviors. Whatever successes these patients experience are still met with depression, guilt, or psychosomatic ailments. Whatever pleasures they are offered are met with scorn, rejection, reluctance, and disinterest. Whenever they meet kind and supportive caregivers, doctors, or acquaintances, they are uninterested, instead seeking out people likely to be rejecting. One of our older patients reported in therapy the mantra that he was "born to fail," which he habitually made come true.

Another common pattern is that of the aging martyr who has sacrificed herself throughout her life, often accompanied with bitterness and regret. The consequences of such martyrdom often become more pronounced in later life. One of our patients had a long history of giving large sums of money to a heroin-addicted daughter who chronically refused treatment. During middle age when the patient was working, she could afford these contributions, but in later life she lost her home and could not afford her own basic necessities, yet continued the pattern of giving money to her daughter (despite knowing the daughter would buy drugs with the money). The lifelong martyr knows no role except suffering, so therapy, with its purpose to reduce suffering, can be antithetical to this style and very difficult.

As noted, some of the opportunities for self-defeating individuals to exhibit their behavior in later life may be diminished (especially educational and occupational areas). Thus, clinicians who follow the *DSM* criteria strictly may find that a patient fails to meet 5 of the 8 Self-Defeating Personality Disorder criteria, despite a high likelihood of the presence of the disorder. At these times, it may be important for clinicians to keep in mind the current *DSM*'s warning that the criteria are only meant to be a general guide to clinical practice. The criteria are not to be used in cookbook fashion. It is, of course, important that clinicians are aware of all the criteria for a particular diagnosis and the threshold for its application (e.g., must meet 5 of 8 criteria) to avoid inappropriate and idiosyncratic diagnoses. However, the *DSM* notes that limitations of the classification system must be recognized and that all individuals who, for example, meet 5 of the 8 criteria for the Self-Defeating Personality Disorder will not all be alike in the expression of their self-defeating behaviors. The *DSM-IV-TR* specifically states that "the exercise of clinical judgment may justify giving a certain diagnosis to an individual even though the clinical presentation falls just short of meeting the full criteria for the diagnosis as long as the symptoms that are present are persistent and severe" (p. xxxii). Thus, when an older person persistently engages in unambiguous self-defeating behaviors across diverse situations (e.g., with family, peers, doctors, or caregivers), a diagnosis of Self-Defeating Personality Disorder becomes likely, especially given a prior history for such behavior.

Depressive Personality Disorder: *DSM-IV-TR* Appendix B

Clinical Description

The appearance of the Depressive Personality Disorder in *DSM-IV* was not unheralded (Coolidge & Segal, 1998). The *DSM-II*, published in 1968, had at least two personality disorders with many of the features of Depressive Personality Disorder. Whereas the cyclothymic personality included many of the same depressive symptoms as the current depressive personality, the symptoms alternated with periods of elation in the cyclothymic type. But the worry, pessimism, and general sense of futility are nearly identical to current criteria. The *DSM-II* also included the asthenic personality, with such symptoms as lack of enthusiasm and marked incapacity for enjoyment. The latter symptom is nearly identical to a feature listed in *DSM-IV-TR* for the Depressive Personality Disorder, and the lack of enthusiasm symptom is similar to other currently listed features.

The central feature of Depressive Personality Disorder is a pervasive pattern of depressive, pessimistic cognitions and behaviors beginning by early adulthood. The negativism of the individual is thought to be a chronic and unremitting trait and not limited to transient states, nor are the symptoms thought to be elicited only in response to depressing news or events in the individual's life. The person's mood is characterized by a general sense of gloom and joylessness. There is not necessarily a sense of apprehension, as that would connote the person anticipates dread or catastrophe in the near future. With the depressive personality type, it is as if they know dread and catastrophe are certain, so there is no need for apprehension. Their gloominess pervades their sense of self and extends to others. They have a very low self-esteem and a pervasive sense of worthlessness. This describes the individual who experiences life through a gray filter.

People with Depressive Personality Disorder seek out others who would reinforce their lowly self-image and avoid those who argue with them and try to bolster their negative perceptions. This choice of others might also maintain and perpetuate the person's negative self-image and would do little to counter

Table 5.3   **Research Criteria for Depressive Personality Disorder (*DSM-IV-TR*, Appendix B)**

A. A pervasive pattern of depressive cognitions and behaviors beginning by early adulthood and present in a variety of contexts, as indicated by five (or more) of the following:

    (1) usual mood is dominated by dejection, gloominess, cheerlessness, joylessness, unhappiness

    (2) self-concept centers around beliefs or inadequacy, worthlessness, and low self-esteem

    (3) is critical, blaming, and derogatory toward self

    (4) is brooding and given to worry

    (5) is negativistic, critical, and judgmental toward others

    (6) is pessimistic

    (7) is prone to feeling guilty or remorseful

B. Does not occur exclusively during Major Depressive Episodes and is not better accounted for by Dysthymic Disorder.

Source: From *Diagnostic and Statistical Manual of Mental Disorders,* fourth edition, text revision, American Psychiatric Association, 2000, Washington, DC: Author. Copyright 2000 by American Psychiatric Association. Reprinted with permission.

or ameliorate their overly negativistic worldview. These people might even join groups of other individuals who share their pessimistic views, such as end-of-the-world cults, although many depressive people are prone to isolation. Their cheerlessness and unhappiness tend to drive others away. When interviewed, patients with Depressive Personality Disorder are often critical of their own behavior and self-derogatory. They freely admit their feelings of guilt and remorse for their current state of affairs. As noted, these negative feelings would also extend to others, so no one would escape their negativistic and critical evaluations and judgmental scrutiny. Some evidence suggests that these chronic depressive traits are heritable and begin before early adulthood (e.g., Coolidge, Thede, & Jang, 2001). Table 5.3 lists the *DSM-IV-TR* diagnostic criteria for Depressive Personality Disorder.

Potential Age-Bias of Criteria

Because most of the symptoms of the depressive type center around negative mood states and pessimistic, critical attitudes (and not behaviors that require high energy or stamina), there is little reason to think that older adults would not manifest the symptoms as they are delineated in the manual. One possible diagnostic bias may occur in cases when others incorrectly view the older person's gloominess and negativity as a normal part of aging and not recognize it as part of a lifelong pathological pattern of pessimism and unhappiness.

Theorized Pattern in Later Life and Possible Impact of Aging
The aging process is challenging enough, so one can imagine the outcome of a characteristically dour and self-flagellating person. Little is definitively known about the depressive personality type in general, and even less knowledge is available about the effects of aging. Nonetheless, we see two possibilities for the depressive type. The counterintuitive hypothesis might be that people with Depressive Personality Disorder are likely to do as well as anyone else as they age because any of the negative effects of aging might be seen as confirming their lifelong held suspicions that life is a gloomy and cheerless place and continues to be so: "You work hard and then you die." The negative events that have been created by older depressive patients as a consequence of their self- and other-critical behaviors appear to them as a constant, which in contrast to psychologically healthier older adults does not necessarily suddenly upset or surprise the depressive patients. Poor treatment, neglectful care, deteriorating health, and ageism may be seen as something the aging depressive patient expected and anticipated. In contrast, the other hypothesis is that many of the symptoms of the Depressive Personality Disorder might exacerbate as a reaction to some of the "slings and arrows" that physical and mental declines bring with advanced age. Thus, it is possible for features of Depressive Personality Disorder to be more prominent in the elderly when they have not been blatantly characteristic earlier in life.

To some extent, people prone to Depressive Personality Disorder features may have their full-blown symptoms kept at subclinical levels by their spouses or occupations. Because mentally healthy adults are able to keep a balanced perspective about the benefits and vagaries of life, people with depressive tendencies may be propped up by those in their lives with healthier attitudes and perspectives. These situations may be the opposite of *folie à deux*. The depressive spouse shares the positive illusions of the healthy spouse, a pattern we label as *joie à deux*. In the situation where the healthy spouse dies first, the depressive person may then revert to more natural depressive traits and symptoms. Although it may appear that the depressive symptoms arose only as a function of the death of the spouse, in reality they have been suspended in a subclinical state by the healthier attitudes of the other spouse. Clinicians may wish to probe depressive patients carefully in such circumstances and interview other family members should these suspicions arise.

Retirement may also exacerbate Depressive Personality Disorder traits, as there are often many naturally positive aspects to one's job or occupation. Those fortunate to have had rewarding job positions and occupations may have had their depressive traits kept at bay by raises, attitudes of healthy coworkers, and other benefits from jobs with self-actualizing potential. With the free time and loss of prestige that often accompany retirement, depressive tendencies may intensify.

Passive-Aggressive Personality Disorder: *DSM-IV-TR* Appendix B

Clinical Description

The Passive-Aggressive Personality Disorder has been in the *DSM* since its inception in 1952. Only in 1994 with the advent of *DSM-IV* was the Passive-Aggressive Personality Disorder removed from Axis II and placed in an appendix. The reasons for its drop in diagnostic status are uncertain; however, Appendix B of *DSM-IV-TR* is intended to foster research that may result in a refinement of the diagnosis and its criteria, so it is possible the type may reappear in revised form in future versions of the *DSM*.

A major problem is immediately evident from an examination of the criteria for the two personality disorders in the appendix of *DSM-IV-TR* (depressive and passive-aggressive). The Passive-Aggressive Personality Disorder's alternate label is *Negativistic Personality Disorder* yet none of the 7 criteria lists negativism as a symptom. Negativism, however, is listed as Criterion 5 for the Depressive Personality Disorder. This anomaly is certain to cause some confusion in the minds of clinicians and researchers who may either be attempting to use the criteria to diagnose either of these disorders or to research potential similarities and differences between the two disorders. Indeed, concerns about construct validity may be one of the reasons the passive-aggressive type was dropped from the official list.

The first *DSM* noted that Passive-Aggressive Personality Disorder was characterized by three types: passive-dependent, aggressive, and passive-aggressive. The passive-dependent type has seemingly evolved into the current Dependent Personality Disorder because the first version of the *DSM* listed feelings of helplessness, indecisiveness, and a tendency to cling childlike to a parentlike figure. The aggressive type appears to share many symptoms of the modern Borderline Personality Disorder such as temper tantrums, recurrent anger, irritability, and destructive behavior. It is the third, passive-aggressive type, that appears to have evolved into the modern Passive-Aggressive Personality Disorder with historical and current features of stubbornness, procrastination, inefficiency, and passive obstructivism.

Most conceptualizations of passive-aggressive individuals suggest that the issue of autonomy versus external control is paramount. They begin to counter their resentment to any restriction of their free will with passive resistance to fulfill even routine social and occupational demands. Ironically, they often feel misunderstood and unappreciated by others and feel they have been unfairly singled out for more than their fair share of the work when the opposite is often true. They will even balk at being asked to do less than their fair share, although they do not view it that way. Thus, they are frequently scornful and critical of authority figures and easily become sullen and argumenta-

Table 5.4 **Research Criteria for Passive-Aggressive Personality Disorder (*DSM-IV-TR*, Appendix B)**

A. A pervasive pattern of negativistic attitudes and passive resistance to demands for adequate performance, beginning by early adulthood and present in a variety of contexts, as indicated by four (or more) of the following:

(1) passively resists fulfilling routine social and occupational tasks

(2) complains of being misunderstood and unappreciated by others

(3) is sullen and argumentative

(4) unreasonably criticizes and scorns authority

(5) expresses envy and resentment toward those apparently more fortunate

(6) voices exaggerated and persistent complaints of personal misfortune

(7) alternates between hostile defiance and contrition

B. Does not occur exclusively during Major Depressive Episodes and is not better accounted for by Dysthymic Disorder.

Source: From *Diagnostic and Statistical Manual of Mental Disorders,* fourth edition, text revision, American Psychiatric Association, 2000, Washington, DC: Author. Copyright 2000 by American Psychiatric Association. Reprinted with permission.

tive when given any task. They are highly envious of others and resent it when others seem to have any good fortune. They tend to complain bitterly to others about their own personal misfortunes and can exaggerate their hardships to gain sympathy, which they then exploit. They also vacillate between their automatic defiance reactions and later become contrite and penitent about their initial behavior. Table 5.4 lists the *DSM-IV-TR* diagnostic criteria for Passive-Aggressive Personality Disorder.

Potential Age-Bias of Criteria

Because symptoms of the passive-aggressive type mostly involve negative mood states, verbal behavioral patterns (e.g., voices complaints, is argumentative, expresses resentment), and the absence of productive behaviors (passively resists fulfilling tasks), it appears that aging per se would not impact the expression of the symptoms. Criterion 5 (expresses envy and resentment toward those apparently more fortunate) may be more easily met among older adults who have experienced the most severe losses with age and are, in fact, less fortunate than most around them. Finally, whereas occupational opportunities to display passive-aggressive behaviors may be reduced somewhat with advancing age, the passive-aggressive individual's opportunities to display resistant behavior in relationships with family, peers, and health care professionals are likely to remain abundant. New demands that appear in the context of aging will likely serve to heighten passive-aggressive reactions.

Theorized Pattern in Later Life and Possible Impact of Aging
A particular challenge for the passive-aggressive person will be increased dependence on health care systems and other institutional organizations. Passive-aggressive behaviors are likely to become more evident as the aging person becomes more reliant on others and is forced to meet the expectations of doctors, caregivers, and congregate living staff. Whereas family members may have long learned to deal with the passive resistance and stubbornness of these individuals, for example by withdrawal, care providers who work with these older persons might be more likely to confront directly such behavior than family members, fostering even greater resistance. The frail passive-aggressive older adult will likely have noteworthy difficulty complying with medication and physical rehabilitation regimes, deriving some degree of power or control by passively failing to comply and making others irritated or perplexed.

As noted throughout this book, many of the stressors that often accompany aging such as physical illness or disability, reduced independence, sensory and cognitive declines, changes in physical appearance, social losses, and financial pressures, frequently serve to exacerbate underlying personality disorder features and traits. The Passive-Aggressive Personality Disorder is probably among the most likely of the personality disorders to become more apparent during the aging process, as the loss of autonomy that often accompanies aging heightens the ambivalence that fuels passive-aggressive traits. Given a far-from-perfect health care system, it seems probable that those who have a history of trouble dealing with external authority figures will have additional problems as they age and become increasing more reliant on those systems.

Inadequate Personality Disorder—A Manifestation of Frontal Lobe Syndrome?

An interesting personality disorder that appeared in the *DSM-II* in 1968 but was dropped as a diagnostic category in 1980 with the publication of *DSM-III* is the Inadequate Personality Disorder. Despite its diagnostic disappearance, we have found it remains clinically relevant and useful in a later life context, and thus we include it in this chapter.

Inadequate Personality Disorder

Clinical Description

The Inadequate Personality Disorder description in *DSM-II* included ineffectual responses to any physical, intellectual, social, or emotional demands placed on the individual. Despite the lack of any real physical or intellectual deficits, these patients appear poorly adapted to their environment, are inept, have poor judgment, are socially unstable, lack physical and emotional stamina, and chronically cannot cope with everyday stress and strain. Detailed, behaviorally specific criteria were not provided for any of the disorders in *DSM-II*.

Our hypothesis is that the inadequate personality disorder may be alternately conceptualized (and labeled) as the *frontal lobe syndrome*. Whereas there is no official *DSM* frontal lobe syndrome, a substantial literature supports many consistent behavioral correlates of frontal lobe damage and dysfunction (see Miller & Cummings, 1999; also see Gazzaniga, Ivry, & Mangun, 2002, for reviews of this literature). There is also provocative evidence that indecisiveness, ineptness, and social misjudgments not only occur after brain insult and injury but may even be highly heritable in the normal population (Coolidge, Thede, & Young, 2000) and possess a bivariate heritability with some personality disorders (Coolidge, Thede, & Jang, 2004). First, we briefly describe some of the characteristics of the frontal lobe syndrome, and then explain how these symptoms may form a reliable grouping of inadequate behaviors without the presence of brain injury or damage.

Since Phineas Gage suffered a severe frontal lobe head injury in 1848 as the result of an iron tamping rod passing through the front section of his skull, scientists have associated personality change to frontal lobe injuries. Gage's personality changes included childishness, erratic behavior, and a definite fall from his position of responsibility (as foreman of a railroad crew) to, sadly, a circus sideshow performer. Within 5 or so decades of Gage's injury, the first frontal lobotomies were being performed that resulted in apathy (if not death) in formerly violent psychiatric patients. In other words, it became well known that frontal lobe insult would reliably result in dramatically reduced spontaneity, creativity, and general social effectiveness.

By the middle of the twentieth century, the behaviors associated with frontal lobe function and dysfunction became known as the *executive functions* of the frontal lobes, and they included the ability to inhibit, plan, organize, strategize, and very importantly, maintain and attain goals. Evidence from a study of twins has suggested that these functions might be highly heritable in normal populations (Coolidge, Thede, et al. 2000). Executive functions were also found to be normally distributed in the population. In other words, some people would be extraordinarily able to plan, organize, strategize, and attain their goals, whereas others would be unable to navigate adequately in society despite adequate intelligence and memory abilities. A subsequent study (Coolidge, Thede, et al., 2004) demonstrated that the executive functions were not only heritable but quite probably shared a common genetic origin with particular personality traits that resulted in personal and social disruption. They found that inherited executive dysfunction would result in personality disorders associated with chronic difficulties in making everyday decisions, inattention to important or relevant stimuli, repeated poor judgments and choices, inadequate planning and organization, and inflexibility. In summary, many of the features of the archaic inadequate personality disorder from *DSM-II* appear to mimic patients with frontal lobe insult and injuries. Moreover, it now appears that there is normal variation in the cluster of these behaviors without any evidence of frontal lobe injury or disease. Thus, the validity of a diagnosis of Inadequate Personality Disorder may be empirically and theoretically justified. Features of this type are certainly seen in clinical practice with individuals simply unable to cope with the demands of the late-life stage.

Potential Age-Bias of Criteria

Because the Inadequate Personality Disorder diagnosis was dropped from *DSM-III* in 1980 and because no criteria were listed for it in *DSM-II* (only a short list of common features), there is little room to examine potential problems with the disorder. Throughout our clinical experiences, however, we have found patients who seem to meet the original picture for Inadequate Personality Disorder in *DSM-II* or at least show some features of the disorder. The reader should note that it is entirely justified to use the *DSM-IV-TR* diagnosis *301.9 Personality Disorder Not Otherwise Specified* for those persons whose behavior does not meet criteria for any specific personality disorder yet whose behavior is chronic and causes significant distress or impairment in their current social milieu, such as would be seen by the inadequate type.

Theorized Pattern in Later Life and Possible Impact of Aging

The pattern we have seen clinically on several occasions is for the person with features of this disorder to become more inadequate and dysfunctional in later life. Indeed, the cognitive and physical declines associated with normal aging seem, in some cases, to further limit the effectiveness of patients who have a lifetime history of marginal social and occupational functioning. One of our patients, a 76-year-old woman, had a long history of psychiatric problems labeled as "depression." She dropped out of high school because she "could not handle" the stress associated with academic assignments. She married after a brief courtship and had three children. Despite not ever having a job outside the home (her husband supported the family), the patient reportedly had minimal responsibilities for cooking, cleaning, managing the household, and raising the children. A sister of the husband largely assumed these duties for the family, although with some resentment. The patient told a story of being "taken care of" by her husband (and after his death, by her children) and achieved only a minimal amount of social success throughout life. Her later years were characterized by even greater despondency and helplessness, especially in adjusting to a new community after a daughter moved the patient to be nearer to her.

It might be expected that the inadequate personality type would have drifted from job to job that appeared to be obviously below their intellectual capabilities. Their occupation, should their job history be relatively stable, might also be far beneath what would appear to be their potential. The patient's indecisiveness might also extend to interpersonal issues such as the choice of friends and even self-concept. It would not be surprising that such patients would have dim or nonexistent views of their place in the world and who they were and are. They would not have been expected to have led creative or spectacularly successful lives. These inadequacies might even become more apparent should the person have married someone far more competent and achieving; on that person's death, it might be expected that the person with Inadequate Personality Disorder might be unable to attain even minimal self-sufficiency (e.g., paying the bills, shopping, cooking, and cleaning). This pattern was evident in our example.

Because there is reasonable evidence that this general cluster of inadequate and insufficient behaviors might have a strongly heritable basis, traditional psychotherapies might have a weak impact on the patient's ultimate prognosis. A lifetime of failure is difficult to overcome in later life. Cognitive, reasoning, and intellectual declines that accompany the normal aging process might well be much more pronounced in the inadequate personality disordered patient. Should this diagnosis be suspected in an older patient, it will be important for the clinician to provide greater structure than is typical with most older patients. Behavioral treatment approaches may be more beneficial to the patient than traditional insight-oriented therapies, with an emphasis on support, encouragement, and arrangements for resources.

Epidemiology and Comorbidity

6

chapter

In this chapter, we discuss the epidemiology and comorbidity of the personality disorders with special emphasis on later life. In the mental health field, *epidemiology* is defined as the study of the frequency and distribution of psychiatric disorders in a population. Epidemiological research is crucial to the understanding of rates of disorders as well as how they vary according to social, cultural, and individual factors (e.g., socioeconomic status, ethnicity, religion, gender, age). Psychiatric epidemiology typically focuses on the following primary variables:

- *Prevalence* refers to the proportion of a population that has a disorder at any point in time. Prevalence data for most mental disorders are summarized in the text of the *DSM-IV-TR*.

- *Incidence* refers to the number of new cases of a disorder that occur in a specific period (1 year is a common incidence cycle). Notably, incidence and prevalence are related: As incidence for any mental disorder increases (or decreases) over time, there will be a corresponding increase (or decrease) in the prevalence of the disorder, although this will be much more gradual.

- *Risk factors* refer to conditions or variables that, if present, increase the likelihood of developing a disorder. For example, childhood adversity (e.g., sexual abuse, chaotic family environment) has been studied as a potential risk factor for a host of personality disorders.

Comorbidity relates to the expressions of psychopathology and can be defined as the co-occurrence of two (or more) mental or physical disorders. Comorbidity is a particularly common occurrence among the personality disorders (McGlashan et al., 2000; Skodol et al., 1999; Zweig, 2003). They are frequently comorbid with each other as well as with diverse clinical disorders on Axis I. This fact often creates diagnostic confusion and complicates intervention.

Epidemiology of Personality Disorders in Later Adult Life

There is a small but growing body of literature about the epidemiology of personality disorders among older persons. Notably, there are fewer studies with older persons than with younger persons. Reported rates for the personality disorders are far more inconsistent and controversial than estimates for more widely studied disorders among older persons, such as schizophrenia, dementia, or major depression. Such inconsistencies likely highlight the difficulty clinicians and researchers have in accurately diagnosing personality disorders among older adults (Agronin, 1994). Prevalence estimates for personality disorders are also known to vary widely due to such factors as differing methodologies, sampling techniques, diagnostic measures, and diagnostic criteria. Another important diagnostic issue in prevalence rates is the tendency among older adults to self-report more personality disorder symptoms when compared with the observations of clinicians (Abrams & Horowitz, 1996). Finally, any prevalence rate can be no more precise than the arbitrary cutoff point between personality traits and personality disorder—the typical distinction depends on the degree of impairment required for a diagnosis (Paris, 2005).

Community and Psychiatric Samples

Surveys conducted in the 1980s found prevalence rates for personality disorders in the older adult community ranging from as low as 2.8% to as high as 11.0% (Cohen, 1990).

Agronin (1994) presented a review of some early epidemiological studies in various European older adult communities and described prevalence rates of 1.8% to 6.0%. However, he noted that many of the diagnoses would not conform to modern *DSM-IV* personality disorder criteria. Weissman (1993) presented somewhat higher estimates of the total lifetime prevalence rates for personality disorders in the general population, ranging from 10% to 13%.

Ames and Molinari (1994) administered a structured interview to 200 community-living older adults (mean age = 72 years), and found a 13.0% prevalence rate. They also noted that, due to the nature of their convenience sample at a senior center, Dependent Personality Disorder may have been over-reported, whereas Schizoid and Avoidant Personality Disorders may have been underreported. When they compared these rates with a sample of 797 younger adults given the same structured interview, they found a prevalence rate of 17.9%. Cohen et al. (1994) used a semistructured psychiatric examination to study personality disorders in a community-dwelling sample of 810 people. They found that older adults (defined in their study as 55 years old and older) had a 10.5% personality disorder prevalence rate, whereas younger people had a 6.6% rate. Another finding was that Antisocial and Histrionic Personality Disorders were both much less prevalent in the older than in the younger subjects. Segal, Hersen, et al. (1998) administered the self-report Personality Diagnostic Questionnaire-Revised (PDQ-R) to 189 community-dwelling older adults (mean age = 76 years) and found that 63.0% of the respondents met criteria for at least one personality disorder diagnosis. They proposed that their high prevalence rate was likely an artifact of the PDQ self-report measure which is known to be overly sensitive to pathology. This is discussed further in Chapter 9. The high prevalence also possibly reflects that sample participants were attending a senior center and, as such, may have been more likely to seek out this kind of social service because of existing personality and interpersonal problems.

To evaluate the prevalence issue from a statistical perspective, Abrams and Horowitz (1996) conducted a meta-analysis of 11 studies of prevalence rates in older adults (defined as age 50 years old and older) from 1980 through 1994 and reported an overall rate of 10% with a range from 6% to 33%. Interestingly, in the three studies that also included under-50 age groups, the overall prevalence for personality disorders was higher among the younger groups at 21% with a range from 17% to 30%. However, in all three studies there was no significant difference in the rate of personality disorders between younger and older adults. Abrams and Horowitz also found no gender differences in their older group and, contrary to their expectations, greater prevalence rates were found in outpatient or community settings than in inpatient settings. They also found consensus methods, defined as agreement among a number of clinicians, and chart reviews to yield higher rates of personality disorders compared with structured interviews.

Our recent empirical research (Coolidge, Segal, & Rosowsky, 2006) on a sample of 681 purportedly normal and healthy, community-dwelling adults ages 18 to 89 revealed that an older group ($N = 114$; age range = 60 to 89 years) had a prevalence rate of 11% (13 of 114 participants) for at least one personality disorder scale on the self-report form of the Coolidge Axis II Inventory (CATI; Coolidge, 2000). These rates are almost identical to those reported by Abrams and Horowitz (1996; older persons' prevalence rates = 10% and 11%, theirs and ours, respectively; younger groups' prevalence rates = 21% and 20%, theirs and ours, respectively).

A number of studies have also reported prevalence rates among older adults in mental health settings. In a retrospective chart review of a mixed sample of inpatient and outpatient older persons, Mezzich, Fabrega, Coffman, and Glavin (1987) found that 5.1% had a personality disorder diagnosis. Casey and Schrodt (1989) reviewed charts of 100 consecutive admissions to a geriatric psychiatry unit and found that 7% received a diagnosis of personality disorder that was determined by psychiatrist ratings. In a larger retrospective study, Fogel and Westlake (1990) ascertained the prevalence of personality disorders in 2,332 older inpatients suffering from major depression. Again, diagnoses were assigned by attending psychiatrists, and the results indicated a 15.8% personality disorder rate. Among older inpatients, Molinari, Ames, and Essa (1994) found a 33% prevalence rate based on clinical interviews that increased to 58% when structured interviews were used. Among depressed older adult psychiatric inpatients, Molinari and Marmion (1995) reported a 63% prevalence rate. Among older inpatient veterans, Kenan et al. (2000) found a 55% prevalence rate.

It is important to note that the prevalence rates for personality disorders in cases where an Axis I diagnosis may have been the precipitating factor in an outpatient or inpatient admission may be greatly underestimated. As explained later in this chapter, some clinicians may focus on signs and symptoms that are more obviously manifested and noted (e.g., mood, anxiety, and somatoform disorders). In some cases, the underlying maladaptive personality traits may be overlooked. Nevertheless, despite some diagnostic barriers among younger and older personality disordered individuals, some studies have documented high prevalence rates of personality disorders in clinical settings serving adults of all ages. Turkhat (1990) found that approximately 50% of clients seeking psychotherapy services have a diagnosable personality disorder, whereas Jackson et al. (1991) documented that 67% of patients in a state mental hospital had at least one personality disorder.

Although personality disorders among long-term-care residents have been infrequently studied, some older studies provide interesting data. Teeter, Garetz, Miller, and Heiland (1976) reported that almost 11% of nursing home residents had a personality disorder diagnosis, and Margo, Robinson, and Corea (1980) found that 15% of referrals to nursing homes were for personality problems.

The Debate about Stability versus Change for the Personality Disorders

Whereas the extant cross-sectional data suggest some tendency for personality disorders overall to be less prevalent in older persons, a different issue is the stability or change in personality disorder signs and symptoms across the life span. Definitive data are lacking about this issue, and in fact, there is some controversy in the geropsychological literature about whether personality disorders decline or mellow with advancing age (Coolidge et al., 1992; Molinari, Kunik, Snow-Turek, Deleon, & Williams, 1999; Segal & Coolidge, 1998; Segal, Hersen, Van Hasselt, Silberman, & Roth, 1996; Segal et al., 2001). The *DSM-IV* (American Psychiatric Association, 1994) was the first version of the manual to include a specific section (along with cultural and gender topics) on the developmental issue of aging in the diagnosis of personality disorders. This trend was continued in *DSM-IV-TR*. Regarding their course, the *DSM-IV-TR* states:

> *[B]y definition, a Personality Disorder is an enduring pattern of thinking, feeling, and behaving that is relatively stable over time. Some types of Personality Disorders (notably Antisocial and Borderline Personality Disorders) tend to become less evident or to remit with age, whereas this appears to be less true for some other types (e.g., Obsessive-Compulsive and Schizotypal Personality Disorders). (p. 688)*

A commonly held belief is that Cluster B personality disorders burn out by middle age, whereas disorders in Clusters A and C show little improvement over time (Paris, 2005). An understanding of the underlying dimensions tapped by the clusters may explain this hypothesis. Trait impulsivity and erratic forms of acting out associated with the Cluster B personality disorders are more likely to decline with advancing age than the cognitive peculiarities and anxiety/fearfulness that typify the personality disorders in Clusters A and C, respectively.

In contrast to the notions of decline or stability of personality disorders, several researchers have suggested that, in some cases, personality disorders (most notably Borderline and Obsessive-Compulsive) may actually worsen or exacerbate in later life (Rose, Soares, & Joseph, 1993; Rosowsky & Gurian, 1991, 1992; Siegel & Small, 1986; Segal et al., 2001). Due to the heterogeneity of individuals with personality disorders, each of these patterns (burnout and stability) may be true for different individuals with the same personality disorder. We have noted a third possibility in many patients: Personality disorder symptoms are most pronounced during early adult life, decline in middle age, and then become exacerbated again in later life (the "reverse-J curve"), especially in response to age-related stressors. This trend was first noted in a classic community study of personality traits, although categorical personality disorders were not evaluated (Reich, Nduaguba, & Yates, 1988). The prevalence of dramatic and (to a lesser extent) anxious personality disorder traits declined up to 60 years of age, with a slight upturn in later years. In contrast, odd or eccentric traits did not change with age.

In another early cross-sectional study, Coolidge et al. (1992) examined age differences in personality disorders between a sample of community-dwelling older adults (age range = 61 to 78 years) and younger adults (age range = 16 to 58 years) with the self-report form of the CATI (Coolidge & Merwin, 1992). Results showed that the older adults were significantly higher on the schizoid and obsessive-compulsive scales than the younger adults; there were no age differences on the dependent and avoidant scales; and younger adults were higher on the remaining scales (antisocial, borderline, histrionic, narcissistic, paranoid, passive-aggressive, schizotypal, sadistic, and self-defeating). These results of age-related elevations for obsessive-compulsive and schizoid scales were replicated with larger samples (Segal et al., 2001). In a similar cross-sectional study using the self-report Millon Clinical Multiaxial Inventory (MCMI; Millon, 1981b), Molinari et al. (1999) also reported a higher rate of Obsessive-Compulsive Personality Disorder in older versus younger psychiatric inpatients, but they did not find any age effect for Schizoid Personality Disorder. Rather, the older inpatients were higher than younger inpatients on the dependent personality scale. Finally, Kenan et al. (2000) reported that among inpatient veterans, older adults obtained a lower frequency (55%) of personality disorder diagnoses than middle-aged adults (69%), who in turn were lower than young adults

(76%). For specific personality disorders, younger patients were more likely to receive a diagnosis of Borderline Personality Disorder than older patients, but older patients were more likely to receive a diagnosis of Narcissistic Personality Disorder than younger patients.

Tyrer (1988) has offered another perspective with which to understand the types of changes likely to be seen in the personality disorders over time. He suggests that mature forms of personality disorder such as obsessive-compulsive, paranoid, schizoid, and schizotypal will likely remain stable with age, whereas the more immature or flamboyant forms of personality disorders such as antisocial, borderline, histrionic, and narcissistic will likely decrease with age. His categorizations have garnered some empirical support (described earlier in the cross-sectional studies) and there is certainly some anecdotal support for his observations. The social functioning of many of our older adult patients (particularly those with Cluster B personality disorders), appears improved compared with the severe interpersonal and occupational difficulties characteristic of their earlier years. Some of these patients have shown the pattern of their symptoms becoming muted or burned out in later life. Conversely, we have seen just as many patients with the opposite pattern—symptoms of their personality disorder pathology become exacerbated or hardened in later life, usually in reaction to the accumulation of age-related losses or stressors associated with aging (described in Chapters 2 to 5), and in cases in which traits adaptive at one point in life become maladaptive in the later life context (described in Chapter 10).

If true age changes for some personality disorders are confirmed with further research, intriguing questions emerge: Why do some personality disorders decline with age while others intensify? Are such changes simply artifacts of age-related changes in activity level, impulsivity, and sociability? Or does evidence of change represent inadequate diagnostic criteria for detecting geriatric variants of the disorders and poor measurement of some personality disorders in the aged (Agronin & Maletta, 2000)? Another possibility hints at an organic phenomenon: To what extent do the abnormal behavioral changes associated with aging reflect underlying changes in neural substrate, hormonal, or chemical neurotransmitter functioning in the brain? Systematic research is necessary to clarify clinical manifestations and develop clearer profiles of each personality disorder in the aged. Longitudinal studies following personality disordered individuals into later life are needed to assess true age-changes over time in symptoms of personality disorders (and not age-differences in symptoms that are detected by cross-sectional studies).

It is expected that the Collaborative Longitudinal Personality Disorders study (McGlashan et al., 2000), which is in process, will yield valuable and rich data on the natural course of personality disorders. As we have emphasized and described earlier, some symptoms are robust, some appear in muted form in the aged, and some are irrelevant. To the extent that these observations are empirically validated, the development of elder-specific diagnostic criteria will become more pressing. At the present moment, however, when evaluating and diagnosing personality disorders among older people, clinicians are encouraged to recognize and be sensitive to potential age-biases in the *DSM* system.

Establishing prevalence rates for the personality disorders and their course across the life span is not a simple task. Prevalence rates vary as a function of the mean age and age range of the sample, where the sample was gathered (e.g., community-dwelling, inpatient psychiatric, outpatient psychiatric), the criteria used (e.g., different versions of the *DSM*, *ICD-10*), the measurement device (e.g., self-report, structured interview, psychiatric examination), and the nature of the cutoff between traits and disorder. Whereas the National Institute of Mental Health Epidemiological Catchment Area (ECA) programs (Krupnick et al., 1996) were successful at providing quality epidemiological data for many mental disorders, the personality disorders were not included for study (with the exception of Antisocial Personality Disorder).

Although cross-sectional studies that have examined personality disorders are intriguing and suggest a general diminution of most types of personality disorders together with an intensification of a few personality disorders in later life, definitive research about the long-term course of individual personality disorders is lacking. Important research issues include whether these differential cross-sectional rates are a reflection of true changes in personality disorders across the life span (through longitudinal studies), whether these differing rates are an artifact of some kind of measurement bias (such as clinical diagnostic bias, self-report bias, or poor suitability of some criteria among older persons) or cohort effects, and whether there are differences in subthreshold cases across the adult life course (*subthreshold* means that the person meets some but not enough of the *DSM* criteria for an official personality disorder diagnosis). To provide the substantive data desired by researchers in the field requires large-scale longitudinal studies with standardized, objective, and validated diagnostic instruments to investigate the prevalence of the full-range personality disorder in later life and to address in a rigorous manner the questions about age-related changes. Such studies are infrequently conducted, largely due to pragmatic concerns (e.g., time involved and cost). Instead, longitudinal studies of a few specific personality disorders have been completed and are discussed later in this chapter.

Epidemiology and Gender

Another important epidemiological issue concerns the extent to which gender differentially affects the prevalence of personality disorders among older adults. According to the *DSM-IV-TR*, three personality disorders (borderline, dependent, and histrionic) are more prevalent in females, and six personality disorders (antisocial, paranoid, schizoid, schizotypal, narcissistic, and obsessive-compulsive) are more prevalent in males. Sadistic Personality Disorder was also thought to be more common in males, whereas Self-Defeating Personality Disorder was thought to be more prevalent in females. No information was provided by the *DSM* for the Passive-Aggressive Personality Disorder regarding gender. Finally, the Depressive Personality Disorder was thought to occur with equal frequency in both genders.

It is unclear to what extent these gender differences apply to older individuals because most studies from which these data are summarized did not include older adults. At least one study of community-dwelling older persons (Segal, Hersen, et al., 1998) failed to find support for the claims in *DSM-IV* regarding gender differences for the personality disorders. Instead, results suggested that older females were more likely to be diagnosed with Avoidant and Schizoid Personality Disorders compared with older males. No gender differences were identified for the remaining personality disorder diagnoses. Our recent study (Coolidge et al., 2006) of 114 older adults (31 males, 83 females) generally supported the Segal, Hersen, et al. (1998) findings regarding limited gender differences for most of the personality disorders, at least in community samples. We found only two significant elevations for males compared with females. They were on the antisocial and sadistic personality scales and both had moderate effect sizes. On the 12 other personality disorder scales, there were no significant differences between the genders.

Course and Prognosis for the Personality Disorders

In general, we would not expect a dramatic diminution of personality disorders over time because personality disorders, de facto, are robust and not expected to change greatly. Given recent evidence for their heritability (Coolidge, Thede, et al., 2001; Torgersen et al., 2000) and the *DSM-IV-TR* definition of personality disorders as enduring patterns of inner experience and external behaviors that are pervasive, inflexible, and stable over time, their chronicity is not surprising. Much more has been written about two specific personality disorders (antisocial and borderline) than the others.

One of the first outcome studies of Antisocial Personality Disorder was performed by Robins (1966). In a 5-year follow-up of 82 adults diagnosed with Antisocial Personality Disorder, she found that 61% showed no improvement and 5% had committed suicide. In another study with a 5-year follow-up interval, Maddocks (1970) found that 80% of 59 antisocial men had not improved. Black, Baumgard, Bell, and Kao (1995) further demonstrated the morbidity associated with the Antisocial Personality Disorder diagnosis, as nearly 24% were found to be dead after varying follow-up intervals of 16 to 45 years. Of course, some of these deaths might have been expected over a period as long as 45 years; however, the study also points to the dangers of interpreting course, outcome, or prognosis from cross-sectional studies.

We noted earlier in several cross-sectional studies that the mean level of antisocial behavior is significantly diminished in older groups. As just noted, a contributing factor is selective mortality: The core and associated features of the antisocial personality disorder, including drug abuse, impulsivity, aggressiveness, and novelty-seeking, will over many years lead some to a premature death. Besides selective mortality, an important question is: To what extent does personality change explain the lower rates of criminality in later life? In a classic study using a large sample (Harpur & Hare, 1994), male offenders ranging in age from 16 to 70 years were assessed with the Hare Psychopathy Checklist, which has two factors. The primary findings were that scores on Factor 2 (largely measuring socially deviant behaviors, impulsivity, and sensation-seeking) decreased sharply with age, whereas scores on Factor 1 (largely measuring affective and interpersonal features) remained stable. These findings provide evidence that the core personality traits associated with the antisocial personality (e.g., manipulativeness, callousness, egocentricity, and incapacity to experience empathy, guilt, and remorse) remain constant across the life span although the overt behavioral expressions dramatically decrease with age.

Paris (2003) has similarly noted that a lessening of impulsive and erratic behaviors over the course of a lifetime does not mean that the antisocial individual is cured or has grown out of the diagnosis. The underlying psychopathology is likely to remain present even though some of the behavioral manifestations are likely to change with advancing age. Although Paris noted that in later life people with Antisocial Personality Disorder are less likely to commit violent crimes or be as physically dangerous, they often remain very difficult people. In fact, an emerging crisis facing the prison system is the growing number of older prisoners, some whom have "aged-in-place" in prison and others who have entered (or reentered) the system in later adulthood (Aday, 2003).

A diagnosis of Borderline Personality Disorder also has a generally poor prognostic implication. There have been strong suggestions of a history of childhood trauma as a precipitating event for the development of this disorder (e.g., Millon & Davis, 1996). However, not all borderline patients have a history of trauma and not all individuals with trauma develop the disorder. Also, many personality disordered patients other than Borderline Personality Disorder do have trauma history as well as do adults without a personality disorder. Early traumatic brain injury as a precursor in Borderline Personality Disorder has also been proposed (e.g., van Reekum, 1993). Similar to the finding regarding childhood physical and sexual abuse, some borderline patients have a history of brain injury, but others do not (Coolidge, Segal, Stewart, & Ellett, 2000). Millon and Davis concluded that there are likely many paths to the development of the Borderline Personality Disorder, and for all the personality disorders. One of these factors for the borderline type is genetics. Coolidge, Thede, et al. (2001) found a correlation of .70 for borderline traits in 70 monozygotic twin pairs and a correlation of .39 for these traits in 42 dizygotic twin pairs. The overall heritability of the Borderline Personality Disorder was 76%.

In Perry's (1993) review of the course of personality disorders, Borderline Personality Disorder was the most widely studied. The major findings are summarized as follows. An important caveat, however, is that because most of the reviewed studies focused on younger and middle-aged adults, extrapolations into later life are unknown:

- An average of 6.1% (range 3% to 9%) of individuals with Borderline Personality Disorder died by suicide in an average of 7.2 years of follow-up. Suicide was less common among the other personality disorders.

- The greatest risk for suicide was in the immediate 1 to 2 years after initial diagnosis.

- The natural history is suggestive of some at least some remission. At 10-year and 15-year follow-up, 52% and 33%, respectively, remain with a definite or probable diagnosis of Borderline Personality Disorder. This is not to suggest that the remitted cases are cured, but rather that the patients no longer meet the diagnostic threshold although they are likely to continue experiencing several residual symptoms and can still have significant functional impairment. In fact, the average psychosocial impairment was moderate after a mean of 9.5 years of follow-up.

In studies of schizoid adolescents and young adults, Wolff (1995) found that a strong majority are still diagnosed schizoid and/or schizotypal in follow-up periods of up to a decade after initial diagnosis. However, she used a broad definition of schizoid behavior that often included aberrant thinking and intense focus on single ideas or subjects. The latter two symptoms are more suggestive of Schizotypal Personality Disorder and Asperger's syndrome, respectively. Nonetheless, Wolff's studies seem to confirm the suspicion that Schizoid Personality Disorder (and/or Schizotypal Personality Disorder) tend to be chronic and unremitting from late adolescence at least into early adulthood.

Studies of the long-term outcome and course of other personality disorders such as histrionic, narcissistic, obsessive-compulsive, avoidant, and dependent are sparse. Paris (2003) is one of the few researchers to address the outcomes of these other personality disorders even if he relied primarily on clinical studies and cross-sectional data. Paris postulated that older histrionic patients are likely to draw attention to themselves through somatic and hypochondriacal complaints rather than with their customary sexual seductiveness and physical charms. In some cases, they may become overreliant on cosmetic surgery as a consequence of their overestimation of physical attractiveness and their quest for youthfulness. It also seems likely that the superficiality of their emotional and social attachments is likely to become more distressing and ego-dystonic as they find themselves less capable of managing others and obtaining attention through physical attractiveness and seductiveness, especially from those people who are much younger than they are.

Paris (2003) and Kernberg (1976) also speculated about the course of Narcissistic Personality Disorder, suggesting that some narcissists may become more interested in therapy as they age. Their charming, bold, manipulative, and self-assured style may become less rewarded with advancing age. As their professional and familial powers over others diminish with retirement and other aspects of advanced aging (e.g., sensory losses), and as their physical prowess declines, it seems likely that they will seek attention, power, and reinforcement through relationships with their therapist and other professionals who fill their need for attention. It may also be predicted that as their disappointments with their customary search for accolades and valuation of their worth by others diminishes with age, individuals with Narcissistic Personality Disorder might become significantly depressed and anxious, and like aging individuals with Histrionic Personality Disorder, they may exhibit somatic and hypochondriacal complaints.

In the few studies of the course of Cluster C personality disorders (avoidant, obsessive-compulsive, dependent), Seivewright, Tyrer, and Johnson (2002) and Tyrer and Seivewright (2000) over a 12-year follow-up found that most of these patients did not improve with age. In fact, they found that their tendency toward anxiety and strong need for control tended to increase over time. The data from Reich et al. (1988) are also suggestive of a slight increase in anxious personality disorder traits in later life. Finally, as noted later in this chapter, patients with Cluster C personality disorders are prone to experience a diverse array of comorbid Axis I disorders, with anxiety, mood, and somatoform disorders particularly common.

In summary, it is relatively common for clinicians to offer somewhat bleak prognoses for the personality disorders, but the picture does not necessarily have to be this grim. First, many inroads are being made into the psychopharmacological treatment of personality disorders (Soloff, 1998), particularly targeting the cognitive/perceptual, emotional, and impulse dyscontrol symptoms associated with the disorders. There are also many partially successful medications for the anxious, depressive, and obsessive manifestations of personality disorder symptomatology. These medications do not in any sense cure the underlying personality disorder or character structure. They can, however, remove barriers to psychotherapy so that standard psychotherapeutic techniques (e.g., cognitive-behavioral, psychodynamic approaches) may be more likely to succeed. Second, new and innovative psychotherapies are continually being developed in psychology, some specifically targeting personality disorders (Linehan, 1993; Millon, 1999). Although it still seems unlikely that the higher-order factors (e.g., temperaments) that help shape personality disorders will be dramatically or radically changed, the *expressions* of these temperaments can sometimes be reformed, massaged, sublimated, or reexpressed in ways that are less troubling for the patients and their families, including those in later life. Traits can also be redirected to more adaptive contexts, a concept demonstrated in several of our case examples presented in earlier chapters. And, although *groups of people* with personality disorders may on average show little change over time, the potential for *individuals* to change, adapt, and grow over time is much greater.

As for the stability of personality traits over time, individuals differ in the degree to which their attributes and behaviors are enduring and pervasive. Millon and Grossman (2006) note: "[E]ach individual displays this durability and pervasiveness only in certain of his or her characteristics; that is, each of us possesses a limited number of attributes that are resistant to changing times and situational influences, whereas other of our attributes are more readily modified" (p. 16). Furthermore, traits, whether adaptive or maladaptive, only have a probabilistic influence on behavior. People who possess any trait are not unfailingly consistent in expressing it (Costa & McCrae, 2006). Applying this concept to individuals with personality disorders, Pincus (2005) states, "Clearly, these patients do not walk around like robots emitting the same behaviors over and over again regardless of the situation (or interpersonal situation)" (p. 133). The fluctuation of personality disorder symptomology can inform psychotherapeutic intervention—strategies can take advantage of stable periods and work to reestablish adaptive functioning during particular times of deterioration or crisis (Pincus, 2005).

Comorbidity: General Issues

The comorbidity of personality disorders with other psychiatric disorders and with other personality disorders presents a special challenge and problem for clinicians and researchers. Since the multiaxial system was created, the *DSM* has inadvertently put personality disorders in a somewhat secondary status by placing them on Axis II, an afterthought to an Axis I assessment. It has even been suggested that clinicians have long been trained to focus on Axis I pathology, as if it is more important than identifying Axis II personality disorders (e.g., Paris, 2003). Paris has also noted that it is all too common to see a diagnosis on Axis I or multiple diagnoses on Axis I with the notation, *799.9 Diagnosis Deferred on Axis II.* Yet, whereas Axis I anxiety attacks or depressive episodes may be relatively transitory, all the personality disorders are characterized by their chronicity and pervasive impact on the individual's life. Thus, focusing diagnosis and subsequent treatment plans on adventitious, episodic Axis I pathologies without consideration of patients' special vulnerabilities due to their poorly developed personality structures is a mistake, one that invites psychotherapeutic failure.

The mounting evidence suggests that the consequences of failing to identify and attend to personality disorders among older patients are steep, including a lengthier therapy, more frequent treatment failures, and unnecessary complications to the therapeutic relationship (Sadavoy, 1999). A further complication is that because older patients have likely exhibited their dysfunctional personality traits for much of their adult life (and in some cases may have benefited from their interpersonal style), it is increasingly likely that they will not view their personality as part of the problem and may not even be cognizant of any personality pathology. Many problems that occasion a mental health evaluation in personality disordered older persons may be overshadowed by the signs and symptoms of an Axis I pathology, such as depressive episodes, anxiety problems, or somatoform disorders. Perhaps even worse, the problems may be seen as stemming directly from Axis III medical problems rather than being identified as manifestations of an underlying personality disturbance.

There is a confluence of factors for many clinicians' reluctance to diagnose personality disorders, particularly in older persons. Some prominent reasons include the lack of awareness of the problem in the older cohort (Kroessler, 1990) and the poor fit of some diagnostic criteria among older adults (Rosowsky & Gurian, 1991). Another reason for the reluctance of clinicians to diagnose personality disorders may be the negative connotations associated with them such as their chronicity, their immalleable genetic temperamental basis, and their generally poor prognoses. For some clinicians, a personality disorder diagnosis perhaps means admitting defeat before even beginning therapy (e.g., Paris, 2003), and the prognosis might seem even more hopeless in the face of advancing age. As discussed later in this book, it is critically important for clinicians to be aware of Axis II personality disorders and their traits or features and include them in the case formulation and treatment planning.

Comorbidity of Personality Disorders with Clinical Disorders and with other Personality Disorders

The comorbidity of Axis II personality disorders with Axis I clinical syndromes is common (Sadavoy, 1999; Zweig, 2003). Table 6.1 presents a list of possibilities based on our clinical experience, research, and suggestions provided in the text of the *DSM-IV-TR*. In one of our previous studies (Coolidge, Janitell, & Griego, 1994) in a sample of 83 community-dwelling older adults (*M* age = 70 years; range = 60 to 92

Table 6.1 **Axis II Personality Disorders with Likely Comorbid Axis I and Axis II Disorders in Older Adults**

Axis II Personality Disorders	Axis I Clinical Syndromes	Axis II Personality Disorders
Antisocial	Substance-Related Disorders Schizophrenia and other Psychotic Disorders Mood Disorders Sexual Disorders Impulse Control Disorders	Sadistic Borderline Paranoid Passive-Aggressive Schizotypal Narcissistic Self-Defeating
Avoidant	Mood Disorders Anxiety Disorders Somatoform Disorders Eating Disorders	Dependent Depressive Passive-Aggressive Schizotypal Obsessive-Compulsive Self-Defeating
Borderline	Substance-Related Disorders Schizophrenia and other Psychotic Disorders Mood Disorders Sexual Disorders Impulse Control Disorders	Passive-Aggressive Depressive Self-Defeating Dependent Antisocial Paranoid
Dependent	Mood Disorders Anxiety Disorders Somatoform Disorders Eating Disorders	Passive-Aggressive Avoidant Self-Defeating Borderline Depressive
Depressive	Mood Disorders Anxiety Disorders Somatoform Disorders Eating Disorders	Borderline Self-Defeating Passive-Aggressive Dependent Avoidant
Histrionic	Mood Disorders Anxiety Disorders Sexual Disorders Impulse Control Disorders Somatoform Disorders Eating Disorders	Narcissistic Borderline Dependent Passive-Aggressive

(continued)

Table 6.1   *(Continued)*

Axis II Personality Disorders	Axis I Clinical Syndromes	Axis II Personality Disorders
Narcissistic	Mood Disorders Anxiety Disorders Substance-Related Disorders	Antisocial Sadistic Borderline Histrionic Paranoid
Obsessive-Compulsive	Obsessive-Compulsive Disorder Mood Disorders Eating Disorders	Depressive Avoidant Self-Defeating Schizoid Dependent Paranoid Narcissistic
Paranoid	Substance-Related Disorders Schizophrenia and other Psychotic Disorders Mood Disorders Sexual Disorders Anxiety Disorders Obsessive-Compulsive Disorder	Narcissistic Sadistic Schizoid Schizotypal Borderline Avoidant
Passive-Aggressive	Mood Disorders Anxiety Disorders Somatoform Disorders Oppositional Defiant Disorder	Borderline Histrionic Paranoid Depressive Dependent Antisocial Avoidant
Sadistic	Schizophrenia and other Psychotic Disorders Mood Disorders Sexual Disorders Anxiety Disorders	Antisocial Paranoid Narcissistic Passive-Aggressive Schizotypal
Schizoid	Schizophrenia and other Psychotic Disorders Mood Disorders	Schizotypal Avoidant Obsessive-Compulsive Paranoid

Table 6.1   *(Continued)*

Axis II Personality Disorders	Axis I Clinical Syndromes	Axis II Personality Disorders
Schizotypal	Schizophrenia and other Psychotic Disorders Mood Disorders Anxiety Disorders	Paranoid Schizoid Passive-Aggressive Self-Defeating Avoidant Borderline
Self-Defeating	Mood Disorders Somatoform Disorders Anxiety Disorders	Passive-Aggressive Depressive Borderline Dependent Paranoid Schizotypal Avoidant

years), we found that depression (as measured by Beck's Depression Inventory) and anxiety (as measured by Spielberger's State-Trait Anxiety Scale) were highly comorbid with personality disorders as an aggregate. We found that 18% of the sample met the criteria for at least one personality disorder (self-report form of the CATI), 25% were mildly, moderately, or severely depressed, and 16% were moderately to severely anxious (trait anxiety). We concluded that there is a danger for clinicians to focus their diagnoses on symptoms that can be medicated or treated in a short course of psychotherapy instead of on the more chronic manifestations of personality disorders, the latter of which are more likely to have a pervasive effect on the individual's functioning and remain unabated if not targeted directly.

In other clinical studies, Kunik et al. (1993) evaluated depressed older adult inpatients and found that 24% also had a comorbid personality disorder diagnosis. Similarly, Thompson, Gallagher, and Czirr (1988) reported that 33% of depressed older adults participating in a psychotherapy outcome study were comorbidly diagnosed with a personality disorder. Molinari and Marmion (1995) used a structured personality disorder scale to assess personality disorders in elderly patients with mood disorders, reporting a 63% comorbidity rate. Similarly, personality disorders were commonly comorbid among older (58%) and younger (66%) adults suffering with a chronic mental illness (Coolidge, Segal, Pointer, et al., 2000). In one of the few studies of personality disorders among older persons with clinically significant anxiety, Coolidge, Segal, Hook, and Stewart (2000) found that 61% met criteria for at least one personality disorder. This latter finding converges with Sadavoy's (1999) impression that because personality disordered individuals likely have difficulty modulating their worry, intense anxiety can be triggered. The primary effect of a comorbid personality disorder in a patient with diverse types of clinical disorders is that treatment will be more complicated, longer, and less effective than in similar patients without personality disorder pathology. We examine this issue more fully later in this book.

Regarding the comorbidity of personality disorders with other personality disorders, our study (Coolidge et al., 2006) of community-dwelling people over 60 years of age (total $N = 114$) demonstrated that those with at least one clinical personality disorder elevation, 27% (4 of 11 participants) had two or more personality disorders. In contrast, the younger sample ($N = 512$; age range = 18 to 50) had a 20% prevalence rate (104 out of 512 participants) of at least one clinically elevated personality disorder scale. Approximately 47% (53 of 114 participants) of those with at least one clinically elevated personality disorder scale had two or more personality disorder scales. Many studies have recorded the comorbidity of personality with other personality disorders in younger populations (e.g., McGlashan et al., 2000; Oldham et al., 1992), and there is no reason to think this pattern will change dramatically as a mere function of growing older. It is even possible for the comorbidity to become worse in later life, especially in cases in which previously adaptive styles and behaviors become maladaptive over time and vulnerabilities, previously hidden, become uncovered. The presence of a dementing illness in individuals with a personality disorder warrants other special considerations.

Personality Disorders and Dementia

Perhaps the ultimate overarching task in late life is that of life review; looking back over one's life, reflecting on it, and making meaning from the journey. Erik Erikson's (1963) influential developmental theory posited a conflict between ego integrity and despair, with the successful outcome being the achievement of wisdom. As clinicians, we recognize that there can be many hurdles along the way. Wisdom might be a possible outcome, but simply becoming old does not guarantee its achievement.

There are certain essential requirements to negotiate this developmental task. One is an adequately intact cognitive infrastructure to support the process of life review. This assumes a degree of memory intactness, as well as the capability of abstract reasoning, judgment, and insight. As a dementing illness progresses, the capability for this becomes progressively limited and ultimately lost.

Another requirement is a characterological infrastructure that supports and enables the ability to take one's self—one's life—as object, to reflect on and analyze it. This requires that the individual is capable of both achieving an internal focus and tolerating the affect this engenders. The individual with a personality disorder who also has dementia is thus doubly, and synergistically, compromised.

Normal aging of the brain does not greatly alter one's personality, but organic brain disease does. When brain pathology serves to alter one's premorbid personality, the individual can present with what appears to be a personality disorder and almost meet criteria for a diagnosis. However, for a diagnosis of a personality disorder, the traits need to be present by early adulthood. Although the diagnosis can be difficult, the temporal factor is key.

When an individual with a personality disorder develops dementia, the effect can be to increase the degree of the personality disorder, to decrease it, or to neutralize (or cancel) it. The dementia process causes changes in premorbid personality in general. Personality changes often occur even before the dementia is diagnosed, and typically appear to correspond with the progression of the dementia. In general, dementia tends to induce an increase in self-centeredness and a decrease in flexibility. The latter can increase the maladaptive expressions of a personality disorder. The self-centeredness (reflecting increasing difficulty in creating novel responses and set-shifting) can also exacerbate premorbid personality traits, especially those defining Cluster B personality disorders. Paranoia and schizophrenic-type withdrawal are also frequently observed.

As the dementia progresses, generally the individual's personality is perceived, and described by family members, as being *less than* prior to the onset of the dementia. The individual is described as being less outgoing, less assertive, less task focused, and less conscientious than he had been historically. (Unfortunately, hostility often appears to hold up as a stable, dementia-resistant trait.) Caregivers frequently report that the personality changes in the individual with dementia are experienced as more burdensome than the memory deficits or the physical requirements of the caregiving (Williams, Briggs, & Coleman, 1995).

How might we understand the relationship between dementia and personality changes? They can reflect the actual degeneration of discrete areas of the brain (e.g., the hippocampus) and association areas. They can reflect the effects of coexisting medical conditions or medications the individual is taking. Thyroid dysregulation and poorly controlled diabetes, for example, can have significant effects on the personality. Steroids and psychotropic medications, often prescribed to older adults, can induce marked personality changes. The organic brain pathology can exaggerate premorbid personality traits such as repetition and perseveration superimposed on the individual with Obsessive-Compulsive Personality Disorder. What is less often considered, but highly relevant, is the effect of feedback from others as experienced by the dementing brain. Consider how a predisposition to paranoid suspiciousness and distrust, anxiety, or dependency can be enhanced, or unmasked, as the dementia declares itself and progresses.

Conclusions

Why is the study of epidemiology and comorbidity of personality disorders so important in later adult life? Clinicians have historically been reluctant to diagnose personality disorders for a confluence of reasons. Regardless of the age of the patient, part of the resistance may stem from the very concept of personality disorders. Because their defining characteristics include pervasive, maladaptive, and inflexible behaviors that cause significant impairment and distress and are generally *stable over time*, clinicians may consciously avoid making personality disorder diagnoses because of negative connotations, bleak prognoses, and fiscal disincentives. Prior to 1980, another problem was that there were neither specific criteria for the personality disorders nor a specific threshold for their diagnosis (e.g., 5 of 8 criteria must be met for a diagnosis). With the advent of the multiaxial *DSM-III* in 1980, polythetic criteria and an overall diagnostic threshold were specified. Placing personality disorders on Axis II, however, inadvertently separated them from other clinical syndromes and relegated them to a secondary status, leading to the often used demarcation, *799.9 Diagnosis Deferred on Axis II*. Ironically, a diagnosis of mental retardation is also currently placed on Axis II, with the inference that both of these classes of syndromes (mental retardation and personality disorders) become evident by adolescence or much earlier and have a chronic and unremitting life course.

We have also highlighted the dangers in overemphasizing the Axis I disorders at the expense of minimizing or ignoring personality-based factors. The identification of comorbid Axis I disorders is important, but if these symptoms are largely caused by the underlying personality pathology, then the medications and psychotherapies targeting overt manifestations are unlikely to make major inroads into the pervasive disruption in the person's life. With an appropriate diagnosis on Axis II for these patients, therapeutic changes are more likely, especially if the medications for their depression, anxiety, or aberrant thinking make them more amenable to psychotherapeutic interventions. With creative and innovative therapies being introduced frequently in clinical psychology and coupled with empirically tested and well-honed older therapies, the prognosis for the personality disorders could likely be more sanguine.

The recognition that personality disorders often occur comorbidly not only with Axis I clinical syndromes but also with other personality disorders is important because clinicians must resist the inclination to settle on single personality disorder diagnosis without examining the near equally likely circumstance that two or more personality disorders may coexist. We have presented in Table 6.1 the most likely occurring comorbid Axis I clinical syndromes and Axis II personality disorders with each personality disorder. We have also listed the comorbid personality disorders in decreasing likelihood of their comorbidity (based on our empirical study, Coolidge et al., 2006) where this evidence was available.

Finally, we reemphasize a major point of our discussion. Despite the overall high probability that medication, psychotherapy, or their combination will not change genetically determined temperaments underlying personality disorders, these interventions can be highly successful in changing the behavioral manifestations of personality disorders such that significant improvements can take place in the patients' and their families' lives. Even after a lifetime of the disruptive behaviors and difficult relationships that are associated with personality disorders, older adults can be as amenable to treatment as younger adults. It is for these reasons that the greater recognition and understanding of the prevalence and comorbidity of personality disorders in later adult life are important. We strongly encourage further research in these areas.

7

It has been said that there is nothing more practical than a good theory. It was Albert Einstein who stated that "It is the theory that decides what we can observe." These ideas can be applied to our understanding of theoretical approaches to psychopathology and psychological treatment.

The role of theory in clinical practice simply cannot be understated. Early in the treatment process, the clinician must begin to develop a coherent case conceptualization (commonly called a case formulation). Although there is no universal approach to this process, the formulation can generally be described as the clinician's theoretical analysis of the current case, typically addressing the questions: What has caused the person's present difficulties (symptoms) to develop? And what maintains those symptoms? The formulation is thus a set of educated hypotheses about the etiology of the person's problems, which must be grounded in defined theories of the particular disorder or clinical construct of interest.

The case formulation is crucial because it drives treatment: It helps the clinician think critically about the interventions that should be applied and those that should not. Throughout treatment, the case formulation is often revised and reconsidered depending on how the patient is responding. We firmly believe that without a case formulation, treatment is likely going to fail, and this is especially true with personality disorders.

Since publication of *DSM-III,* in 1980, when the personality disorders were placed on Axis II (separate from the clinical syndromes), personality disorder research has undergone unprecedented growth in the breadth and quantity of empirical studies and in studies that have attempted to account for the etiology and origins of personality disorders.

Etiological theories of personality disorders are nearly as numerous as the paradigms that attempt to describe behavior in general psychology. Focusing on five major paradigms, which have contributed strongly to the advancement of knowledge after decades of personality disorder research, we speculate about possible applications of these paradigms to aging individuals. In this chapter, we examine the cognitive, psychoanalytic, and interpersonal models, which are all prominent psychologically based perspectives for personality disorders. Each of these seeks explanations for personality disorders in the immediate phenomenological and social world of an individual. In Chapter 8, we discuss two prominent biological theories of personality disorders (the evolutionary and neurobiological paradigms).

Cognitive Theories of Personality Disorders

It may be useful to define what is meant by the various terms *cognitive theory, behaviorism, cognitive therapy,* and *cognitive-behavioral therapy* (CBT). Theories of cognition are as old as the original foundations of psychology. Cognitive psychology was originally the study of internal mental processes. Wilhelm Wundt, a German psychologist and arguably the founder of psychology, used a method, in 1879, called *introspection* in which his subjects would be asked to reflect inwardly on their thought processes and respond outwardly with their observations. Hermann Ebbinghaus, also a German psychologist and Wundt's contemporary, published seminal experimental studies of learning and memory beginning in 1885. For approximately the next 4 or 5 decades, these studies would be subsumed under the rubric *experimental psychology.*

Beginning in the 1920s, John Watson, an American psychologist, founded the theory of behaviorism, which formally rejected Wundt's method of introspection, psychoanalysis, and any theory or practice that addressed unobservable or unmeasureable traits or processes. Watson and behaviorism's subsequent proponents, like American psychologist B. F. Skinner, argued that psychology could only advance scientifically if it confined itself to observable behaviors that can be readily measured or counted. Skinner maintained this uncompromising stance until his death in 1990. He is considered to be the progenitor of *operant conditioning,* which holds that an organism's behaviors can be created and controlled by contingent reinforcement and punishment. Behaviorism had also earlier adopted the work of Russian physiologist Ivan Pavlov (1849–1936) who observed that natural behaviors (like fear) could be brought under control by new (novel) stimuli. The study of these procedures was called *classical conditioning.* Operant and classical conditioning became the two main theoretical pillars of behaviorism, although role modeling and imitation were added later.

However, there was growing discontent with the behaviorism paradigm because important mental processes such as language and grammar production, attitudes, beliefs, and desires were all largely ignored or considered unscientific endeavors by radical behaviorists. Eventually, their harsh stance led to the development of the broader discipline, cognitive psychology, which reembraced the study of internal mental processes and broadened to include learning and memory, intellect, attention, perception, reasoning, problem solving, creativity, as well as mental representations and symbols. More recently, many in this paradigm have recognized that the empirical methods and experimental designs of cognitive psychology have great application to the study of any mental state, its representations, and such processes as the manifest productions of introspection and phenomenology. Perhaps most important, these practitioners developed a set of techniques and strategies to aid in the treatment of psychological distress and mental disorders.

Cognitive Therapy Basics

Cognitive therapy is a type of short-term psychotherapy that involves the recognition of distorted, illogical, or unhealthy thoughts with the goal of replacing them with less distorted and more logical and adaptive ones. The approach was typified in the 1950s and 1960s by Albert Ellis, who created Rational Emotive Behavioral Therapy, and Aaron T. Beck, who claims the specific rubric Cognitive Therapy. With the adoption of many of the behavioral techniques applied to psychopathological behaviors (e.g., use of homework assignments, trying out and evaluating new behaviors, role-playing and behavioral rehearsal, exposure strategies, and using positive and negative reinforcement to increase adaptive behaviors) in the cognitive therapy paradigm, the term *cognitive-behavioral therapy* became the more general term in the field. Indeed, the overlap between cognitive therapy and cognitive-behavioral therapy is great.

Beck, Ellis, and other cognitive-behavioral therapy proponents make similar suppositions. For example, these approaches assume that an individual's thinking and thought patterns are intimately connected to his or her feelings and behaviors. The theory suggests that an event, in and of itself, is not the cause of an emotional response, but rather it is how the individual *interprets* or *perceives* that event (i.e., cognitive processes) that causes an emotional reaction. Consider the death of a loved one as an example. It might be assumed that this death would automatically make someone sad and despondent, but that is not always the case. An older person who has died of a long, painful, and debilitating disease might not provoke the same feelings in their respective loved ones as would the death of a young healthy person in the prime of life. Indeed, in this example, whether we experience relief or intense despair depends on the meaning that we attach to the death. Thus, according to the theory, our attitudes and beliefs about an event give rise to our emotions and not the events themselves. It should be emphasized that this central concept is by no means a recent one: Centuries ago, Phrygian Stoic philosopher Epictetus (circa 101 A.D.) expressed his view in *The Enchiridion,* stating that "Men are disturbed not by things, but by the view which they take of them" (Epictetus, c. 101/1955). Modern-day cognitive theorists embrace this ancient notion that our thoughts profoundly influence our affect and behavior. Two important corollaries to this central tenet are that (1) cognitions can be monitored and changed and (2) by changing our thinking patterns or our attitudes or perspectives about an event, we can exert desirable changes in emotions and behaviors, even in situations in which we have little or no control over the external precipitant (Dobson & Dozois, 2001).

Cognitive-behavioral therapy is a time-limited approach and is considered a short-term psychotherapy, particularly in contrast to much longer treatments such as psychoanalysis or Jungian therapy. Cognitive-behavioral therapy is highly instructional and patients are frequently given homework assignments outside of the therapy sessions, which can also shorten the therapeutic process. Cognitive-behavioral therapy is also more akin to those who practice behavioral therapy in that, although the therapeutic relationship is deemed important to therapeutic outcomes, the relationship itself is not seen as the primary curative factor. Cognitive-behavioral therapists do believe in a trusting relationship between therapist and patient; however, they believe that a successful therapeutic outcome occurs when their patients learn to identify unhealthy thinking patterns and then alter their thoughts accordingly. Cognitive-behavioral therapists, therefore, emphasize the recognition of irrational and harmful thinking and the learning of self-counseling skills. The therapist and patient set goals collaboratively and then monitor progress toward the goals. Cognitive-behavioral therapists listen, encourage, and help patients learn and apply methods to challenge negative thinking, whereas the patient's role is to express concerns and implement the self-counseling techniques learned in treatment.

Application to Personality Disorders

Pretzer and Beck (1996) believe that cognitive therapy has particular value in the treatment of personality disorders. Interestingly, Beck is one of the very few theorists to offer an ultimate explanation for personality disorders from an evolutionary perspective and also to offer specific therapeutic interventions for their amelioration. Beck's theorizing follows the traditional evolutionary explanations (which are expanded on in Chapter 8). Simply put, Beck (1992) theorizes that the origins of many modern personality disorders developed from specific conditions in the ancestral environment that are now maladaptive in the present environment. He labeled these behaviors, which were successful in the ancestral environment, *primeval strategies.* For example, persons with Antisocial Personality Disorder exhibit the primeval strategy of predation. Persons with the Histrionic Personality Disorder exhibit the primeval strategy of exhibitionism. Obsessive-compulsive persons exhibit the primeval strategies of creating rituals and order. However, understanding personality disorders from a primeval perspective does not obviate the need for interventions or make these interventions any less successful. It does, however, provide a greater theoretical perspective for the understanding of personality disorders, emphasizing that something about the exhibited behavior has some possible adaptive function, at least at some point in the past. Whether the distant past or the more recent past (i.e., childhood) is a greater influence on the dysfunctional behavior is an important point of debate.

Pretzer and Beck (1996) noted that persons with personality disorders pose significant problems for therapists because the pervasiveness, chronicity, and range of their symptoms often make their problems difficult to conceptualize clearly. Because cognitive-behavioral techniques are problem focused, Pretzer and Beck note that they may be used to alleviate current stress and to accomplish deeper changes necessary for future successes.

As noted earlier, cognitive therapies are theoretically based on a phenomenological paradigm—that events themselves do not directly cause our emotions but rather that emotions are caused by our attitudes and reaction to those events. In practice, cognitive therapy is highly pragmatic and strongly emphasizes individualized effective treatments. This approach hypothesizes common underlying misperceptions in people (of all ages) with personality disorders. The identification of the patient's particular misperceptions is crucial for cognitive therapy to proceed. Commonly occurring misperceptions include (a) all-or-none thinking (i.e., seeing personal qualities or situations in absolutist black-and-white terms, and failing to see the shades of gray in between), (b) catastrophizing (i.e., perceiving negative events as intolerable catastrophes—making mountains out of molehills), (c) labeling (e.g., attaching a global label to oneself, "I am a loser," instead of referring to a specific action or event, "I did not handle that particular situation very well"), (d) magnification and minimization (i.e., exaggerating the importance of negative characteristics and experiences while discounting the importance of positive characteristics and experiences), (e) personalization (i.e., assuming one is the cause of an event when other factors are also responsible), and (f) "should" statements (using *should* and *have-to* statements to provide motivation or to control behavior).

Underlying these specific logical errors or cognitive distortions are *schemas* or core beliefs held by people that influence their perceptions and thoughts at the conscious level. Schemas are often expressed as unconditional evaluations about the self and others, including beliefs that "I am incompetent," "I am defective," "I am unlovable," "I am special," "Others are hurtful and not to be trusted," "Others need to take care of me," and "Others must love and admire me." Schemas are generally thought to be formed early in life and tend to persist if no conscious effort is made to identify, examine, and challenge them (Dozois, Frewen, & Covin, 2006). Some examples of cognitive distortions and schema relevant to personality disorder pathology include:

- An individual with Paranoid Personality Disorder is prone to habitually and chronically perceive others as deceitful, abusive, and threatening.
- An individual with Borderline Personality Disorder is prone to sort people into categories of either "all good" or "all bad."
- An individual with Histrionic Personality Disorder often labels what another might consider a minor hassle as a real threat and also perceives him or herself as lacking the resources to cope.
- An individual with Obsessive-Compulsive Personality Disorder tends to be a slave to "shoulds" and "oughts," which he and others must fastidiously and uncompromisingly adhere.
- An individual with Dependent Personality Disorder sees herself as weak, incompetent, and inadequate, requiring constant reassurance, nurturance, and direction.

A cognitive therapist will evaluate his or her patient for their specific misperceptions, attitudes, assumptions, schemas, and interpersonal strategies and generally use a different intervention strategy with each type of personality disorder and person with a specific type of personality disorder (Beck, Freeman, & Associates, 2003).

Many cognitive therapists have developed empirically tested approaches for dealing with the various personality disorder groupings. For example, cognitive-behavioral therapist Marsha Linehan has developed an approach specifically for treating the Borderline Personality Disorder, called dialectical behavior therapy (DBT), which is discussed in Chapter 10. Other cognitive-behavioral interventions have been developed for the full spectrum of personality disorders (Beck et al., 2003; Pretzer & Beck, 1996; Young, 1999; Young, Klosko, & Weshaar, 2003) although empirical support is in the nascent stages. Interestingly, Young's approach has a developmental perspective in which he delineates five different unhealthy developmental environments in which a child might be raised, each of which contributes to creation of a discernable number of distinctive core beliefs, called Early Maladaptive Schemas. Research should address the question of whether (or to what extent) these core beliefs remain constant or change throughout the life span.

Cognitive therapies have done little to address specifically the issues associated with aging and personality disorders, although some cognitive therapists have begun to address general aging issues that may have some application to older persons with personality disorders (e.g., Reinecke & Clark, 2004). The individualized treatment approaches that cognitive-behavioral therapists have developed should, however, adapt well to the unique challenges that older persons with personality disorders present. An excellent reference for CBT approaches with older adults has recently been published (Laidlaw et al., 2003), and although the book focuses largely on treating clinical disorders and problems, some strategies can apply directly to the treatment of personality disorders among older adults.

Psychoanalytic Theories of Personality Disorders

Psychoanalytic accounts of the origins, diagnosis, and treatment of personality disorders fit well into the contemporary research and literature of personality disorders. When Freud (1899/1913) originally conceived of psychoanalysis, he grounded it firmly in the sciences of his time, particularly the work of Charles Darwin. Although Freud did not specifically elaborate on the effects of natural selection and Darwinian processes for normal and abnormal psyches, he recognized the effects instincts and temperaments had on the developing and adult personality structure and afforded them a central status. To his credit, he also recognized the importance of environmental features interacting with these instincts and temperaments to produce long-lasting psychological effects. Thus, in Freudian theory, early childhood experiences and parenting styles interact with heritable factors and, therefore, play dominant roles in the final form of the adult psyche.

Freud can also be credited with developing some of the earliest theoretical foundations of personality disorders such as the Dependent, Passive-Aggressive, Borderline, Narcissistic, Histrionic, and Obsessive-Compulsive Personality Disorders. Besides their instinctual bases, he viewed these personality disorders as emerging from unsuccessful resolutions of the psychosexual stages of development he posited. We now examine the psychoanalytic concepts relevant to the formation and maintenance of these and other personality disorders.

Provinces and Instincts of the Psyche

Freud's three provinces of the psyche (i.e., ego, id, and superego) are all household names. He postulated that they performed their functions through a form of psychic energy derived directly from instincts. He defined an instinct as an inborn and innately compelling directive in psychological processes rooted in organic or biological determinants. Later in his life, Freud divided instincts into two categories: life and death. Life instincts become mental representatives of all bodily needs, which require satisfaction through survival and reproduction (better known as the sex instinct). The life instincts' principal agent is the ego, and according to Freud, the ego owed its very existence to the need for satisfying bodily needs and making realistic transactions with the environment. The ego also transforms or sublimates death instincts that serve the ends of life rather than the ends of death. All life instincts are driven by a very well-known form of psychic energy—the libido (although earlier in his writings he proposed the libido denoted only sexual energy).

Freud apparently developed his notion of death instincts based on the terrible destructions of World War I and through his very realistic fears of future destruction through another world war. His notion of a death instinct was, however, entirely consistent with his core idea that behavior consisted of innate and environmental stimuli. Death instincts, therefore, were built into living matter in the very earliest transmutations of inorganic forms into life forms. The goal of the death instinct was ultimately to return matter into its inorganic, lifeless form. While writing *The Future of an Illusion,* he even vilified any benevolent Providence and the beginning of any kind of higher existence after death (Freud, 1928). The goal of the death instinct for Freud was extinction.

Neuroses, Psychoses, and Personality Disorders

Freud called his earliest conception of neurosis *neurasthenia,* and he saw all neurasthenias as rooted in sexual difficulties. Later, he differentiated the neurasthenias into different types, such as anxiety, hysteria, melancholia, narcissistic, obsessional, sexual, and war neuroses. He maintained that neuroses had no specific etiologic factor but that their nucleus, regardless of neurotic type, was the Oedipal conflict (or presumably Electra conflict for women) during the phallic stage. Neurotics, in general, had the common symptom of anxiety, either manifest or latent. When *DSM-III* adopted a more behavioral approach than the formerly psychoanalytically based *DSM-II,* it dropped the specific term *neurosis* but not the essential idea that a group of disorders had at their core the symptom of anxiety. Notably, some of Freud's other neuroses were later categorized by the *DSM* as personality disorders, such as narcissistic (Narcissistic Personality Disorder), obsessional (Obsessive-Compulsive Personality Disorder), and melancholia (Depressive Personality Disorder). In summary, many of Freud's neurotic types serve as clear prototypes for modern personality disorders.

Freud's conception of psychosis also plays a fundamental role in modern psychoanalytic interpretations of the more severe personality disorders: Schizoid, Schizotypal, Borderline, and Paranoid Personality Disorders. Contemporary psychoanalysts (e.g., Kernberg, 1996) view psychoses as a crisis in identity fusion and diffusion in the integration of self and others. There is a prominence of primitive ego defenses such as projection, denial, and omnipotence. In high affective states, there is a severe loss of reality testing often resulting in a lack of differentiation between self and object representations. A splitting often occurs under these conditions to protect psychotic persons from their perceived chaotic and aggressive conditions. According to Kernberg, the current cluster of symptoms of the Borderline Personality Disorder typifies the psychotic personality organization.

Kernberg (1996) has attempted to classify modern personality disorders into psychoanalytic schema. He views the interrelationships among personality disorders as varying along several continua. First, personality disorders may vary from mild to extreme severity. He considered Obsessive-Compulsive and Depressive Personality Disorders in the mildest category and characteristic of the neurotic personality organization. The Dependent, Histrionic, and Narcissistic (some of the better functioning narcissists) Personality Disorders were considered by Kernberg to be more severe than mild but less severe than extreme, and he considered them to be in the "high" borderline personality organization. Kernberg viewed the Paranoid, Schizoid, Schizotypal, Borderline, Antisocial, and Narcissistic (some of the more malignant narcissists) Personality Disorders in the "low" borderline personality organization. By high personality organization he meant that these people could achieve some satisfactory social and occupational adaptational levels, whereas people in the low category more often could not.

Kernberg (1996) views one of the benefits of psychoanalytic conceptions of personality disorders as allowing a combination of both the categorical and dimensional criteria, such as viewing modern personality disorders as groups of categories along a severity dimension. Kernberg also argues that psychoanalytic theory also has the advantage of viewing personality disorders from a developmental perspective in that varying levels of temperamental affective and aggressive states interact with parents and culture to shape the ultimate expressive symptomatology of personality disorders.

Psychoanalytic Theory and Aging

Freudian theory is preeminently a theory of early childhood, yet given many of Freud's adult life experiences, this is somewhat ironic. From about 4 years before the publication of *Interpretation of Dreams* in 1899, Freud began describing himself as old in letters to his friend Wilhelm Fliess (even though Freud was only 40 at the time). He became very depressed and remained so for years after the death of his aged father Jacob in 1896. Nearing the age of 60, Freud agonized over the fate of his adult sons in World War I. Thus, throughout his later adult life, he struggled with his feelings of being old and unproductive. Nevertheless, psychoanalytic theory and Freud's own psychoanalytic practice with young and older adults always kept its clinical eye toward early childhood as the root of any adult problem.

Formally, at least, Freud did address at least one theoretical aspect of aging—death. As noted earlier, he did hypothesize a death instinct, *thanatos,* and clearly mocked those who held beliefs of life after death, a beneficent divine Providence, and the belief that eventually good is rewarded and evil is punished. For Freud, belief in a god or gods and other religious ideas were formed through the ego defense of reaction formation in the face of what he viewed as the crushingly superior force of nature. In his own life, particularly over the last 2 decades while he suffered greatly from jaw cancer, he nevertheless remained stoic and productive, even if he remained highly self-critical. It is perhaps unfortunate that Freud and psychoanalytic theory did not formally address the issues that aging and death pose for adjusted and maladjusted persons.

A Brief Note about the Humanistic Approach

In contrast to the more conflict-based and mechanistic infrastructure of the psychoanalytic theories, the humanistic theory describes the individual's innate drive to achieve more evolved developmental trajectories, including affective, cognitive, interpersonal, and behavioral domains. This theory perhaps speaks more to personality resilience than pathology. Abraham Maslow

(1954), for example, posited a sequence of needs and motivations, the meeting of which served to organize the individual. These ranged from the most basic (i.e., life supporting) through the most highly evolved (i.e., altruism, actualization, and self-transcendence). Due to the emphasis on positive development, this approach offers little theoretical clarification of the personality disorders, although it remains a popular force in promoting warm, encouraging, and authentic relationships, which are viewed as essential features of most psychotherapies (for clinical and personality disorders alike).

Interpersonal Theories of Personality Disorders

Interpersonal theories tend to have a broad theoretical perspective, including interactions with others and the effects that culture, gender, and environmental factors have on the individual psyche and outward behavior. Such theorists as Harry Stack Sullivan, Abraham Maslow, Carl Rogers, Sidney Jourard, Timothy Leary, and Lorna Smith Benjamin may be good representatives for aspects of interpersonal theories, but psychoanalyst Karen Horney developed one of the premier, time-tested, interpersonal theories. Her theory addressed the continuum of psychologically healthy and unhealthy as well as cultural and gender issues, yet her simple language allowed easy access by nonprofessionals. Furthermore, one of Horney's biographers (Paris, 1994) described that what Horney wrote of as *neuroses* should now best be conceived of as modern personality disorders. For our exposition, we focus on Horney's model.

Karen Horney was born in Germany on September 16, 1885. She was trained as a medical doctor and underwent psychoanalysis herself with Karl Abraham who was a close friend and associate of Freud. From 1915 to 1932, she worked as a psychoanalyst in private practice and later taught and practiced psychoanalysis at the Berlin Psychoanalytic Institute. She moved to the United States to direct the Chicago Institute for Psychoanalysis and then moved to New York City in 1934 to practice and teach at the New School for Social Research. She is best remembered for a number of creative and insightful books, *The Neurotic Personality of Our Time* (1937), *New Ways in Psychoanalysis* (1939), *Our Inner Conflicts* (1945), *Neurosis and Human Growth* (1950), *Feminine Psychology* (a collection of her writings published posthumously, 1967), and *Final Lectures* (1987).

Because of her strong objections to some traditional Freudian ideas, such as inherited temperaments, penis envy, and the death instinct, she was expelled from the New York Psychoanalytic Institute in 1941. She then cofounded her own group, the Association for the Advancement of Psychoanalysis. She expanded her ideas far beyond the borders of traditional psychoanalysis and also had interests in Zen and oriental philosophies. She died in New York City on December 4, 1952, at the age of 67.

Horney's Interpersonal View of the Personality, Personality Disorders, and the Basic Conflict

Horney's major disagreement with traditional Freudian theory was over the Freudian concept of instincts in personality development and the genesis of psychopathology. Horney thought that environmental, social, and family relationships played a much stronger role in the development of the normal and abnormal personality than did Freud. Central to her thinking was the concept of a basic conflict or basic anxiety, which Horney (1945) defined as:

> *the feeling a child has of being isolated and helpless in a potentially hostile world. A wide range of adverse factors in the environment can produce this insecurity in a child: direct or indirect domination, indifference, erratic behavior, lack of respect for the child's individual needs, lack of real guidance, disparaging attitudes, too much admiration or the absence of it, lack of reliable warmth, having too much or too little responsibility, overprotection, isolation from other children, injustice, discrimination, unkept promises, hostile atmosphere, and so on and so on. (p. 41)*

To cope with these environmental disturbances, Horney thought that all children would develop ways of coping along three dimensions: a child can move toward people (Compliant type), against them (Aggressive type), or away from them (Detached type). She further postulated that the three ways of coping are not mutually exclusive, such that a child may use two or more ways of coping at the same time. Given particular environmental circumstances, a child may come to rely on one way of coping, and this style might become their predominant mode of behaving. Horney thought these predominant modes crystallized into neurotic trends, resulting in one of the three neurotic types: Compliant, Aggressive, or Detached.

Horney's Description of Types

Compliant Type (Moving toward People)

Compliant types have a strong and compulsive need for affection, approval, belonging, and human intimacy. They need a partner on whom they can regularly rely for help, protection, and guidance. Their urge to satisfy these compulsions is so strong that they often forget what their own real feelings are because they become so sensitive to their partner's feelings. They become so unselfish and self-sacrificing that they have a warped view of their own needs and feelings. They are so compliant and overconsiderate that they tend to see everyone as trustworthy and nice when, in fact, some people are not. This discrepancy frequently leads Compliant types into disappointment, failure, and a deepening sense of insecurity. They become unassertive, uncritical, unable to make even reasonable demands on others, and unable to strive for and achieve their own personal goals. Of the Compliant type, Horney (1945) wrote:

> Also, because his life is altogether oriented toward others, his inhibitions often prevent him from doing things for himself or enjoying things by himself. This may reach a point where any experience not shared with someone—whether a meal, a show, music, nature—be-

comes meaningless. Needless to say, such a rigid restriction on enjoyment not only impoverishes life but makes dependence on others all the greater. (p. 53)

Horney summarized the Compliant type as having some of these essential characteristics: pervasive feelings of weakness and helplessness and a strong tendency to subordinate oneself to someone else, which leads to inferiority, and a strong dependence on others, including rating oneself completely by what other people think. In the modern diagnostic system (*DSM-IV-TR*), Horney's Compliant type is similar to the Dependent Personality Disorder and the Self-Defeating Personality Disorder (from the *DSM-III-R*).

Aggressive Type (Moving against People)

Horney saw Aggressive types as viewing all people as hostile, so they adopt a "tough" appearing life stance. Interestingly, Horney thought that Aggressive types were exacerbations of the Darwinian concept where only the fittest survive and the strong annihilate the weak. Aggressive types, therefore, see it as essential that they pursue only their self-interests and learn to control and manipulate others. Horney believed that the Aggressive type's other neurotic features, such as compliance needs or detachment needs, might ultimately shape their outward behavior. For example, if an Aggressive type also had strong compliant features, their outward behavior might use indirect methods such as being oversolicitous or getting others obligated to reciprocate. If an Aggressive type is concurrently inclined toward detachment, they will also be inclined to indirect methods rather than open domination or aggression, because the latter brings them into uncomfortable contact with others.

Horney proposed that Aggressive types also have a strong need to excel, to be successful, and to be acknowledged by others as powerful, dominant, and supreme. In this respect, the Aggressive type is as dependent on others as is the Compliant type. Aggressive types need others to affirm their supremacy.

They need to exploit and manipulate others. Feelings are viewed as a weakness. Love is mostly irrelevant. An Aggressive type will more typically marry to improve their social standing, prestige, or wealth. They also have great difficulty admitting to any weaknesses or fears. Horney thought they were consequently likely to find "drastic" ways of attempting to control their fears. For example, Aggressive type parents might throw their children in the water, in a sink-or-swim attitude, to teach their children to swim. Some Aggressive types practice putting their fingers over a flame to teach themselves to overcome pain and the fear of pain.

Although Aggressive types appear to be fearless and uninhibited, Horney thought they actually were as inhibited as the Compliant type. The Aggressive type's inhibitions center about the expression of emotion, forming friendships, love, sympathy, and empathy. They become highly contemptuous of those who do share their emotions, because Horney thought that Aggressive types are actually highly ambivalent about the expression of emotions. They despise its free expression in others because they view it as a sign of weakness (that they themselves might still possess), yet its expression leaves others vulnerable, which Aggressive types should welcome. Horney thought the resulting inner struggle left the Aggressive type as conflicted and confronted by their basic anxiety as any of the other major neurotic types. The Aggressive neurotic trend is present to a great extent in the modern Antisocial Personality Disorder (e.g., in their hostile affect), Paranoid Personality Disorder (e.g., in their emotional coldness and brutal rationality), Borderline Personality Disorder (e.g., in their intense anger), and the Narcissistic Personality Disorder (e.g., in their desire for power and manipulation of others). Indeed, empirical support for the relationships between Horney's neurotic types and personality disorders and their features has recently been reported (Coolidge, Moor, Yamazaki, Stewart, & Segal, 2001; Coolidge, Segal, Benight, & Danielian, 2004).

Detached Type (Moving Away from People)
Horney proposed that this neurotic trend did not just involve an estrangement from other people but also an alienation from oneself. As Horney (1945) wrote:

> *that is a numbness to emotional experience, an uncertainty as to what one is, what one loves, hates, desires, hopes, fears, resents, believes. . . .*
>
> *Detached persons can be quite like the zombies of Haitian lore— dead, but revived by witchcraft: they can work and function like live persons, but there is no life in them. (p. 74)*

Horney thought that Detached types strive both consciously and unconsciously to distance themselves from others, particularly in regard to any emotional ties or bonds, including loving, fighting, cooperation, or competition. She thought they also have a strong need to be self-sufficient, and one way to reduce their reliance on others is to reduce their general wants and needs. Horney (1945) wrote:

> *He is inclined to restrict his eating, drinking, and living habits and keeps them on a scale that will not require him to spend too much time or energy in earning the money to pay for them. He may bitterly resent illness, considering it a humiliation because it forces him to depend on others. (p. 76)*

Detached types were also thought to have a strong need for privacy. They prefer to work alone, live alone, and even eat alone. Horney believed that Detached types express a kind of hypersensitivity to any kind of obligation or coercion, no matter how subtle. For example, she proposed that Detached types might even resist the physical pressure of such things as "collars, neckties, girdles, shoes." In the current *DSM-IV-TR*, the Schizoid Personality Disorder has many of the same features as Horney's Detached type.

The Resolution of Neurotic Conflict

Horney did not think these neurotic trends could be changed simply by evasion, willpower, rational thinking, or coercion, but she did think they could be changed through psychoanalysis. An analyst might help a patient to discover the roots and conditions that brought that patient's particular personality dimensions into existence. Horney thought that the overall goals of therapy would vary depending on the patient's particular expression of their conflicts. However, she thought that patients must learn to assume responsibility for themselves and feel active and responsible for their decisions and the consequences of those decisions. Patients should also develop an inner independence, which might involve establishing their own hierarchy of values and apply these values to their own lives. Ultimately, patients would come to develop spontaneity of feeling where they would become aware and alive with feeling; they also develop the ability to express these feelings yet have a feeling of voluntary control over them. Finally, Horney proposed that the most comprehensive formulation of a goal of therapy should be wholeheartedness. Horney (1945) wrote:

> to be without pretense, to be emotionally sincere, to be able to put the whole of oneself into one's feelings, one's work, one's beliefs. (p. 242)

Horney, Feminist Psychology, and Humanism

Although Horney is most often associated with the psychology of feminism, by the mid-1930s, she had evolved into a more general humanist. She became interested in the liberation of both sexes and less concerned with the study of their differences. In 1935, she delivered the following public lecture:

> First of all we need to understand that there are no unalterable qualities of inferiority of our sex due to laws of God or nature. Our limitations are, for the greater part, culturally and socially conditioned. Men

who have lived under the same conditions for a long time have developed similar attitudes and shortcomings.

Once and for all we should stop bothering about what is feminine and what is not. Such concerns only undermine our energies. Standards of masculinity and femininity are artificial standards. All we definitely know at present about sex differences is that we do not know what they are. Scientific differences between the two sexes certainly exist, but we shall never be able to discover what they are until we have first developed our potentialities as human beings. Paradoxical as it may sound, we shall find out about these differences only if we forget about them.

In the meantime what we can do is to work together for the full development of the human personalities of all for the sake of general welfare. (as cited in Paris, 1994, p. 238)

Horney, Aging, and Personality Disorders

As noted earlier, Horney's neurotic types are now best described as personality disorders. She did not directly address changes as a function of aging in her three personality types or three personality dimensions. However, she did address the interpersonal issue of aging for the two sexes and thought that women suffered more greatly than men as a function of aging because of a cultural bias toward the erotic attractiveness associated with youthfulness. She thought men who were frightened and depressed by the prospects of becoming middle aged could be considered abnormal, because that was an unusual response compared to men's typical responses to middle age. However, for women, she felt it was a more common response because of society's emphasis on youthful physical attractiveness; Horney found this natural outcome abhorrent and that an age-phobia was "pathetic." In women, it was even more pernicious for two reasons: First, aging fears in women stifle their development when they are younger and create great insecurity; ironically, this is when they are seen as physically attractive by their cultures. Second, as women age into their 30s and 40s, these anxieties and depression about aging create an unnecessary and unhealthy jealousy between mothers and daughters that frequently spoils their relationships.

Horney emphasized that aging is a problem for both men and women, but that it becomes an increasingly desperate problem if either gender holds youth and erotic attractiveness as chief values. She felt all people would suffer the loss if the important qualities of maturity like poise, independence, autonomy of judgment, and wisdom were not core societal and personal values. If society's core values remain youth and attractiveness, according to Horney, beginning in people's 20s, insecurity begins to rob people of their worth, and she considered insecurity the greatest evil of her time and culture.

Conclusions

In this chapter, we have reviewed the cognitive, psychoanalytic, and interpersonal paradigms of personality disorders and aging. Cognitive theories of personality disorders tend to be framed through individuals' phenomenological world, yet their treatment of personality disorders tends to be grounded in precise behavioral assessment techniques. Thus, cognitive-behavioral assessment and interventions are ideally suited to aging persons with personality disorders. The assessments and interventions are not yet uniquely developed for groups of older persons with personality disorders, as cognitive-behavioral theorists have done for some personality disorder types like the borderline category. However, because of the emphasis on the individual phenomenological world of any person with a personality disorder, the special issues associated with aging can be appropriately assessed and treated.

Psychoanalytic theorists have also tended to ignore the particular challenges that aging poses for people with personality disorders. In general, psychoanalytic thought has always focused itself on childhood roots for adult personality problems. Freud generally ignored aging issues from his psychoanalytic perspective; ironically, he appeared to suffer greatly from his own aging issues, and he appeared to view himself as old well before his time. Kernberg, a contemporary psychoanalytic theorist, proposes that psychoanalysis still has much to offer in the diagnosis and treatment of personality disorders. The main techniques of psychoanalysis—free association, dream analysis, and the interpretation of the transference reaction—would still be highly appropriate to some of the issues of older persons with personality disorders.

Horney's interpersonal theory of neurotic types (i.e., personality disorders) perhaps addressed issues of aging more directly than the other two theories in this chapter. Horney also saw that two aging issues, a cultural bias toward the erotic attractiveness associated with youthfulness and the dependent emphasis of qualities associated with maturity, like poise, independence, autonomy of judgment, and wisdom, as critical to the mental health and growth of women. She recognized that both sexes had to be liberated at the same time to have the full development of all human personalities.

We have also seen that each of these major theories of personality disorders presented in this chapter tend to be somewhat deficient when addressing many of the specifics of personality disorders and aging. One argument could be made in their favor and that is general personality trait research has shown an overriding stability of most traits, including some traditionally abnormal ones such as neuroticism and psychoticism (e.g., Heatherton & Weinberger, 1994). However, research has also shown that individual variation in personality traits and disorders tends to be large, exceeding well-known influences on the personality, such as gender, by a factor of 30.

Regarding theories of personality, one size does not fit all. We continue to struggle to arrive at a unified theory that supports our understanding of the origin, maintenance, and presentation of personality pathology. Old theories each contribute, and must be integrated, but cannot stand alone, perhaps especially as they relate to older adults. For this population, we need to consider cohort and historical moments juxtaposed to developmental stages. The current stage and context need also to be considered in the theoretical analysis. What is being asked of the personality so that it presents as disordered?

Finally, we want to emphasize the point that personality disorders appear to be a final expression of many factors, including significant genetic and constitutional factors, which we address in Chapter 8. Studies of heritability support the existence of infrastructure factors. Psychodynamic factors and early environments also play an important role in shaping personality (healthy and disordered). From very early in life, a history of neglect, abandonment, inconsistent and fragile attachments, trauma, and abuse can lead to disordered styles of relating to the others and the world. Whereas most of the research in this area has focused on Borderline Personality Disorder showing that people with borderline personality are likely to have had early trauma experiences (Stone, 1993), it is likely that diverse unhealthy, unduly stressful, chaotic, or abusive early environments often play at least some role in the formation of each specific type of personality disorder.

Because a theoretical understanding of the older personality-disordered patient is crucial for guiding interventions, let's reconsider the quotes offered at the beginning of this chapter. As Einstein suggested, a theory is limiting if we adhere dogmatically to one particular perspective and all that we "see" is "filtered through the particular lens" of that theory: Some important details of the case may be overlooked or not given appropriate weight. We therefore encourage clinicians to become well versed in a variety of theoretical perspectives, knowing that the ability to look at older patients and their problems from different vantage points can be very useful.

Theories of Personality Disorders: Evolutionary and Neurobiological

8

Chapter

Theories may provide *ultimate* or *proximal* explanations for behavior, particularly in the evolutionary paradigm. Ultimate explanations attempt to understand behavior based on our long evolutionary history in our remote ancestral environments. Proximal explanations seek understanding in our immediate biological and social environments. In this chapter, we examine both ultimate and proximal biological explanations for personality disorders (the evolutionary and neurobiological theories, respectively). These biological theories are perhaps most useful in providing foundations for understanding the origins of personality disorders but they are less useful for the purposes of case conceptualization and informing treatment.

Evolutionary Theories of Personality Disorders

Current evolutionary psychologists have drawn heavily from the earlier theory of sociobiology as expounded by E. O. Wilson in his influential 1975 book. Wilson based the premise of sociobiology on Charles Darwin's book *Origin of the Species* published in 1859. Darwin's central thesis revolved around the process of natural selection, which Darwin once summarized as "multiply, vary, let the strongest live and the weakest die." Yet, Darwin's theory could not readily explain behaviors such as altruism, particularly in cases where the altruistic organism died in the process. For example, Darwin was puzzled by a group of insects that produced no descendants. How could a whole caste of ants be sterile? He vaguely suspected that it had something to do with the survival of the whole family of ants, all of the castes. Darwin likened it to making a well-flavored soup where the individual contributions are lost, although he worried that his failure to explain the phenomenon would be fatal to his whole theory.

Basic Concepts of Evolutionary Theory

Sociobiology came to posit at least three mechanisms to account for such altruistic behaviors: (1) kin selection, (2) kin altruism, and (3) reciprocal altruism. Kin selection proposes that survival be examined from the point of view of the gene: There are numerous examples in the animal kingdom where an organism sounds a warning call or in one way or another exposes itself to a predator. These acts are typically labeled *altruistic,* because it appears that the organism is unselfishly concerned with the welfare of others, even to its own detriment. Sociobiologists prefer to label it a *selfish act* because that organism is simply helping exact copies of its own genes to survive and propagate. Furthermore, the term *kin selection* implies that the organism is more likely to commit this act when the other organisms are highly related to it and less likely when they are distantly related or not related. Thus, altruistic acts are more likely when the relationships are parent-child, sibling-sibling, cousins, distant relatives, strangers, and different species, in decreasing order of probability.

When an organism sounds a warning call even if it has not yet reproduced itself, its close relatives may survive to reproduce. Thus, the gene for self-sacrifice will survive, probably in at least half, if not more, of the organism's siblings. The life of the self-sacrificial animal is short but not that much shorter (in evolutionary time) than those animals that survive. However, the gene for self-sacrifice will survive for a long time, perhaps millions of years, because this gene is ultimately selfish. By perishing at the right time, copies of itself will survive and flourish.

Evolutionary psychologists, thus distinguish between *kin altruism* (i.e., offering to help relatives) and true altruism, or their preferred label *reciprocal altruism* (i.e., helping someone unrelated). Thus, nepotism (i.e., people in power giving jobs to their relatives) has a biological basis according to evolutionary psychologists. The concept of kin altruism allows us to explain Darwin's dilemma about the sterile ants. If the sterile ants spent their time helping fertile ants to survive and reproduce (and they do), some of the genes of the sterile ants would also survive in the survival machines of the fertile ants.

Reciprocal altruism (i.e., good deeds done for nonrelatives) is viewed by evolutionary psychologists as simply another form of genetic selfishness, based on the idea that humans who cooperate with one another are more likely to survive than those who do not. In the ancestral environment, it may have meant that those humans who cooperated in a hunt were more likely to have been successful than solo hunters, and those humans who protected their families in a larger group were more likely to survive from an attack than solo families. Thus, it is no small irony that the Golden Rule is also the basis for reciprocal altruism: Do unto others as you would have them do unto you. Reciprocal altruism invokes doing a favor for a nonrelative because they may return the favor. Because reciprocal altruism may have played such a central role in the survival of the ancestral families in securing protection and food, it is not surprising that evolutionary psychologists have strongly emphasized its role.

Evolutionary psychologists emphasize that natural selection typically favors a predominant behavioral pattern yet allows alternative or dissimilar patterns to develop and persist. These patterns (both the predominant and alternatives) are called *evolutionary stable strategies* (ESS). They further purport that an optimal and stable ratio develops between the predominant and alternative patterns. In our original example, this means that the ratio of fertile ants to sterile ants develops and stabilizes over time. If the population of ants became dominated by the sterile ants, it would create an inherently unstable structure and would more than likely become extinct.

To explain further the development of ESS, British biologist John Maynard Smith coined the term *frequency-dependent selection*. Frequency-dependent selection states that the value of a trait will decrease as its frequency in the population increases. In practice, this means that natural selection places an upper limit on the predominance of any trait, which allows for an alternative and usually dissimilar behavioral trait. To relate this concept to personality disorders, evolutionary psychologists would posit that people with Antisocial Personality Disorder traits could persist in the gene pool as an alternative pattern to the predominant pattern of a culture's members practicing kin altruism and reciprocal altruism. However, it could not be a predominant pattern because not everyone, nor even a majority of societal members, could practice cheating and neglectful parenting and have that culture survive. From this basic foundation of evolutionary theory, we now examine clusters of personality disorders from an evolutionary psychology perspective; Recall, however, the evolutionary approach can be most useful in understanding the origins of dysfunctional personality traits in society, not the specific causes of personality disorder in any one individual.

Application to Antisocial, Histrionic, Narcissistic, Dependent, and Avoidant Personality Disorders

Evolutionary psychologists speculate that this seemingly disparate group of personality disorders might have developed in the ancestral environment because of varying ESS with regard to status hierarchies (which are characteristic of nearly all primates). A status hierarchy implies that organisms living in groups fall along a continuum from dominant to submissive. By evaluating the success of fighting or submitting, individuals maximize their outcomes for obtaining mates, food, or other resources. It is thought that some inherent genetic predispositions drive people to their natural place in a group status hierarchy. For example, inheriting an above average tendency for aggression and a below average tendency for avoiding harm might place an organism closer toward the dominant end of the status hierarchy. Those with the opposite tendencies would be closer to the submissive end of the status hierarchy. By not challenging every other organism for a place in the status hierarchy, organisms are able to maximize their resources, in part, by not wasting them on unnecessary competition.

Evolutionary psychologists propose that individuals with either Antisocial Personality Disorder or Histrionic Personality Disorder "cheat" their way into the status hierarchy. For example, the antisocial person disregards and violates the rights of others with chronic patterns of aggression, deceitfulness, irresponsibility, and a lack of remorse. The *DSM-IV-TR* states that its prevalence rate is 3% in males and 1% in females, and these rates are relatively invariant across the world. Evolutionary psychologists suspect that antisocial persons often steal the resources of others rather than earn them by their place in the status hierarchy. Antisocial men may fake their parental investment so as to fool women into thinking they will be stable fathers when they will not be. Antisocial women may fool men who are actually high in parental investment to impregnate them despite the women's lack of commitment to the relationship or the children. In both cases, antisocial genes are passed on.

Individuals with Histrionic Personality Disorder also "cheat" their way into the status hierarchy but by different strategies. Histrionic people are excessively emotional, flamboyant, and attention-seeking, and this pattern occurs more frequently in females. By exaggerating their sexuality, they attract spouses. By exaggerating their needs and wants through excessive emotional displays, they gain resources they would not ordinarily gain in the hierarchy.

Evolutionary psychologists propose that even in the ancestral environments (say 100,000 years ago) natural selection may have begun to favor the one man-one woman reproductive dyad. Yet, frequency-dependent selection allowed the development of some alternative forms. Some men, perhaps with natural predilections against hard work, parental investment, and faithfulness found it easier to steal resources rather than earn them. Some found it easier to force or trick women into sex: The greater their abilities to aggress against, deceive, or mislead others, the greater their success at reproduction. In the ancestral environment, abandoning a pregnant woman may not have been as successful a reproductive strategy as staying with her and providing her and the child with resources. However, abandoning 5 or 10 pregnant women may still allow a few of the resulting children to survive to reproductive age, ensuring the survival of antisocial genes. A population might never be able to support 50% of its members being antisocial, because too many children would likely be abandoned and not reach reproductive age themselves. Such a population would perish quickly. However, frequency-dependent selection would have allowed some stable percentage, such as our present 3% and 1% antisocial prevalence rates for males and females, respectively.

With regard to the Antisocial Personality Disorder, evolutionary psychologists might postulate that natural selection places a lower *upper limit* on women than it does on men. They base this difference on men and women's differing reproductive strategies. A woman who abandons her child shortly after birth has less chance of passing on her genes than a man who abandons his child shortly after birth. A woman's strategy of promiscuity and child abandonment must not have been successful in the ancestral environment. Nonetheless, an alternative ESS of Antisocial Personality Disorder has persisted in women but only at about one-third the prevalence rate for men.

Thus, the modern *DSM* Antisocial Personality Disorder criteria of deceitfulness, irresponsibility, and a lack of remorse all had useful consequences for reproduction. Deceitfulness allows antisocial men to steal others' resources, to impregnate other men's mates, and to have that man raise that child as his own. Their irresponsibility and lack of remorse allows them to abandon their children without hesitation. The latter is also true of antisocial women, although it appears to be a much less successful evolutionary strategy in women. The emotions (primarily guilt and sympathy) that evolved to prevent cheating either did not develop or were diminished to the extent that they did not prevent cheating. Women with antisocial and histrionic traits may have used their deceitfulness to deceive men high in parental investment into thinking they would be good and faithful mates and mothers. Their irresponsibility and lack of remorse would also allow them to leave their children with a man with high parental investment. Indeed, some men, but not all, may be successful at raising these abandoned children to reproductive age, thus passing on the antisocial and histrionic genes of the mothers.

People with features of Narcissistic Personality Disorder are perhaps, on the surface, more clearly related to ancestral status hierarchies than the other disorders in this group. Narcissistic persons are attracted to power, have a high need for admiration, and lack empathy. They often abuse people whom they feel are beneath them, especially if these attacks also build up the narcissist. They often exaggerate their own successes while they denigrate or greatly envy the successes of others. The basis of the Narcissistic Personality Disorder is one of status and its maintenance. They are also seen as cheaters by evolutionary psychologists because their self-centeredness and lack of empathy means that they will take advantage of others and be poor reciprocators.

The Dependent Personality Disorder and Avoidant Personality Disorder can also be viewed as disorders of the ancestral status hierarchy. Dependent persons are known to make excessive attachments to another person in the status hierarchy. Through their exceptional submissiveness, they avoid all the dangers of competition in the hierarchy. A negative consequence of this strategy, however, is that they are subject to abuse and domination by their partner. A similar pattern is seen among avoidant persons. They actively avoid social situations and competition. They should not necessarily be seen as submissive, however, because they choose not to participate in the status hierarchy. Theoretically, this means that they must maintain and survive without the benefits of the group, and although it is a low frequency solution, it survives and persists, nonetheless, in modern societies.

Application to Borderline Personality Disorder

The *DSM-IV-TR* states that people with Borderline Personality Disorder have a chronic pattern of instability in interpersonal relationships, impulsivity, intense anger, suicidal attempts, and stress-related dissociative episodes. Borderline Personality Disorder has an early adult onset, and may occur three times more in females than males. On the surface, it appears that individuals with these features would not have much reproductive success. However, according to the *DSM-IV-TR*, its prevalence rate is about 2% in general populations throughout the world, 10% of all patients in outpatient settings, 20% among psychiatric inpatients, and 30% to 60% of all patients with a suspected personality disorder. Thus, it is a relatively common personality disorder despite this array of seemingly negative elements.

One reason for its persistence from an evolutionary perspective may be that, although Borderline Personality Disorder may be highly heritable, an adult onset in contemporary society might have meant that in the ancestral environment reproduction might have taken place at a much earlier age. Thus, this array of features may not have yet been present when that individual was selecting a mate or attempting to keep a mate. From this perspective, Borderline Personality Disorder symptoms may not have had any particular evolutionary value but they did not hinder reproduction because of their later adult onset in the ancestral environment. Indeed, this explanation might be true for most, if not all, of the personality disorders. Their adult onset might not have hindered early (e.g., adolescent) reproduction. However, the consistency of the cluster of symptoms in the Borderline Personality Disorder and other impulsive types appears to require another explanation.

One possibility for the general impulsivity in affectivity, cognition, and behavior in the Borderline Personality Disorder may reside in the nature of impulsivity itself: Impulsivity in the ancestral environment might have had some positive consequences (e.g., Jensen et al., 1997). Jensen et al. postulated that ancestral environments might have varied along several continua including safe versus not safe, resource-rich versus resource-impoverished, and time-optional versus time-critical. In environments that were unsafe, impoverished, and time-critical, they argued that humans' survival may have depended on hypervigilance, rapid-scanning, quickness to fight or flee, and motorically high activity (e.g., to forage or move to a warmer climate). Jensen et al. reasoned that not all environments may have been harsh and not all individuals would have needed these extreme symptoms. However, they hypothesized that in the harshest environments, traits that allowed some individuals to fight or flee quickly and to be "response-ready" may have ensured the survival of group members who were more docile or placid. Again, frequency-dependent selection might have allowed such "deviant" behavior but also placed an upper limit on its prevalence.

A seemingly tougher symptom to explain from an evolutionary perspective is suicidal behavior common among people with Borderline Personality Disorder. One proposed explanation is based on the supposition that depression and low self-esteem have some latent adaptive value. For example, when failing in an attempt to obtain a mate or resource through competition, individuals may temporarily suspend aggressive behaviors, allowing them to reevaluate their behavioral goals and strategies, perhaps resulting in greater success in later endeavors. This time-out period may also allow individuals to lower their expectations resulting in fewer disappointments and unsuccessful and dangerous challenges in the status hierarchy. Lowered expectations and a drop in the status hierarchy may also result in self-protection because that individual may be less likely to be perceived as a threat by more dominant individuals. Regarding actual suicidal behavior, Torgersen (1994) has suggested that suicidal acts among the extremely depressed, terminally ill, or some aged persons are a form of kin altruism—with their death, siblings, and close genetic relatives have more resources.

Application to Paranoid Personality Disorder

According to the *DSM-IV-TR*, people with Paranoid Personality Disorder are hypervigilant, distrustful, suspicious, and pathologically jealous. As noted, Jensen et al. (1997) hypothesized that hypervigilance might have been adaptive in ancestral environments where conditions were unsafe, there were few resources, and time was of the essence. They further proposed that such "response ready" individuals would be at an advantage over more contemplative or phlegmatic individuals, particularly in primitive battlefield situations.

For males in the ancestral environment, distrustfulness, suspicion, and jealousy might have been of adaptive value in reproductive relationships to help ensure that any resulting children from a sexual union were from that male and not some other male. From a female's perspective, these same traits might have helped to ensure that a male mate did not share precious resources with other females. Because these personality disorder traits seem to be highly heritable (and additive), individual differences in the magnitude of these traits is to be expected. The Paranoid Personality Disorder is also one of the more prevalent personality disorders, thus, perhaps reinforcing the notion of the value of hypervigilance and jealousy in the ancestral environment.

Some evolutionary psychologists (e.g., Stevens & Price, 1996) even argue that the paranoid disposition is a trait that all humans share to some extent. They postulate that life has always taught us to expect trouble. They hypothesize that typical social interactions keep our suspicions at bay and reinforce our trust in others. In those individuals where their paranoid predispositions are higher than normal, their paranoia and suspiciousness further isolates them from social interactions that might otherwise ameliorate their paranoid tendencies.

Application to Schizoid, Schizotypal, and Avoidant Personality Disorders

Individuals with Schizoid Personality Disorder are highly detached from nearly all social relationships and have a restricted range of emotions in interpersonal interactions. A schizoid person is the quintessential loner, who appears aloof, cold, and remote to others. Even when pressed into relationships, they do not appear to enjoy them, including sexual interactions. Individuals with Schizotypal Personality Disorder share two of the same criteria as the Schizoid Personality Disorder: (1) constricted affect and (2) a lack of close confidants. Like schizoid persons, schizotypal persons have serious social and interpersonal difficulties. Unlike schizoid persons, schizotypal persons have in addition eccentricities in their thinking and reasoning, such that they find highly personal meanings in meaningless events (ideas of reference) and have odd beliefs and speech or magical thinking. Like the Schizoid and Schizotypal Personality Disorders, individuals with Avoidant Personality Disorder are also socially inhibited. Avoidant Personality Disorder traits also include negative evaluations of self and great restraint in social and interpersonal relationships, which are both longed for and feared.

Some individuals who are either forced into seclusion (by the death of their family) or who socially or interpersonally withdraw for other reasons may function at least semi-normally by themselves; sometimes they even do original work on their own. One factor for that success might be that their seclusion may foster conditions that allow or generate creativity and originality (e.g., fewer social or emotional distractions).

Another factor is that diseases (particularly fatal ones) may have been transmitted more readily with increasing social interaction. A schizoid, schizotypal, or avoidant individual in the ancestral environment, who reluctantly participated in social or sexual unions, might have been subsequently much less susceptible to diseases that were socially transmitted. It might also be possible that the restricted emotional expressions in these individuals (having "poker faces") would make them less vulnerable to manipulation and being taken advantage of when engaging in reciprocal altruistic acts.

In summary, evolutionary psychologists believe that personality disorders persist because of frequency-dependent selection. Behavior traits that do not predominate and have rather low prevalence rates survive because individuals with these traits found adaptive niches in the ancestral environment.

Evolutionary psychologists have not yet directly addressed the issue of personality disorders and aging, but numerous general evolutionary theories of aging exist. Kirkwood (2000) suggested that aging and senescence were the price humans paid for their evolutionary success. Indeed, our somatic cells age while our genes have the potential to be immortal. Bouchard and Loehlin (2001) observed that evolutionary psychologists, although addressing the evolutionary adaptiveness of personality disorder traits in the ancestral environment, have not yet adequately studied personality disorders in the evolutionary perspective in regards to aging.

Neurobiological Theories of Personality Disorders

Evolutionary psychologists' explanations for current behavior based on the evolution of behavior in time-distant ancestral environments are said to be *ultimate* explanations. They use the word ultimate in the primary sense of furthest back in time, remote, or distant. Neurobiological theories of behavior are said to be *proximal* explanations, in the sense that they are closely and directly linked to our current biological functioning. From a proximal neurobiological perspective, the present evidence that personality disorders have a neurobiological basis is beyond question. Debates now center on such issues as the extent of the contribution of genes to personality disordered behavior and the malleability and limits to the amelioration of personality disorders. Also of question are what particular interventions are necessary for changing personality disordered behavior and whether these interventions change across the life span.

Now let us explore the parameters of what is meant by a biological basis for a personality disorder. The major parameter for a biological basis of any behavior is genes. Genes are actually locations along chromosomes, which are structures inside the nucleus of cells. A particular gene location consists of a double strand of deoxyribonucleic acid (DNA), which is made up of only four amino acids—adenine, thymine, cytosine, and guanine. These amino acids accomplish two main tasks: First, their own replication (and thus, survival of the greater organism); second, the coding of larger protein molecules, which in turn control nearly all other functions of living organisms, including such basic tasks as respiration, heart rate, blood pressure, and digestion and such higher level functions as survival, intellectual endeavors, and personality traits.

Heredity patterns focus on the different forms of genes called *alleles*. A person's specific combination of alleles is called a *genotype*. The observed behavior of an individual as a result of his or her genotype is called a *phenotype*. There are at least three major forms of genotypic transfer: (1) major dominant gene transmission, (2) recessive gene transmission, and (3) additive gene transmission. There are also other genetic reasons for particular phenotypes that are not transmitted from parents to their children such as new mutations (that can subsequently be heritable) and changes in chromosomes (e.g., extra chromosomes or repeated DNA sequences).

One of the most well-known examples of a pathological phenotype due to a major dominant gene is Huntington's disease (HD). This progressive dementing disorder causes major dysfunction in intellectual and memory processing and eventually death. Huntington's disease is caused by a single dominant allele. These individuals inherit one dominant allele (coding for the disease) and one normal (but recessive) allele. Because the two alleles each split during reproduction, the children of HD individuals have a 50-50 chance of inheriting the dominant allele, thus 50% of the children of an HD parent will inherit HD.

The second major form of genetic transmission is due to two recessive alleles that can only express themselves in the presence of an alike, recessive, but pathological allele. If a person carries only one pathological recessive allele, this person will not have a noticeable pathological phenotype; however, by definition, they are called carriers of the disease. Reproduction with another carrier will result in a 25% likelihood that their children will exhibit the pathological phenotype, a 50% likelihood that their children will be carriers of the disease, and a 25% likelihood that their children will neither exhibit the phenotype nor be a carrier for the disease. It is estimated that over 1,500 diseases or pathological conditions are caused by recessive alleles.

The third form of genetic transmission is less well known than the other two but accounts for millions of phenotypic traits, diseases, and conditions. This form is called *additive genetic transmission,* which involves multiples genes (i.e., polygenic; see DeFries, McGuffin, McClearn, & Plomin, 2000, for an overview of genetic transmission). Most complex human traits, both physical (e.g., height) and psychological (e.g., intelligence), are thought to be influenced by multiple genes. These phenotypic traits are typically measured quantitatively along some scale or dimension. Interestingly, their measurements in large groups of people often produces a normal distribution (i.e., a bell-shaped curve) with most people scoring in the middle of the dimension and fewer people toward either end of the scale. For quantitative phenotypic traits with a polygenic cause, it is not often easy to identify a point along the scale where individuals above a certain point are said to be pathological and individuals below that point are not. Nonetheless, personality disorder research conventionally measures personality disorders dimensionally yet often treats them as discrete groups or categories (Millon & Davis, 2000).

Thus, personality disorders likely have a heritable polygenic basis, which is at least as strong as other influences. The two most traditional experimental sources for the evidence of the heritability of complex human traits such as personality disorders comes from (1) family studies where the number of affected individuals is traced in single families over generations and (2) twin studies of identical (monozygotic or MZ) and fraternal (dizygotic or DZ) twins. In twin studies, if a trait is more alike (i.e., has greater concordance) in MZ twins than in DZ twins, the trait is thought to have a genetic basis. The concordance rates are measured with correlation coefficients (r) where a coefficient of 1.00 indicates that a pair of twins (or two individuals) are absolutely the same on a trait, 0.00 indicates no relationship whatsoever between the twins, and −1.00 indicates that the twins are exactly opposite on the trait. Thus, in twin studies, a genetic influence is indicated where the MZ twin correlation is greater than the DZ twin correlation. The MZ correlation value has been used as a rough estimate of proportional influence of genes to the variability in that trait. For example, if a trait has a correlation of .62 in a group of MZ twins and a correlation of .25 in a group of DZ twins, the overall heritability of the trait can be estimated to be .62, thus 62% of the variability in the trait may be due to heritable influences. It is also important to note a common error in the interpretation of the heritability coefficient. A trait that is said to have a heritability of .62 does *not* mean that 62% of the trait is heritable. It does mean that in this polygenic trait, 62% of the *variability* of individual scores when measured on the trait is attributed to genetic influences.

Whereas most personality disorders have long been noted to run in families (e.g., Millon & Davis, 2000), the evidence for their heritable basis from twin studies has only recently been empirically demonstrated. The first of these was an adult twin study by Torgersen et al. (2000) who interviewed 92 MZ twin pairs and 129 DZ pairs using a structured interview for personality disorders. They found a median heritability correlation of .59 for 10 personality disorders ranging from .79 for Narcissistic Personality Disorder to .28 for Avoidant Personality Disorder.

Coolidge et al. (2001), in a study of 70 MZ twin pairs and 35 DZ twin pairs of children ranging from 5 to 17 years old, used a parent-as-respondent inventory (Coolidge Personality and Neuropsychological Inventory; Coolidge, Thede, Stewart, & Segal, 2002) designed to assess the 12 personality disorders and their features from *DSM-IV-TR*. They found a median heritability correlation of .75 for the 12 personality disorders with a range of .81 for Dependent Personality Disorder to .50 for the Paranoid and Passive-Aggressive Personality Disorders.

In a provocative article, Turkheimer (2000) proposed three laws of behavior genetics relating to polygenic causes. The first law is that multiple sources of evidence appear to show that all complex human behavior is heritable, at least to some extent. The second law is that the effect of genes on our behavior is usually greater than the effect of our common family influences (i.e., *shared environment*). The third law states that a substantial portion of the variation in complex behavioral traits is not accounted for by the effects of genes or family influences (i.e., *nonshared environment*). The two twin studies previously cited (Coolidge et al., 2001; Torgersen et al., 2000) appear to follow all three of Turkheimer's laws. All of the personality disorders appear to be at least somewhat heritable and some appear to be highly heritable, thus outstripping the impact of any shared or nonshared environmental influences. Typical twin study analyses include an estimate of the overall heritability of a trait, the relative differential influence of genes, the family environment in which the twins are raised (i.e., shared environment), and the unique experiences to which each twin might individually be exposed (i.e., nonshared environment). The latter statistical estimates are made using a technique known as structural equation modeling (see Neale & Cardon, 1992, for additional details). Both the Torgersen et al. and Coolidge et al. studies found that the predominant heritability model was one that included only additive genetic influences and unique or nonshared influences. Surprisingly, the effects of a family's influence on the formation of a personality disorder appeared to be the least influential.

Let's examine Turkheimer's third law with regard to these previously mentioned personality disorder studies: A substantial portion of the variation in personality disorder traits is not accounted for by the effects of genes or family influences. Genetic researchers label this factor the nonshared environmental influence, and it accounts for the reason siblings and twins are different although raised in the same family. The entire system in which a complex trait arises is characterized by a high degree of interactivity. This means that genes and environmental influences will interact with other genes and environmental influences to make simple interpretations of these separate factors almost absurd. For example, whereas a personality disorder might have nearly equally heritable and environmental contributions, particular genetic influences might predispose an individual to select a particular environment that affects the expression of that and other genetic and environmental influences.

Although all three sources of influence are involved in this interactivity, the interpretation of the nonshared environmental influences present a particularly thorny problem to psychologists, particularly in light of Turkheimer's third law. However, it does not mean that what a family teaches a child does not matter or does not affect the child's later adult personality. It may, however, indicate how siblings can be different despite being raised in the same family because the unique individual environments of each child and that child's peers may be a more potent cause of the later developmental outcomes of the child than the shared ones. However, the results of a meta-analysis of a plethora of studies designed to objectively assess these unique experiences of individuals are daunting. The meta-analysis revealed that nonshared environmental influences are exceedingly difficult to assess and quantify (e.g., Turkheimer & Waldron, 2000). Indeed, the results have been labeled the *gloomy hypothesis*, suggesting it may be the nonshared environmental influences that are too unique, unsystematic, capricious, and/or serendipitous to measure quantitatively—although we are likely to hear about these unique influences from our patients during treatment. Because of a high degree of interactivity between genetic and environmental influences, these unsystematic nonshared environmental influences are exposed to equally unsystematic genetic processes.

For psychologists interested in personality disorders, this may mean that additive genetic factors have the greatest influence on the formation of personality disorders. This may obviate some guilt in the family members or parents of individuals with personality disorders, but it clearly stops there. So what if a personality disorder has a genetic basis? Until highly successful biochemical genetic treatments or other biochemical interventions are developed, therapists are left to guess what the individual nonshared environmental factors might be in the formation of a particular personality disorder in an individual. Currently, there is no acceptable quantitative method for estimating these influences, leaving the assessment of these influences to the therapist's intuitions. It also leaves the necessity of these evaluations to a successful therapeutic outcome to the intuition and training experiences of the therapist. But the results of these neurobiological studies are not totally in vain. Preliminary data suggests that personality disorders are heritable (at least to some degree), but demonstrating a strong genetic basis does not invalidate or negate attempts to explain familial, environmental, and intrapsychic features that promote and maintain personality disorders. Indeed, as is true for most mental disorders, an inclusive biopsychosocial model is most appropriate for understanding the origins of the personality disorders, and, perhaps most importantly, for informing interventions.

Conclusions

In this chapter, evolutionary theories of personality disorders strive to provide ultimate explanations for personality disorders and they view the behavior of personality disordered individuals as having persisted from adaptations to the ancestral environments. These behaviors, which may have had adaptive value in the ancestral environment, have become maladaptive in the current environment. We have also seen that aging and senescence are viewed as the price humans have paid for their evolutionary success. Evolutionary psychologists' primary theoretical concerns focus on reproductive success and various acts of altruism. Although there are evolutionary theories of aging, evolutionary theorists have yet to address specifically how aging and personality disorders may relate in an evolutionary perspective.

From a neurobiological perspective, there is a strong contribution of genetic factors in the creation and maintenance of most personality disorders. Unique environmental factors may play an important but apparently secondary role in the proximal origins of personality disorders. The gloomy hypothesis suggested that these unique environmental factors may be too unsystematic, as of yet, to assess in their relationship to personality disorders. Perhaps, surprisingly, the least influential factor in personality disorders is that of shared environmental influence—that is, the effects of being raised in the same family as our siblings. This is not to suggest that family influences, family values, and early childhood experiences do not play any role in the creation of personality disorders; however, the current research suggests that our genetic predispositions and unique experiences play greater roles. Much more work, both theoretical and empirical, needs to be done in this area. Replication of twin studies with larger samples assessed with comprehensive structured interviews for personality disorders is one important avenue.

Assessment

9

Chapter

Assessment is a key component of any psychotherapeutic undertaking. Without an accurate and thorough understanding of the nature of the patient's problems, it may be difficult for the clinician to conceptualize the case, select targets for treatment (done collaboratively with the patient if possible), and develop a treatment plan. We view assessment as part of the treatment process, not as a separate clinical task to be completed as a precursor to treatment. Assessment should be considered an ongoing process in which hypotheses are continually being developed, tested, and refined as treatment progresses.

Identification and assessment of personality disorders is critical because they exert significant clinical impact and need to be incorporated into the treatment planning (Dougherty, 1999; Millon & Davis, 2000; Paris, 2003; Rosowsky & Dougherty, 1998; Rosowsky, Dougherty, Johnson, & Gurian, 1997). We concur with Paris who concluded that "early diagnosis of a personality disorder has a great clinical advantage. If you know this much about a patient, you will not be surprised when he or she presents treatment difficulties or fails to respond to methods that are effective for others. You can also adjust your expectations to chronicity" (p. x).

Compared to Axis I clinical disorders, the assessment of personality disorders is known to be particularly challenging and fraught with difficulty. Clinicians and researchers alike have struggled with their ability to accurately diagnose personality disorders and distinguish one personality disorder from another (Coolidge & Segal, 1998; Westen & Shedler, 2000; Widiger, 2005). Unfortunately, this process tends to be even more complicated among older individuals (Dougherty, 1999; Sadavoy, 1996; Sadavoy & Fogel, 1992). The criteria sets for the personality disorders simply do not fit older adults as well as younger adults (Agronin & Maletta, 2000; Rosowsky & Gurian, 1991). As we described earlier, some clinicians may not think to diagnose personality disorders in their older patients, despite evidence of having "difficult" patients on their caseloads.

Another important issue concerns the reliability of personality disorder diagnoses. In general, reliability of measurement refers to consistency, replicability, or stability (Segal & Coolidge, 2006). In psychiatric diagnosis, reliability refers to the extent of agreement between clinicians concerning the presence or absence of particular disorders, which is often called inter-rater reliability. Reliability is highly important because if different clinicians cannot agree on specific diagnoses, those diagnostic categories are, at best, of limited value and, at worst, virtually meaningless (Segal & Coolidge, 2003).

Notably, inter-rater reliability has historically been poor for the personality disorders (see Mellsop, Varghese, Joshua, & Hicks, 1982; Spitzer, Forman, & Nee, 1979) although diagnostic practices have improved in recent years. Nonetheless, research has documented lower reliability rates for the personality disorders compared to almost all of the major Axis I disorders such as Major Depression, Panic Disorder, and Schizophrenia (Grove, 1987). Poor reliability of diagnosis for the personality disorders is a problem across the life span. An important contributing factor to unreliability has to do with the actual diagnostic criteria for the personality disorders because many of the criteria lack behavioral anchors (thus requiring some level of judgment on the part of the clinician), the criteria sets lack a mechanism for specifying severity in diagnostic categories, and some criteria overlap among different personality disorders (Zweig & Hillman, 1999). Another source of unreliability is that patients rarely present with the classic homogenous signs of one particular personality disorder; rather, it is common for them to have some signs and features of several personality disorders (Oldham et al., 1992; Paris, 2005). This is also true across the life span, which makes accurate diagnosis of personality disorder difficult at any age.

An important point to emphasize about the assessment of personality disorders is that it cannot be conducted "in a vacuum." A full evaluation of episodic clinical disorders and the patient's current mental state should be a part of the comprehensive assessment. Given that the report or description of enduring personality characteristics can be seriously compromised in a patient who is experiencing acute psychopathology or distress, this is not surprising. And the presence of some clinical disorders can exacerbate the patient's typical personality. Indeed, the aim of all personality assessment measures is to rate the respondent's typical, habitual, and lifelong personal functioning rather than acute, temporary, or ephemeral states. Making the distinction between "state" versus "trait" is an important part of the diagnostic process, one which has significant implications for case formulation and intervention.

Thorough and careful assessment has long been a hallmark of geropsychological practice (Qualls & Segal, 2003; Segal, Coolidge, & Hersen, 1998), a development which was necessitated by the types of complex cases commonly seen in clinical practice. Older adults presenting for mental health treatment are much more likely than younger adults to have significant comorbid health issues, real catastrophic losses (e.g., death of a spouse), complicated histories, and numerous other psychosocial stressors. Older adults are also less familiar with psychological testing and assessment, which can make them anxious and fearful about the process and perhaps unmotivated to cooperate. All of these issues complicate the assessment of personality problems among older adults. In this chapter, we discuss five primary elements that should be considered pieces of a thorough assessment of personality disorders among older patients: (1) chart/records review, (2) clinical interview of the patient, (3) interview with informants, (4) self-report objective personality inventories, and (5) semi-structured interviews. For each approach, we identify and discuss issues and challenges in evaluating older adults. Before proceeding, we want to emphasize that an understanding of the patient's normal and maladaptive personality traits is critical to the therapeutic process. Mental health clinicians do not treat disorders or problems; rather, we treat people with disorders and problems and, thus, an understanding of the person we are treating is essential.

Chart/Records Review

In some clinical contexts in which older patients may be evaluated (e.g., nursing homes and rehabilitation hospitals), charts or records may be available. In long-term care settings in which patients have had lengthy stays, these charts may be voluminous. In cases where records are accessible, it behooves the clinician to thoroughly examine them as part of the assessment process. A review of such records may show important behavioral patterns of the patient that are observed by members of the treatment team. Such patterns may give clues to personality disorder features shown by the patient, especially if the same traits are seen by different professionals. For example, passive and helpless behaviors might be noted by nursing staff and activity directors, suggesting a dependent personality style. Aggressive, haughty, and indignant behaviors in another resident may point to the presence of narcissistic, borderline, or paranoid features. Noncompliance with treatment may be due to several factors (e.g., cognitive impairment or depression), but it may also indicate personality pathology (e.g., passive aggressive or antisocial traits), and this possibility should be explored.

Records from mental health professionals who have previously treated the patient can also be important sources of assessment data. Due to the chronicity and severity of their problems, many personality disordered older adults have received treatment at an earlier point in life; in some cases, they have had multiple experiences with psychotherapy. It is crucial to ask patients about their past treatment history, and if the patient has previously consulted a mental health professional, the clinician should ask the patient to sign a "release of information" form so that records can be requested by the present clinician and released by the former clinician. This task is often easier said than done. It has been our experience that many older adults with personality disorders refuse to grant permission to request records. In essence, they are telling the clinician at the outset of treatment that they will not cooperate with treatment despite their desperate need for assistance. We recommend that the reasons for their refusal be gently explored, and this may give some noteworthy clues to the type of personality disorder present.

Should treatment records be obtained, they should be carefully reviewed with particular emphasis on diagnostic formulations (which should be examined closely in the present case) and on identifying aspects of the prior treatment(s) that seemed particularly effective (if any exist) and particularly ineffective (usually some ineffective aspects will be apparent). At a simplistic level, a long history of multiple treatment failures, especially those indicated by the patient dropping out of treatment prematurely and having consistent difficulties forming a bond with the clinician, should point to the possibility of an underlying personality disorder. Understanding what did and did not work in previous treatment may also be valuable in orchestrating current treatment. Specifically, if a particular type of intervention seemed effective (e.g., activity planning or challenging negative self-statements), the clinician may strive to recreate these aspects (so the clinician does not have to "reinvent the wheel"). Conversely, aspects of treatment that previously were ineffective should be avoided (so as to not "reinvent a flat tire"). Hypothesis and hunches about the patient's psychopathology generated from a review of charts or records should be followed up during conversations with the patient, and this topic is discussed next.

The Clinical Interview of the Patient

When meeting an older patient for the first time, the clinician often forms some preliminary impressions of the patient as a person. How does the person come across? Is he or she formal or relaxed? Aggressive or shy? Entertaining or bland? Patently bizarre or seemingly ordinary? Does the patient take some initiative in the session or passively wait for the clinician to provide the structure? These initial impressions and clinical intuitions are followed up on during the clinical interview in which the clinician strives to gather important data about the patient's problems and the patient as a person.

An important part of the clinical interview is to take a thorough history of the patient. One issue is that older adults with a diagnosis of a personality disorder typically have a long and complicated history of problems and conflicts. One positive aspect of this is that clinicians are often presented with a wealth of information from which to raise diagnostic hypotheses. Patterns of interpersonal difficulties sometimes emerge, which can help the clinician pinpoint the specific nature of personality disorder pathology. The negative aspect to a long history of problems is that it takes a great deal of time, energy, and focus to sort through without becoming overwhelmed. Older patients with personality pathology may also have difficulty accurately reporting on their behaviors from many decades ago in part because of the long interval and in part because of inaccurate attention to historical detail and compromised self-perceptions.

In some cases, the personality disorder pathology is quickly noticeable during the interview. For example, some narcissistic patients are demanding, immediately challenging of the therapist's professional qualifications and ability to understand their unique problems, and they tend to brag. One of our patients, a narcissistic older man, started the intake session by reporting that he had terminated prematurely several recent consultations with other psychologists when he realized that he was "smarter" than the clinicians and was wasting his time with inferior people. Another one of our patients began the consultation by offering his professional resume in exchange for one of ours. Most people with Schizotypal Personality Disorder are also easy to identify—their unusual dress and language and their palpable social discomfort are immediately noticeable. Some other examples include: histrionic patients who make an immediate impression with their provocative and flamboyant behavior, dramatic dress, and overly emotional presentation; paranoid patients who are brazenly distrustful and defensive during the interview; and dependent patients who are helpless and sycophantic. It is important for clinicians to monitor their emotional reactions to the patient because this often gives valuable diagnostic clues and helps clinicians to understand the types of feelings and reactions that the patient probably engenders in others in the patient's life. We return to this important concept of countertransference later.

In other cases, however, it is not as easy to identify the dysfunctional personality. During the interview, the patient may focus excessively on symptoms of an Axis I disorder. Consider, for example, a patient who can speak at length about his or her severe depression and physical problems but not reveal much about him- or herself as a person. One way to investigate potential personality disorder pathology is to specifically focus the interview on the patient's functioning in the social arena. By asking the patient to describe his or her relationships with significant others, friends, and family members over time, the social impairment associated with a personality disorder often becomes apparent. It is important to understand if the social dysfunction is of a long-standing and pervasive nature, which is required for a personality disorder diagnosis, or if it is merely a transient, even expectable, reaction to social losses and current stressors. Consider the example of an older woman who presents with severe loneliness, isolation, and apathy. If the evaluation reveals that her loneliness is due to the recent death of her husband and her subsequent relocation to an assisted living facility away from many lifelong friends in her old neighborhood, the possibility of personality pathology is less likely. However, if the evaluation reveals a lifetime history of alienating others, the prospect of a personality disorder becomes more likely. To the extent that the history reveals social problems that have been recurrent or consistent throughout much of adult life, a personality disorder is probable.

Another strategy to detect personality disorder pathology among older adults is to evaluate the extent to which specific "triggers" exacerbate the patient's emotional distress. Triggers refer to specific social circumstances that habitually cause problems for the patient. Examples of common triggers include: situations in which the person has to fend for him- or herself and cannot rely on others, having to deal with authority figures, needing to ask for help, needing to cooperate with medical professionals, having to be assertive with family members or care professionals, reacting to abandonment (whether real or perceived), and social rejection. It can be enlightening to ask patients if their emotional symptoms (e.g., depression or anxiety) tend to develop or worsen after specific social stressors. To the extent that psychological symptoms and problems are related to chronic deficiencies in managing interpersonal relationships, a personality disorder diagnosis is likely.

The assessment of how an individual copes can also reveal clues about his or her personality organization. Most patients who seek psychotherapy do so because their ability to cope has been temporarily outstripped or overwhelmed. In some cases, the person's ability to cope is shored up with treatment and no further intervention is required. However, people with personality disorders tend to have *significant and chronic deficits in their usual coping strategies,* and they show patterns of ineffective coping throughout much of the life course. Thus, when patients present with a long-standing pattern of poor coping, especially with minor or typical challenges associated with life, then a personality disorder should be suspected. Problems with coping in one particular instance (e.g., an older man overwhelmed by the death of his spouse of 60 years) can be expected and easily understood. Problems with coping that seem pervasive and chronic are often signs of a personality disorder.

Another potentially challenging assessment issue relates to the extent to which the personality disorder symptoms have been "hidden" for much of adult life. As noted earlier, it is likely that most cases of personality disorder in later life reflect the continuation of the same disorder from earlier adulthood into old age. In these instances, the clear and consistent pattern of dysfunction can be readily understood. However, other cases of personality disorder may appear to be new in later life, and these can perhaps be conceptualized as representing a deterioration of more adaptive personality traits in vulnerable older adults, likely due to an accumulation of stressors in old age. In these instances, the older patient does not present with a long history of interpersonal problems or with a pattern of regressing after specific social triggers. Essentially, the personality pathology has been hidden or contained by significant others in the person's life who compensated for the person's difficulties and prevented any real dysfunction or distress from occurring. This so-called invisibility of some personality disorders is examined further in Chapter 10.

A final issue regarding the clinical interview with older patients is that all psychosocial data gathered during the interview must be viewed in the context of physical health. The nature, severity, and impact of the patient's current medical illnesses should be thoroughly assessed by the clinician. This information is vitally important because many medical problems, some common to older adults, are known to cause psychiatric conditions (American Psychiatric Association, 2000). In some cases, older adults present with exacerbations or deteriorations in their personality traits due to a dementing illness. According to Zarit and Zarit (1998), common personality changes associated with dementia include increased aggressiveness, anger, impulsivity, disinhibition, dependency, and apathy. Besides dementia, however, a host of neurological and other medical conditions are known to cause personality changes and these are summarized in Table 9.1. If there is no evidence of dysfunctional personality traits through much of adult life, or if the negative personality traits are caused by an underlying organic illness, a personality diagnosis is not warranted. In these cases, a more appropriate *DSM-IV-TR* diagnostic option is Personality Change Due to a General Medical Condition.

It is also imperative to assess the patient's use of medications because many medications commonly taken by older adults are known to cause psychological symptoms. For example, some antihypertensive drugs and steroids can induce depressive symptoms, some stimulants and steroids can cause maniclike symptoms, and some analgesics, bronchodilators, and anticonvulsants can cause anxiety symptoms (American Psychiatric Association, 2000). Because older adults consume a disproportionate amount of prescribed and over the counter medications (due to age-related increases in the frequency of many chronic medical conditions), they are at increased risk for adverse drug effects. Detrimental consequences can occur because of harmful drug interactions and the build-up of medication in the body due to slower metabolization rates associated

Table 9.1 **Neurological Diseases, Insults, and Other General Medical Conditions Known to Cause Personality Changes**

Head trauma

Environmental toxicants (e.g., lead, cadmium, mercury, ethanol)

Brain tumor

Dementia

Cerebrovascular disease/Stroke

Huntington's disease

Epilepsy

Systemic lupus erythematosus

Pernicious anemia

Endocrine conditions (e.g., hypothyroidism, hypoadrenocorticism, hyperadrenocorticism)

Infections (e.g., meningitis, encephalitis)

with normal aging. Older adults are encouraged to bring a complete listing of medications to the clinical interview, both prescribed and over the counter. An alternative strategy is for the patient to bring in the bottles of current medications from which the clinician can compile a listing (the "brown-bag" review). Due to the significant effects that medical illness and medications can have on psychological functioning, a referral for a thorough medical workup is always indicated if the patient has not recently been medically evaluated.

Interview with Informants

As an adjunct to interviews with the patient, collateral interviews with people who know the patient well may be enlightening. Informants may be spouses, children, other family members, health care providers, or professionals from the patient's living setting (e.g., assisted living or nursing home staff). Individuals who have regular contact with the patient can offer a unique perspective because they see the patient in varied social contexts and, in some cases, they may have known the patient for many years and can speak about lifelong patterns of behavior, the longitudinal course of the disorder, and degree of social impairment in the patient. Thus, informants can provide valuable diagnostic data (especially longitudinal observations) that can help resolve the state/trait distinction about specific criterion behaviors. Often, it is advisable to interview the patient and the close informant conjointly. Rather than hearing about troublesome interactions from the patient or the informant, the clinician can *directly observe* the interactional patterns in the consulting room, and this can be enlightening. As an example, in an individual interview, one of our older male patients came across as aggressive and angry. During a conjoint interview with his wife, however, the patient appeared more docile and timorous and was deferential to his wife during the meeting. Because personality disorder symptoms can ebb and flow over time and can be amplified or dampened when certain peo- ple are around (e.g., the patient's spouse or children; Mroczek, Hurt, & Berman, 1999), assessment of the patient in multiple contexts and across different occasions is necessary.

Another advantage of collateral interviews is that patients with personality disorders tend to lack insight into their own maladaptive personality traits (Paris, 2003) and distort facts about their strengths and limitations. Personality-disordered patients are typically unaware of having a mental illness, whereas significant others are often acutely aware of the pa- tient's problems. It is common that the patient's self-report of the problem may not match the report from others, and as such, clinicians must evaluate all sources of data to make their own judgments. A final advantage to interviewing significant others is that the patient's level of social support can be evaluated and, if appropriate, significant others may be involved in the treat- ment process.

In cases where it is unclear from the clinical and/or collat- eral interview if the patient has significant features of a person- ality disorder, or in cases where it is probable that the patient has significant personality dysfunction but it is not clear which specific personality disorder might be present, further assess- ment using standardized measures is advisable.

Self-Report Objective Personality Instruments

Clinical psychology has a long and rich tradition of assessing di- mensions of personality using self-report personality tests (Segal & Coolidge, 2004). Several popular multiscale instru- ments have been designed specifically for the assessment of personality traits and personality disorders among adult re- spondents. At present, there is no specific inventory designed for older adults. The current instruments can be appropriately used with older adults, although some modifications and con- siderations are necessary. One issue is that older persons (espe- cially those in the oldest-old cohort) are less familiar and experienced with taking psychological tests, so we recommend that the purpose of personality testing be carefully explained to older patients to reduce anxiety about and resistance to the process (e.g., "this test will tell us about you as a person, which will be very helpful as we proceed with treatment together"). Routinely encouraging the respondent to be honest and cooperative with the assessment process is also advised. Because the popular personality inventories are all lengthy, fatigue can also be a problem with older patients. It is important for clinicians to monitor the patient and, if necessary, break the testing session up into smaller sessions.

An important benefit of some self-report inventories is that they provide standardized scores for a multitude of *DSM*-based personality disorders. By looking at the relative elevations of the personality disorder scales, diagnostic hypotheses can be developed that should be further evaluated during subsequent clinical interviews or semi-structured interviews with the patient. Other advantages are that the inventories are unaffected by examiner biases and they provide a glimpse of the patient's intrapsychic world from the patient's perspective. A common limitation of the inventories is that they are tied to the diagnostic criteria in the *DSM*, and as we described earlier, some criteria for the personality disorders do not apply well to older people. Limitations in the diagnostic criteria reflect important limitations of the assessment instruments, especially as they are administered to older adults. Another general concern is that people afflicted with personality disorders often have difficulty perceiving themselves and their behaviors objectively, and as a consequence, accurate self-identification of problems may be difficult (Dougherty, 1999).

Although many personality disorder instruments are available to the clinician and researcher, a review of all of them is beyond the scope of this chapter. With these caveats in mind, we now provide a description of three popular multiscale self-report personality disorder instruments: the Millon Clinical Multiaxial Inventory-III, the Personality Diagnostic Questionnaire-4+, and the Coolidge Axis II Inventory. Personality disorders covered by

Table 9.2 **Personality Disorders Covered by the SCID-II, IPDE, SIDP-IV, PDI-IV, DIPD-IV, MCMI-III, PDQ-4+, and CATI**

Personality Disorders	Semi-Structured Interview					Self-Report Inventory		
	SCID-II	IPDE	SIDP-IV	PDI-IV	DIPD-IV	MCMI	PDQ	CATI
Cluster A								
Paranoid	X	X	X	X	X	X	X	X
Schizoid	X	X	X	X	X	X	X	X
Schizotypal	X	X	X	X	X	X	X	X
Cluster B								
Antisocial	X	X	X	X	X	X	X	X
Borderline	X	X	X	X	X	X	X	X
Histrionic	X	X	X	X	X	X	X	X
Narcissistic	X	X	X	X	X	X	X	X
Cluster C								
Avoidant	X	X	X	X	X	X	X	X
Dependent	X	X	X	X	X	X	X	X
Obsessive-Compulsive	X	X	X	X	X	X[a]	X	X
Other Personality Disorders								
Mixed or Personality Disorder NOS	X	X	X	NO	NO	NO	NO	NO
Sadistic *(DSM-III-R)*	NO	NO	NO	NO	NO	X[a]	NO	X
Self-Defeating *(DSM-III-R)*	NO	NO	X	NO	NO	X	NO	X
Depressive *(DSM-IV-TR* Appendix B)	X	NO	X	X	X	X	X	X
Negativistic[b] *(DSM-IV-TR* Appendix B)	X	NO	X	X	X	X	X	X

[a] In the MCMI-III, Obsessive-Compulsive is called Compulsive; Sadistic is called Aggressive/Sadistic.

[b] Negativistic = Negativistic [Passive-Aggressive].

these instruments are reported in Table 9.2. We also describe the Minnesota Multiphasic Personality Inventory-2 (MMPI-2) as well as a popular dimensional measure of normal personality, the Revised NEO Personality Inventory. Although the MMPI-2 and the NEO are not personality disorder instruments per se, they both can be useful in understanding maladaptive personality traits.

Millon Clinical Multiaxial Inventory-III

One of the most widely acclaimed leaders in the personality disorder field is Theodore Millon who in the late 1970s began developing one of the first standardized self-report measures of personality disorders called the Millon Clinical Multiaxial Inventory (MCMI; Millon, 1983). The MCMI was created to evaluate personality disorders according to Millon's own theory of personality psychopathology, but it was generally consistent with *DSM-III* conceptualizations of personality disorders. The MCMI was subsequently revised and renamed the MCMI-II (Millon, 1987) to match changes in Millon's theory and changes in the *DSM-III-R.* The most current version is the MCMI-III (Millon, Davis, & Millon, 1997), which is largely aligned with *DSM-IV,* although there are some subtle differences in conceptualizations of some personality disorders.

The MCMI-III is a 175-item, true-false, self-report inventory that is widely used in research and clinical activities for the assessment of personality disorders and clinical syndromes. The Axis II (personality disorder) scales are linked to Millon's comprehensive theory of personality, which is anchored broadly and firmly to evolutionary theory. In contrast, the Axis I (clinical disorder) scales are not explicitly derived from Millon's theory and essentially represent *DSM* constructs.

The MCMI-III includes 11 Clinical Personality Patterns scales: Schizoid, Avoidant, Depressive, Dependent, Histrionic, Narcissistic, Antisocial, Aggressive/Sadistic, Compulsive, Negativistic (Passive-Aggressive), and Self-Defeating Personality Disorder. Three Severe Personality Pathology scales are also included and these are: Schizotypal, Borderline, and Paranoid Personality Disorder. Each represent more advanced stages of personality pathology with episodes of psychosis. Additionally, 7 Clinical Syndromes scales (Axis I related) are provided, covering moderate clinical presentations (e.g., Anxiety, Somatoform, Dysthymia, Alcohol Dependence) whereas 3 Severe Syndromes scales denote more serious clinical disorders (Thought Disorder, Major Depression, and Delusional Disorder). The MCMI-III has a Validity Index (3 items of an improbable nature) and 3 Modifying Indices (Disclosure, Desirability, and Debasement) designed to detect deviant test-tasking attitudes defensiveness or exaggeration of problems (Millon et al., 1997).

An important component of the MCMI-III is that it is designed for adults being seen in mental health settings and, thus, should not be used in nonclinical populations or distorted results will emerge. Specifically, the test will likely severely over-pathologize if given in nonclinical settings. Administration is either by paper and pencil or computer administered. The MCMI-III must be computer scored during which raw scores for each scale are converted into Base Rate scores, which differ by gender (Millon et al., 1997). The MCMI's have been the focus of over 500 research publications and the MCMI-III ranks among the most widely used testing instruments in clinical practice. The MCMI-III has a wealth of data supporting its psychometric properties (see recent review by Millon & Meagher, 2004). At present, Millon has no plans to develop an MCMI-IV.

Personality Diagnostic Questionnaire-Fourth Edition Plus

The Personality Diagnostic Questionnaire has been through several revisions since its inception and the latest edition is called the Personality Diagnostic Questionnaire—Fourth Edition Plus (PDQ-4+; Hyler, 1994), which is consistent with the *DSM-IV*. The PDQ-4+ assesses the 10 standard personality disorders in the *DSM-IV* and the "plus" indicates that the measure also assesses Passive-Aggressive Personality Disorder and Depressive Personality Disorder in Appendix B of the *DSM-IV*. The PDQ-4+ contains 99 self-report, true-false items and takes about 30 minutes to complete. It has two validity scales: the Too Good scale measures underreporting of pathological personality traits, whereas the Suspect Questionnaire scale detects lying and random responding.

Due to the excess number of false positives associated with earlier versions of the measure, an optional Clinical Significance scale was designed for the PDQ-4+ to help the clinician assess whether the abnormal traits endorsed by the respondent (a) meet the diagnostic threshold for causing distress or impairment in the person's life, (b) are both pervasive and persistent, and (c) are not due to a current Axis I condition (Bagby & Farvolden, 2004).

The PDQ-4+ has a limited theoretical foundation. Rather, it was designed to be directly linked to the *DSM-IV* and, consequently, each item on the measure corresponds to a single *DSM-IV* diagnostic criterion for a personality disorder. A "true" response to each item indicates that it is to be scored as pathological (and there are no reverse-scored items; Hyler, 1994). Scores are summed to indicate the number of criteria endorsed for each personality disorder, which can be used for tentative diagnosis. In addition, a total score consisting of the sum of all pathological items endorsed can be generated. This total score is an index of overall personality dysfunction (Hyler, 1994). Due to its simplicity, the PDQ-4+ can be hand scored although computer administration and scoring are available. The measure can be used in both normal and clinical populations and provides both dimensional and categorical scores for the disorders. Regarding psychometric properties of the PDQ-4+, the primary concerns seems to be a high false-positive rate and poor validity of the validity scales (Bagby & Farvolden, 2004). However, the measure does seem to have a low false-negative rate. As such, the measure is probably best viewed as a screening instrument in which tentative diagnoses must be followed up by more comprehensive patient assessment. Due to the low false-negative rate, PDQ-4+ might be helpful in ruling out personality disorders. Notably, there is no manual for the PDQ-4+ (which is problematic) and there are no imminent plans to revise the measure.

Coolidge Axis II Inventory

The Coolidge Axis II Inventory (CATI; Coolidge, 2000; Coolidge & Merwin, 1992) is a 225-item, self-report inventory designed and revised to assess personality disorders and many clinical disorders according to the specific diagnostic criteria of *DSM-IV-TR*. Items are answered on a 4-point Likert scale ranging from strongly false to strongly true. The CATI measures all 10 personality disorders in the main text of the *DSM-IV-TR* but it also covers the Passive-Aggressive and Depressive Personality Disorders in the appendix of the *DSM-IV-TR* and the Sadistic and Self-Defeating Personality Disorders from the appendix of *DSM-III-R*.

Items on each personality disorder scale were designed to cover a specific diagnostic criterion from the *DSM*, thus the CATI is essentially atheoretical by design. Validity scales include a 3-item scale to detect random responding and a 97-item scale to detect denial and defensiveness, called the Tendency to Deny Blatant Psychopathology.

Like the MCMI-III, the CATI also provides assessment for many Axis I scales. These include: Depression, Anxiety, Schizophrenia, and Posttraumatic Stress Disorder. The *DSM-IV-TR* Personality Change Due to a General Medical Condition is also evaluated, with scales measuring each of the five subtypes: Apathy, Disinhibition, Emotional Lability, Aggression, and Paranoia. A unique feature of the CATI is that it has an 18-item neuropsychological dysfunction scale for assessing neuropsychological symptoms of brain disease, trauma, and dysfunction, with three subscales assessing language and speech dysfunction, memory and concentration difficulties, and neurosomatic complaints related to brain dysfunction. The CATI also includes a 16-item executive functions of the frontal lobe scale with three subscales measuring poor planning, decision-making difficulty, and task incompletion. Two other features of the CATI make it distinctive. First, a significant-other version of test is available so that informants can rate the clinical and personality disorder features of a person being evaluated (Coolidge, Burns, & Mooney, 1995). As noted earlier, informants may be able to identify abnormal personality traits of which the patient is unaware. Second, a parent-rated version of the CATI is available to assess personality disorders and neuropsychological problems in children and adolescents (ages 5 to 17 years; Coolidge et al., 2002).

Administration of the CATI is either by paper and pencil or computer administered. Scoring must be done by computer (the CATI and its software are available to researchers for free). Raw scores on all CATI scales are translated into T-scores (with a mean of 50 and a standard deviation of 10) based on a normative sample of 1700 adults. According to the CATI manual, T-scores above 70 are indicative of the likely presence of the particular disorder. Provision of standardized scores is important because elevations on the individual personality disorder scales can be compared against each other. Also, the large normative data base from which standard scores are created helps reduce the problem of false positives. Indeed, a respondent must score at least two standard deviations above the mean to be considered to meet the diagnostic threshold. The CATI can be used in both normal and clinical populations because it views personality disorders as dimensional in nature. The CATI has been used in over 100 research publications and the psychometric properties appear strong.

Minnesota Multiphasic Personality Inventory-2

The Minnesota Multiphasic Personality Inventory-2 (MMPI-2; Butcher, Dahlstrom, Graham, Tellegen, & Kaemmer, 1989) is unarguably the most widely used self-report measure of adult psychopathology and personality. In the original MMPI, Hathaway and McKinley (1943) revolutionized the field of personality assessment by creating the inventory through the novel empirical method at that time called *criterion-keying*. In criterion-keying, an item was assigned to a scale if it effectively discriminated a criterion group (e.g., people with clinical depression) from the normative sample (e.g., healthy relatives of patients at the University of Minnesota hospitals). To create the MMPI-2, the original MMPI was significantly revised and restandardized on 2,600 individuals who were generally representative of the U.S. Census. Although the sample included persons up to 85 years of age, older adults were somewhat underrepresented (about 5% of the sample; Graham, 2006).

The MMPI-2 contains 10 clinical scales, 15 content scales, many supplemental scales, and several validity scales. The standard clinical scales include Hs (Hypochondriasis), D (Depression), Hy (Hysteria), Pd (Psychopathic Deviate), Mf (Masculinity-Femininity), Pa (Paranoia), Pt (Psychasthenia), Sc (Schizophrenia), Ma (Hypomania), and Si (Social Introversion) scales. The primary validity scales include L (Lie, intended to detect those claiming excessive virtues), K (Defensiveness, designed as an indicator of the tendency to deny psychopathology), and F (Infrequency, intended to detect exaggerated symptom endorsement). Other validity scales for the MMPI-2 include Back F (Fb), Faking Psychopathology F(p), Variable Response Inconsistency (VRIN), True Response Inconsistency (TRIN), and Superlative Self-Assessment (S) scales. On the clinical scales, older adults tend to obtain higher scores on scales Hs (Hypochondriasis), D (Depression), Hy (Hysteria), and Si (Social Introversion) and lower scores on scales Pd (Psychopathic Deviate), and Ma (Hypomania). According to Graham (2006), these elevations probably do not indicate greater psychopathology among older persons but rather reflect biological maturation and age-graded changes in health problems and energy levels.

Administration is either by paper and pencil or by computer. The MMPI-2 can be hand scored but, due to the complexity and time required, computer scoring is most common. Audiocassette versions are available, which can accommodate those with vision problems or physical disabilities. Raw scores on each scale are converted into T-scores, with 65 and above indicating the clinical range. The MMPI-2 has been translated into 22 languages and is widely used in cross-cultural research. MMPI-related publications since the 1940s are approaching 14,000 and, as such, an enormous database provides psychometric support for the measure (see recent review by Butcher, Atlis, & Hahn, 2004).

Because the MMPI-2 is a measure of symptom profiles, Axis I disorders, and personality traits, it is not intended as a formal measure of *DSM*-based personality disorders. As can be seen from the standard scales, only 1 of the 10 scales (Psychopathic Deviate) is an overt measure of personality pathology (Antisocial Personality Disorder). Although researchers have derived personality disorder scales (Morey, Waugh, & Blashfield, 1985) from the original MMPI items, use of these derived scales in clinical practice is uncommon; they have not been updated since their initial creation nor validated with older adults specifically. Thus, although the MMPI-2 can be helpful in understanding the psychopathology of the younger or older patient, its application for personality disorder assessment is more limited.

NEO Personality Inventory-Revised

A famous historical and current debate in psychology concerns the number of dimensions that most accurately describe the broadest themes in individual differences in personality. For example, famous psychologists Raymond B. Cattell (1946) derived 16 primary dimensions from factor analytical techniques, whereas Hans Eysenck (1960) proposed that trait descriptors can be subsumed under two ubiquitous factors he called Neuroticism and Extraversion. A competing and popular model of personality called the Big-Five suggests that there are five superordinate factors: Neuroticism, Extraversion, Openness to Experience, Agreeableness, and Conscientiousness. These domains are operationalized and measured by the NEO Personality Inventory-Revised (NEO PI-R; Costa & McCrae, 1992).

The NEO PI-R is comprised of 243 self-report items rated on a 5-point scale. It measures the five global factors as well as six facets for each domain. Specifically, the facets for Neuroticism are anxiety, hostility, depression, self-consciousness, impulsiveness, and vulnerability. Facets for Extraversion are warmth, gregariousness, assertiveness, activity, excitement-seeking, and positive emotions. Facets for Openness to Experience are fantasy, aesthetics, feelings, actions, ideas, and values. Facets for Agreeableness are trust, modesty, compliance, altruism, straightforwardness, and tender-mindedness. Facets for Conscientiousness are competence, self-discipline, achievement-striving, dutifulness, order, and deliberation. As can be seen, the five domains provide a general description of personality, whereas facet scales allow more detailed analysis.

Items on the NEO PI-R assess diverse aspects of traits including patterns of thoughts, feelings, and actions. The factors and facets are all scored dimensionally so that an individual may score anywhere on the continuum from low to high on each scale. The NEO PI-R includes 3 validity items and can generally be completed in about 40 minutes. In addition to the self-report format, an observer report version is available in which the target person is rated by others. The NEO PI-R can be hand scored or computer scored. The Big-Five model and its measurement with the NEO PI-R have been evaluated in an impressive array of cross-sectional, longitudinal, and cross-cultural studies using diverse clinical and nonclinical populations (for a full review, see Costa & McCrae, 2006). An advantage of using the NEO PI-R is that it offers an alternative approach to the categorical distinction of normality versus abnormality. A disadvantage is that the NEO PI-R is not a direct measure of personality disorders, although Widiger, Costa, and McCrae (2002) suggest that an understanding of personality pathology can be guided by general personality traits.

Application of Personality Inventories with Older Adults

The MCMI-III, PDQ-4+, CATI, MMPI-2, and NEO PI-R have all been widely used in clinical research and practice with diverse types of individuals, including older adults. One issue is that older persons with visual impairments may have difficulty reading items in the administration booklets, and big print versions of the tests or audiocassette versions should be used when available. A common limitation of the personality disorder inventories (i.e., MCMI-III, PDQ-4+, or CATI) as they apply to older adults is that they are all essentially tied to *DSM* criteria, which may not necessarily capture the unique presentation of some personality disorders in later life. Another significant source of concern with use of these instruments among older adults is that test items may be perceived and interpreted differently by older respondents compared to younger ones due to generational changes in language use, different educational experiences, or age-graded shifts in the relevance of *DSM* criteria (Mroczek et al., 1999).

The clinician should also be aware of some general problems associated with using self-report personality disorder inventories as isolated or stand-alone instruments in clinical practice, including the higher number of false-positive diagnoses and the concern that results, may be more state dependent compared to structured interviews. Advantages of self-report inventories include that they are easy to administer and take less time and clinical expertise than structured interviews. Whereas a significant amount of research has examined the application of the MMPI-2 and NEO PI-R across the adult life span, the limited number of studies applying the MCMI-III, PDQ-4+, and CATI to older populations represents a serious gap in the research literature. Much research is required to establish relevant cutoff scores for these measures with older adult respondents, perhaps by comparing self-report data to that generated by semi-structured interviews. Perhaps the best conclusion to be drawn is that self-report inventories can be very useful for the *screening* of personality disorders among older adults. However, diagnostic hypotheses must be confirmed by other assessment data, typically an interview assessment.

Semi-Structured Clinical Interviews

Over the past 3 decades, numerous structured and semi-structured diagnostic interviews have been created to assist with the differential diagnosis of all standard Axis II personality disorders and all major Axis I clinical syndromes. During such an interview, diagnostic criteria are comprehensively assessed through a consistently applied set of questions and responses that are coded in a replicable fashion. Structured and semi-structured interviews have become widely used in clinical, research, and training applications often serving as the gold standard for diagnosis in these settings. These interviews are an important development in the mental health field because, when used appropriately, they provide a standardized, scientific, systematic, comprehensive, and quantitative approach to the evaluation of mental disorders (Segal, Coolidge, O'Riley, & Heinz, 2006). This has served to enhance diagnostic reliability and validity, especially for the personality disorders (Segal et al., 2006).

The major interviews that focus on a wide range of personality disorders include the Structured Interview for *DSM-IV* Personality, the International Personality Disorder Examination, the Structured Clinical Interview for *DSM-IV* Axis II Personality Disorders, the Personality Disorder Inventory-IV, and the Diagnostic Interview for *DSM-IV* Personality Disorders. These measures are all closely aligned with the *DSM-IV* system and have a semi-structured format, which means that although the initial questions for each personality disorder criteria are specified and asked verbatim to the respondent, the clinician has substantial latitude to follow up on responses. For example, the interviewer may modify existing questions and even devise new questions to more accurately rate the diagnostic criteria. Due to the semi-structured format of these interviews (in contrast to a fully structured format), clinical experience and knowledge of psychopathology are required for competent administration; lay professionals cannot administer them (for further information about diverse structured interview approaches, the interested reader is referred to a comprehensive text by Rogers, 2001).

Next, we describe each Axis II instrument and conclude with some thoughts about their application with older adults. Personality disorders covered by the current version of each instrument are presented in Table 9.2.

Structured Interview for *DSM-IV* Personality

The Structured Interview for *DSM-IV* Personality (SIDP-IV; Pfohl, Blum, & Zimmerman, 1997) covers 14 *DSM-IV* Axis II diagnoses, including the 10 standard personality disorders, Mixed Personality Disorder, as well as Self-Defeating, Depressive, and Negativistic Personality Disorders. Pfohl et al. (1997) recommend that prior to administering the SIDP-IV, a full evaluation of episodic clinical disorders is required. Interestingly, the SIDP-IV does not cover personality problems on a disorder-by-disorder basis. Rather, *DSM-IV* personality disorder criteria are reflected in items that are grouped according to 10 "topical sections" that reflect a different dimension of personality functioning, and these include: interests and activities, work style, close relationships, social relationships, emotions, observational criteria, self-perception, perception of others, stress and anger, and social conformity (Pfohl et al., 1997). It should be noted that these categories are not scored or rated. Rather, they reflect broad areas of personal functioning under which personality disorder items can logically be subsumed.

For the most part, each SIDP-IV question corresponds to a unique *DSM-IV* Axis II criterion. An attractive feature of the instrument is that the specific *DSM-IV* criterion associated with each question is provided for interviewers to easily see and reference. All questions are typically administered to the patient and there are no skip-out options. Most questions are conversational in tone and open ended to encourage respondents to talk about their *usual* behaviors and long-term functioning. Respondents are specifically instructed to focus on their typical or habitual behavior when answering each question, and they are prompted to "remember what you are like when you are your usual self." Based on the responses, each criterion is rated on a scale with four anchor points. A rating of "0" indicates that the criterion was not present, "1" corresponds to a subthreshold level where there is some evidence of the trait but it is not sufficiently prominent, "2" refers to the criterion being present for most of the past 5 years, and "3" signifies a strongly present and debilitating level. The SIDP-IV requires that a trait be prominent for most of the last 5 years to be considered a part of the respondent's personality. This 5-year rule helps ensure that the particular personality characteristic is stable and of a long duration as required by the General Diagnostic Criteria for a Personality Disorder described in *DSM-IV.*

A strong point of the organizational format by personality dimensions (rather than by disorders) is that data for *specific* diagnoses are minimized until final ratings have been collated on the summary sheet. This feature can potentially reduce interviewer biases, such as the halo effect or changing thresholds, if it is obvious that a patient needs to meet one additional criteria to make the diagnosis. Chart records and collateral information from those who know the patient well (when available) can be considered in the ratings of items, and final ratings are made after all sources of information are considered. Ratings are then transcribed onto a summary sheet that lists each criterion organized by personality disorder, and formal diagnoses are assigned. As required by the *DSM,* diagnoses are made only if the minimum number of criteria (or threshold) has been met for that particular disorder.

Minimum qualifications for competent administration consist of an interviewer with an undergraduate degree in the social sciences and 6 months experience with diagnostic interviewing. Moreover, 1 additional month of specialized training and practice with the SIDP is required to become a competent interviewer (Pfohl et al., 1997). Administrators are required to possess an understanding of manifest psychopathology and the typical presentation and course of Axis I and II disorders. Training tapes and workshop information are available from the instrument authors. Overall, 60 to 90 minutes are needed for the patient interview, 20 minutes for interview of significant informants, and approximately 20 minutes to fill out the summary score sheet.

International Personality Disorder Examination

The International Personality Disorder Examination (IPDE; Loranger, 1999) is an extensive-semi-structured diagnostic interview to evaluate personality disorders according to both the *DSM-IV* and International Classification of Diseases, 10th edition (*ICD-10*) classification systems. Impetus for the creation of the IPDE came from the World Health Organization and the U.S. Alcohol, Drug Abuse, and Mental Health Administration in their joint effort aimed at producing a standardized assessment instrument to measure personality disorders on a worldwide basis. As such, the IPDE is the only personality disorder interview based on worldwide field trials. The IPDE manual contains the interview questions to assess either the *DSM-IV* or the *ICD-10* personality disorders. The two IPDE modules (*DSM-IV* and *ICD-10*) contain both a self-administered screening questionnaire and a semi-structured interview booklet with scoring materials.

The IPDE Interview Modules contain questions, each reflecting a personality disorder criteria, that are grouped into six thematic headings: work, self, interpersonal relationships, affects, reality testing, and impulse control (Loranger, 1999). Like the SIDP-IV, disorders are not covered on a one-by-one basis. As such, the intent of the evaluation is less transparent. Another similarity is that respondents are encouraged to report their typical or usual functioning rather than their personality functioning during times of acute psychiatric illness. Prior to the structured interview, a screening of Axis I conditions and the respondent's personal history is recommended.

The IPDE sections typically begin with open-ended prompts to encourage respondents to elaborate about themselves in a less structured fashion. In each module, specific questions are asked to evaluate each personality disorder criterion. For each question, the corresponding personality disorder and the specific diagnostic criterion are listed with precise scoring guidelines.

The IPDE requires that a trait be prominent during the past 5 years to be considered a part of the respondent's personality. When a respondent acknowledges a particular trait, interviewers follow up by asking for examples and anecdotes to clarify the trait or behavior, gauge the impact of the trait on the person's functioning, and substantiate the rating. Items may also be rated based on observation of the respondent's behavior during the session. To supplement self-report, interview of informants is also encouraged.

Each criterion is rated on a scale with the following definitions: "0" indicates that the behavior or trait is absent or within normal limits, "1" refers to accentuated degree of the trait, "2" signifies criterion level or pathological, and "?" indicates the respondent refuses or is unable to answer. Comprehensive item-by-item scoring guidelines are provided in the manual (Loranger,

1999). At the end of the interview, final impressions are recorded on a summary score sheet. Ratings are then collated by hand or computer. The ultimate output is extensive including: presence or absence of each criterion, number of criteria met for each disorder, a dimensional score (i.e., sum of individual scores for each criteria for each disorder), and a categorical diagnosis (i.e., definite, probable, or negative; Loranger, 1999).

The IPDE is intended to be administered by experienced clinicians, such as psychologists and psychiatrists, who have also received specific training in the use of the IPDE. Such training typically involves a workshop with demonstration videotapes, discussions, and practice. Average administration time is 90 minutes. Ample evidence of reliability and validity of the IPDE has been documented (Loranger et al., 1994; Loranger, 1999). Due to the instrument's ties to the *DSM-IV* and *ICD-10* classification systems and adoption by the WHO, the IPDE is widely used for international and cross-cultural investigations of personality pathology.

Structured Clinical Interview for *DSM-IV* Axis II Personality Disorders

The Structured Clinical Interview for *DSM-IV* Axis II Personality Disorders (SCID-II; First, Gibbon, Spitzer, Williams, & Benjamin, 1997) was developed to complement the widely used Axis I version of the SCID (First, Spitzer, Gibbon, & Williams, 1997). The SCID-II has semi-structured format (like the Axis I version) but it covers the 10 standard *DSM-IV* Axis II personality disorders, as well as Personality Disorder Not Otherwise Specified, and Depressive Personality Disorder and Passive-Aggressive Personality Disorder from *DSM-IV* Appendix B (see Table 9.2). The Axis I SCID is commonly administered prior to personality disorder assessment so that the patient's mental state can be considered.

In contrast to the SIDP-IV and IPDE, the SCID-II has a modular approach in which the personality disorders are assessed one at a time. This design is a strength of the SCID-II because administration can be customized easily to meet the unique needs of the user. For example, the interview can be shortened or lengthened to include only those disorders of interest and the order of modules can be altered. The format and sequence of the SCID-II was designed to approximate the flow of experienced diagnostic interviewers.

A useful feature of the SCID-II is that it includes a self-report Personality Questionnaire, which is a 119-item self-report, forced choice yes/no screening component that can be administered prior to the interview portion and takes about 20 minutes. The purpose of the Personality Questionnaire is to reduce overall administration time because only those items that are scored in the pathological direction are further evaluated during the structured interview portion. During the structured interview component, the pathologically endorsed screening responses are further pursued to ascertain whether the symptoms are actually experienced at clinically significant levels. The SCID-II has many open-ended prompts that encourage respondents to elaborate freely about their symptoms. At times, open-ended prompts are followed by closed-ended questions to fully clarify a particular personality disorder symptom. Consistent with its strong link to *DSM-IV,* the formal diagnostic criteria are printed on the interview page permitting interviewers to see the criteria to which SCID-II questions pertain.

During the interview, responses are coded as follows: "?" = inadequate information, "1" = absent or false, "2" = subthreshold, and "3" = threshold or true. Each personality disorder is assessed completely and diagnoses are made before proceeding to the next disorder. Clinicians who administer the SCID-II are expected to use their clinical judgment to clarify responses, gently challenge inconsistencies, and ask for additional information as required to rate accurately each criterion. Collection of diagnostic information from ancillary sources is permitted. Complete administration of the SCID-II typically takes less than 1 hour.

The SCID-II is optimally administered by trained clinicians. Training in administration includes carefully reading the administration booklet and score sheet, viewing videotape training materials that are available from the SCID-II authors, and conducting role-played practice administrations with extensive feedback discussions. The psychometric properties of the SCID-II are strong, and the interested reader is referred to First and Gibbon (2004) for a comprehensive review. For more information on the SCID-I and SCID-II, the interested reader may visit the SCID web site: www.scid4.org.

Personality Disorder Interview-IV

The Personality Disorder Interview-IV (PDI-IV; Widiger, Mangine, Corbitt, Ellis, & Thomas, 1995) is a semi-structured interview for the assessment of the 10 standard personality disorders in the *DSM-IV* as well as the two proposed personality disorders (Passive-Aggressive and Depressive) presented in the *DSM-IV* appendix. The PDI-IV is appropriate for respondents ages 18 years and older and administration time is about 90 to 120 minutes.

A unique feature of the PDI-IV is that it is available in two separate versions, each with its own interview booklet. The PDI-IV Personality Disorders Interview Booklet arranges the diagnostic criteria and corresponding questions by personality disorder. The Thematic Content Areas Interview Booklet organizes the criteria and questions by thematic content. The nine topical areas are: attitudes toward self, attitudes toward others, security of comfort with others, friendships and relationships, conflicts and disagreements, work and leisure, social norms, mood, and appearance and perception. Notably, the questions for each diagnostic criterion are the same in each interview form, but the organization is different. The modular approach easily lends itself to focused and rapid assessment of particular personality disorders of interest to the researcher or clinician. A screening questionnaire is not provided for the PDI-IV.

In the PDI-IV administration book, questions for the assessment of each of the 94 individual personality disorder diagnostic criteria are presented. Direct instructions to interviewers, as well as prompts and suggestions for follow-up questions, are included in each booklet. Space is provided for recording responses to each question. Each criterion is cross-referenced to the *DSM-IV*. During administration, each criterion is rated on the following 3-point scale: "0" indicates not present, "1" indicates present at a clinically significant level, and "2" indicates present to a more severe or substantial degree. A particular strength of the PDI-IV is its comprehensive manual (Widiger et al., 1995) which extensively discusses the history and rationale for each diagnostic question as well as problems that often arise in the assessment of each criterion.

After the interview is completed, the clinician summarizes the responses to individual PDI-IV criteria and plots the overall dimensional profile in a booklet. According to the manual, this profile may help clinicians to rank multiple diagnoses by order of importance and to identify characteristics in the respondent that are relevant to psychopathology and treatment. Notably, the output provided is both a dimensional rating for each personality disorder as well as a categorical rating. Reliability and validity data, as summarized in the manual (Widiger et al., 1995), are solid.

Diagnostic Interview for *DSM-IV* Personality Disorders

The Diagnostic Interview for *DSM-IV* Personality Disorders (DIPD-IV; Zanarini, Frankenburg, Sickel, & Yong, 1996) is a semi-structured interview designed to assess the presence or absence of the 10 standard *DSM-IV* personality disorders as well as Passive-Aggressive Personality Disorder and Depressive Personality Disorder in the *DSM-IV* appendix. Before personality assessment, a full screening for Axis I disorders is recommended. Additionally, an assessment of the respondent's general functioning (e.g., in the areas of work, school, and social life) is advised before administration of the DIPD-IV (Zanarini et al., 1996).

The interview is conducted on a disorder-by-disorder basis. The interview contains 108 sets of questions each designed to assess a specific *DSM-IV* personality disorder diagnostic criterion. The *DSM-IV* criterion is provided in bold below each set of questions for easy cross-reference. The initial question for each criterion typically has a yes-no format which is followed up by open-ended questions to more fully explore the experiences of the patients. Patients are informed that the interview pertains to the past 2 years of their life and that the interviewer wants to learn about the thoughts, feelings, and behaviors that have been typical for them during the 2-year period. Whereas patients are the sole source of information for rating most of the diagnostic criteria, behavior exhibited during the interview is valued and may override patient self-report if there are contradictions. Probing on the part of the administrator is encouraged if responses appear incomplete or untrue.

Each diagnostic criterion is rated on the following scale: "0" indicates absent or clinically insignificant, "1" indicates present but of uncertain clinical significance, "2" indicates present and clinically significant, and "NA" indicated not applicable. After all 108 criteria are rated, final categorical diagnosis for each personality disorder is made based on the number of criteria met. The final output is recorded as "2" indicting "yes" or met full criteria, "1" indicating "subthreshold" (one less than required number of criteria), or "0" indicating "no."

Information about administration and scoring of the DIPD-IV is relatively sparse, at least compared to the other Axis II interviews. The training requirements include at minimum a bachelor's degree, at least 1 year of clinical experience with personality-disordered patients, and several training interviews in which the person observes skilled administrators and then administers the interview. Administration time is typically about 90 minutes. Most notably, the DIPD-IV has been chosen as the primary diagnostic measure for personality disorders in the Collaborative Longitudinal Personality Disorders Study which is a large, multisite, prospective naturalistic longitudinal study of personality disorders and comorbid mental health problems.

Application of Semi-Structured Interviews with Older Adults

Each of the semi-structured interviews has been subjected to extensive empirical evaluation, but their use has been most common among adult respondents. The literature regarding specific application of these instruments with older adults is relatively sparse. A few clinical reports have provided evidence that they can be successfully applied to older adults (e.g., Abrams, Alexopoulos, & Young, 1987; Abrams, Rosendahl, Card, & Alexopoulos, 1994; Schneider, Zemansky, Bender, & Sloane, 1992; Thompson et al., 1988). However, larger reliability and validity studies are warranted, especially with more diverse older adult populations (e.g., medical patients, minorities, or psychiatric inpatients).

Several additional concerns about the application of these semi-structured interviews with older adults should be noted. A common feature among the interviews is that respondents are encouraged to describe their "typical or usual" functioning rather than their possibly altered personality functioning during times of acute psychiatric illness. During the course of the interview, respondents are sometimes asked to describe their behaviors at different points in time, possibly spanning several decades. Such distinctions may be difficult for some older patients to make given their longer histories and the normal cognitive changes associated with aging. In cases where cognitive impairment or a dementing illness is apparent, the task is further complicated.

Another problem with the utilization of structured interviews with older patients is the length of time required for completion. With young patients, administration time for the various interviews typically ranges from 1 to 3 hours. However, administration may take considerably longer with older patients. One reason for this is that older individuals simply have more extensive and complicated histories to review. Some older people also require breaks that may not be needed by younger people: Many older adults fatigue more quickly, and this must be monitored because their responses may become less accurate or rich if they become inattentive or unmotivated. Older adults typically perform their best when given frequent opportunities to stretch, take a brief walk, rest, or use the bathroom. Sometimes, it may be helpful to divide the interview session into several shorter sessions. The length of time required for full administration of structured interviews with older adults impacts the viability of using these instruments in routine clinical practice.

Sensory impairments can also affect the interview evaluation. Older persons with hearing difficulties may misunderstand parts of the query or fail to answer the question entirely. It is often helpful to sit closer to the older patient, face him or her directly, speak slowly and clearly, and reduce background noise in the evaluation room. Lastly, some older adults may respond negatively to the structure imposed by the interviews. In these cases, it is advisable to spend more time developing rapport; reflect more feelings during the interview; allow for more elaboration, venting, and storytelling from the patient about troublesome symptoms or experiences; and explain the purpose and format of the structured interview. Judicious amounts of flexibility and sensitivity are needed during the structured interview with older adults, and this is especially important when personality disorder pathology is also present.

Despite the potential concerns we have noted, semi-structured interviews can and should have an important place in the assessment process. For example, a semi-structured interview may be used with all patients at the beginning of treatment, or it may be administered after a more unstructured clinical interview or self-report objective personality inventory is completed. As noted previously, this requires a significant investment in time and expertise. Using sections of an interview to clarify specific diagnostic hypotheses generated from a clinical interview or a self-report inventory (e.g., only the Borderline Personality Disorder module of the SCID-II may be administered to enable a more comprehensive evaluation of the borderline pathology) is a less time-consuming option. With their premium on diagnostic reliability and comprehensive assessment of criteria, structured interviews can be valuable resources for the geropsychological clinician and researcher.

Conclusions

In this chapter, we provided an overarching process for the clinical assessment of personality disorder pathology among older adults. We described several strategies and examined potential complications with older patients. We offered these guideposts with an important theme in mind: Accurate patient assessment is crucial for case formulation and subsequent treatment planning. We concur with the astute observation reported by Mroczek et al. (1999) that "there is a uniqueness about personality disorders in late life that warrants special measurement" (p. 136). Diverse combinations of the approaches and instruments we suggested, in conjunction with a thorough assessment of episodic mental disorders and attention to the unique context of aging and coexisting medical conditions, will likely provide the rich clinical data that can propel the treatment process with older patients.

Treatment: General Issues and Models

10

Chapter

When considering treatment for the individual with a personality disorder in older age, what is it that we treat? This is an especially relevant question, because the "personality" is the essence of the individual. As clinicians, we treat individuals who are in distress and pain, hoping to improve their quality of life. When an older person comes to us for treatment, what they have been doing, thinking, and feeling for many years no longer works for them. We interpret their distress to mean that what they are being asked to handle is outstripping their ability to cope; changes occurred in themselves that now prevent them from responding as they have formerly. At times, older adults are required to cope with problems or situations with which they have not had experience or for which they lack adequate resources. For example, after losing a spouse, they might be on their own for the first time in their lives. They might enter a new community or need to make new friends and establish a social network for the first time in many years. As their lifelong ways of coping no longer work for them, they become even more distressed, function even less well, and their behavior worsens. This vicious cycle typically makes intervention quite challenging.

Core Features of Personality Disorder Affecting Treatment

The core features of individuals with personality disorders are (a) their reliance on primitive defenses, (b) the rigidity of their character structure and limited affective repertoire, and (c) the effect they have on people with whom they are in close relationship. These features are robust and appear to last a lifetime. Each is discussed next.

Reliance on Primitive Defenses

Decreased autonomy and increased mutual interdependence are both normal and expectable as people grow old. In older age, people come to need and rely more on others, need more actual care, and need to cooperate more with this care. Interdependence and cooperation requires the ability to relate reasonably well to others and to be able to tolerate a degree of intimacy. Being hardy, flexible, and resilient relies on more mature defenses, such as altruism and humor, and the ability to change. Individuals with personality disorders present with profound limitations in these areas. They rely on immature defenses such as repression, denial, and projection. They are vulnerable rather than hardy, rigid rather than flexible—and they have difficulty considering themselves as agents of change; to them, "things" (over which they do not perceive they have much control) just happen. This is why the challenges of aging are so problematic for them, and why they are typically poor candidates for psychological treatments, despite their desperate need.

Understanding these constraints, and recognizing the real and many challenges of aging, it becomes clear that the older individual with a personality disorder is at significant risk of experiencing increased distress and failures in functioning. They may become aware of the need to make a change, but do not know how to go about doing this; generally, they are not people for whom change is congruent or comfortable. Older adults with a personality disorder seek help only when they perceive that change is inevitable, their needs are unmet, or they are becoming increasingly distressed or developing a mental illness. Thus, responding in their usual ways (i.e., resisting change) no longer works for them. In their schema, others are perceived as responsible for their distress, and they typically expect others, or the world, to change for them.

Rigidity of Character Structure and Limited Repertoire

Another core feature of personality disorder is the individual's "Johnny-one-note" quality regarding perceptions, point of view, affect, and behavior. This means that anything that elicits a strong response is experienced as one dominant affect or cognition: All perceptions are colored by the filter of this theme. For some, the cognitive theme is "suspicion." Thus, people and experiences are perceived as threats or potential threats unless proven otherwise. For others, all affect is experienced in the spectrum of "anger," ranging from frustration and annoyance to outright rage. For yet others, relationships are experienced as "hierarchical and judgmental," with the individual always being found wanting. Historically, a dominant affective filter colors their response to others, defining interpersonal relationships as limited or absent, strange or strained, inconsistent or unreliable, disconnected or fused, subordinate or dominant, protective or dangerous. As a consequence, these older adults tell a history of difficult or limited relationships with others.

Effect on Others

Another robust feature is the strong effect those with a personality disorder have on others. This effect is not a response to their pathology but rather is indicative or pathognomic of their pathology. The older individual with a personality disorder has the same effect on others, and on the contexts of care, as does the younger individual with a personality disorder. Context refers here to where they are living, working, living their lives, and who is actively in their lives in these venues. Individuals who as younger adults leave us feeling ineffective and hopeless may evoke these same feelings in us when they are older. Individuals who when younger leave us feeling manipulated and angry may continue to have this effect when they are older. The presenting problem may be different (or maybe not), but our response to the individual will be remarkably consistent. Recognition and identification of this effect can be used diagnostically, and will be addressed further in a discussion of countertransference.

Course of Personality Disorders

Studies and anecdotal reports suggest that the natural course of some personality disorders evidences little change over the life course, whereas others have a more fluctuating course or show marked improvement. As noted earlier, the more dramatic presentations of the Cluster B personality disorders often become less florid in old age. This can be understood in a number of ways. For example, this might reflect selective mortality, whether those with greater pathology die earlier, either through sequelae of risky behaviors or perhaps from actual suicide. Cases may not be recognized because they may not meet diagnostic criteria, showing instead proxy signs and symptoms more appropriate to the late-life context (Rosowsky & Gurian, 1992). The more withdrawn and anxious personality disorder (Clusters A and C) appear to change little over the life course (Livesley, 2004).

Some changes reflect biological maturation. This includes actual brain changes as well as changes in the total organism. For example, impulsivity and the more dramatic and histrionic behaviors take considerable energy, which becomes diminished with age.

Routes into Treatment

Older adults with a personality disorder who seek professional help generally present for symptom relief or to address a specific problem. The problem often reflects interpersonal conflict. They frequently come to treatment secondary to the loss of autonomy and control or on the strong suggestion of another person on whom they must depend (e.g., an adult child, a housing manager, or a primary care physician; Kean, Hoey, & Pinals, 2004). They do not generally self-refer for psychotherapy because their psychopathology is experienced as syntonic.

Other catalysts to their presenting to treatment include usual, age-related events (i.e., physiological and socioenvironmental), as well as special events engendered by their personality disorder (Kean et al., 2004). Usual physiologic changes include illness (both chronic and acute), weakening, general slowing, sensory decrements, reduced energy and stamina, and functional decline. Socioenvironmental changes include losses of significant roles and relationships, context changes, and changes in tasks that are required of them. In addition, there exist stage-appropriate existential catalysts, which may develop from an awareness of mortality and concerns about death and legacy.

Role changes and changes in their relationship network also often serve as catalysts. Changes in health status, especially an awareness of a life-threatening condition, can serve to activate, or reactivate, maladaptive behaviors. These potential catalysts, which lead the patient to present for treatment, all indicate that the stressor has outstripped the individual's ability to effectively cope. Frequently, the level of distress escalates after the loss of a significant person who served specific functions relative to the personality disordered individual and affected the actual symptom presentation of the personality pathology.

Let's consider three major types of these functions: buffering, bolstering, and binding. Recognizing and understanding these functions offers great significance for the treatment plan. If a function that limited the expression of pathology is lost, an effective treatment plan would be wise to introduce compensatory or substitute measures whenever possible.

Function of Buffering

Some individuals serve to buffer, or run interference between the individual and the rest of the world. For example, a wife might serve to interface on her husband's behalf in social encounters and thereby protect him from feedback or responses that might feed into his propensity toward suspiciousness. His Cluster A personality disorder (e.g., Paranoid Personality Disorder) would thus seldom be triggered or exposed. Another frequently observed example is that of the individual with Dependent Personality Disorder who is directed as to how to respond to life's challenges and problems by a dominant and controlling spouse. It is not unusual that dysfunctional behaviors become revealed after the loss of the spouse. The degree of the manifestations of a personality disorder often surprise other family members who were unaware of the function served by the lost spouse.

Function of Bolstering

The individual who bolsters serves to shore up (i.e., potentiate and reinforce) the adaptive traits of the individual with a personality disorder, thereby reducing the expression of maladaptive traits. An example of this would be offering positive reinforcement to the individual with Avoidant Personality Disorder for attending and participating in activities at a local senior center. If the person in his world who has served the functions of supporting, encouraging, or "bringing out the best" is lost, the expression of his personality disorder can be expected to become more apparent.

Another example of bolstering is the individual with Narcissistic Personality Disorder who is naturally limited in his capability to work mutually with others. Modeling and coaching can shape his efforts in a group project: His adaptive skills at being charming, perhaps, and definitely seeking the recognition of others, can be appropriately directed.

Function of Binding

The function of binding refers to the inhibition of the more maladaptive behaviors of the individual with a personality disorder.

With the loss of another who has served this function, it is understandable that the personality disorder will become more apparent or reappear after a comparatively quiescent phase. For example, someone in a close relationship with an individual with Borderline or Narcissistic Personality Disorder may recognize the early warning signs of a rageful explosion and know how to be able to ward these off. Another example might be an adult woman who assists her mother with Avoidant Personality Disorder, disallowing ("binding") the maladaptive fearful and avoidant tendencies by being with her for initial contacts with others, and progressively withdrawing unreasonable support.

These critical functions of buffering, bolstering, and binding can be served by roles as well as relationships. For example, a job which relies on the individual's marked obsessional traits, when lost, might well leave these same traits undirected and unutilized, and the obsessionality then becomes maladaptive (by degree or object). The trait itself is not maladaptive, but the trait is applied in a maladaptive manner (by degree or object). This concept has important implications for treatment planning, and is discussed more fully in Chapter 11.

An Essential Caveat

It is recognized that a personality disorder, while affected by aging, does not disappear in old age (Sadavoy, 1987, 1996; Sadavoy & Fogel, 1992). The personality disorder reflects a lifelong pattern, which is applied to situations across time, task, role, venue, and relationships. Although the specific expressions of the personality disorder might change, the core vulnerability does not. Throughout life, the individual continues to be more sensitive and vulnerable to the stresses of life than his or her nonpersonality disordered counterpart. Even so, there has been relatively little research addressing personality disorders in old age (Agronin & Maletta, 2000), and even less addressing its treatment. Most studies of personality disorders have included younger individuals, with older adults being underrepresented in the sample or not represented at all. Thus, much of what we know and practice with this clinical population may neither be accurate nor appropriate for older adults.

Goals of Treatment

Research findings suggest that many forms of treatment of personality disorders can be equally effective. The guiding principle is the recognition of a personality disorder as being chronic and as defining the essence of the individual. The aim of treatment then is not to cure but rather to reduce distress and improve function. Livesley (2004) has proposed four principles as inherent to personality disorders, each of which needs to be considered in the treatment plan:

1. A personality disorder is central and involves all aspects of the personality structure. Therefore, an effective treatment plan must incorporate a range of interventions and not just be a response to a specific problem. An implication of this is that the treatment indicated is typically long-term rather than brief.

2. There exist core features common to all personality disorders and other features common to specific personality disorders. Therefore, treatment needs to incorporate strategies to manage the personality disorder as a general psychopathology and to offer customized strategies to address the more specific and idiosyncratic manifestations of specific personality disorders.

3. A personality disorder reflects a biopsychosocial etiology. Therefore, interventions need to reflect multiple contributing factors, with the overarching goals of reducing distress and facilitating adaptation and functionality.

4. Adventitious stressors ("psychosocial adversity"; p. 574) impact the personality system and those with personality disorders are especially vulnerable. Therefore, the treatment also needs to address the consequences of these particular stressors. Recall that exaggerated responses to stressors are pathognomic of a personality disorder.

Therapy needs to be reasonable, realistic, and practical (Paris, 2003). What is reasonable and what is not? The individual cannot be recreated or reinvented. His life story cannot be rewritten, and his defensive structure should not be dismantled. This is not because it cannot be done, but because dismantling implies the possibility of him being left without defenses (maladaptive or otherwise), being defenseless, at a stage in life where he may not have the necessary self-resources or time to allow a reconstruction of character. The process of treatment includes assessing the personality traits of the individual, and identifying which are adaptive and which are maladaptive, with the referent(s) of both being clearly identified. These referents elucidate the specific threats and challenges the individual faces, how they are met by his personality traits, and how they may directly contribute to the distress he experiences. These referents can be at the level of the context or system (e.g., when the individual is a patient in a hospital), the level of a group (e.g., a member of a senior center or a family), or the level of a dyad (e.g., in relationship with a spouse or child).

The referent can also refer to a specific task required of the individual for him or her to be appraised as functioning acceptably or adaptively. For example, an individual moving into an assisted living facility after living independently in her own home is now required to regularly participate in a residents' group, where she is expected to voice her concerns and complaints. If she has an Avoidant Personality Disorder, this could be painfully difficult for her. Another example might be a man with Schizoid Personality Disorder who must share a room with other men in a rehabilitation facility. He would likely feel highly anxious with this degree of unfamiliar intimacy and infringement on his personal space. This could be acted out in ways that would interfere with the tasks involved in his rehabilitation program (e.g., refusing group activities or even leaving the program prematurely).

Therapy needs to also identify and address which characteristics or traits of the individual might be adaptive to his current circumstances, and include these in the treatment plan. In other words, it is important to put adaptive traits to use. Doing so serves several functions. Using "adaptive" traits (i.e., giving them a job) reduces the expression of less desirable traits, respecting the concept of reciprocal inhibition. It is always useful to reinforce healthy narcissism, in other words, to make certain the individual has an opportunity to express and is rewarded for expressing that which he most values in himself. Enhancing the positive (or nonmaladaptive) traits increases the probability that the individual will receive positive rather than negative feedback from the environment. It also reduces the strength of the stressor and thereby reduces the challenge to the individual's resiliency.

Any treatment should of necessity be a combination of approaches and strategies to best address the individual's symptoms, her relationship with others, and the context of care. Treatment needs to be clearly relevant to what the individual understands as having a negative impact on her life. If the individual does not understand the relationship between this distress and the treatment offered, she will not sign up for the treatment, or she will sabotage it.

Treatment needs to respect both internal and external individual resources. Internal resources may include time, interest, energy, and money. External resources may include the support and encouragement offered by others. Treatment must appear to be wise to the individual—operationalized as concrete, appropriate, and doable. It also needs to appear to have a low requirement for change and a high probability of achieving the desired results.

Treatment must be perceived as being moderately novel: It must fall somewhere between the appraisal that "I've tried it and it doesn't work" and "This is too strange. It doesn't feel at all comfortable to me." Treatment above all must be seen as being worth the effort to make the required change. The clinician should be aware that change is difficult for people in general and that change may be particularly hard for personality disordered older adults who have used their rigid approach to coping and problem solving for many years, so helping the patient see the potential benefit to change is important. And the benefit must be to the patient, and not merely to other's in the patient's life.

Invisibility of Personality Disorders

Personality disorders are often omitted from a diagnostic formulation, and therefore are not addressed in a treatment plan. There are several ways to understand this omission. There is the assumption that an Axis II disorder is not treatable because it describes the pathology of the individual's characterological infrastructure, which, it is assumed, cannot be significantly altered.

Personality disorder diagnoses are often used as pejorative labels, which serve to close off treatment options. For example, the label "Borderline" is frequently clinical shorthand for a potpourri of negative countertransference reactions to the patient's manipulative and rageful tendencies and noncompliance with treatment.

There are also fiscal disincentives to treating Axis II conditions. Many managed care products discourage what might be lengthy and difficult treatments in favor of highly specific foci for short term treatments. The individual with a personality disorder diagnosis or diagnoses, in the absence of a diagnosable Axis I condition, can be disallowed authorization for more than minimal treatment.

What (Little) Is Known

Although scant research has examined psychological treatments specifically for older adults with personality disorders, some has looked at the treatment of personality disorders of mixed ages, with younger adults being the most heavily represented. The findings can be summarized as follows:

- Those with personality disorders being treated for Axis I disorders have a more complicated course and a poorer outcome than those without personality disorders (Brodaty et al., 1993; Devanand, 2002; Shea & Yen, 2003; Shea et al., 1990; Stek, Van Exel, Van Tilburg, Westendorf, & Beekman, 2002).

- Those with personality disorders develop Axis I disorders earlier in life; have more symptoms, more severe symptoms, longer episodes; and relapse more frequently than those without personality disorders (Abrams, Alexopoulos, Spielman, Klausner, & Kakuma, 2001; Devanand et al., 2000; Fava, Bouffides, Pava, & Rosenbaum, 1996; Trapler & Blackfield, 2001).

- All psychotherapies have been found to be more difficult to conduct when a personality disorder is present, and these patients respond less positively to any intervention or treatment (Agronin & Maletta, 2000; Sadavoy, 1999; Thompson et al., 1988).

- After treatment, those with a personality disorder evidence greater residual/continued negative effect on their level of functioning and quality of life (Abrams et al., 2001; Condello, Padoani, Uguzzoni, Caon, & DeLeo, 2003). This is especially observed in those individuals with more than one personality disorder diagnosis (Condello et al., 2003).

Comorbidity of Axis I and Axis II Disorders

Those with a personality disorder are selectively at greater risk of developing an Axis I disorder, especially mood, anxiety, and somatization disorders (Zweig, 2003). As discussed earlier, we know that Axis I and II disorders commonly coexist in about 20% to 75% of patients (DeLeo, Scocco, & Meneghel, 1999; Oldham, 2001; Widiger & Seidlitz, 2002). Comorbid depression is especially prevalent, with approximately 15% to 30% of older adults diagnosed with depression also having a comorbid personality disorder (Devanand, 2002; Kunik et al., 1994). Most of the personality disorders fall into Cluster C (Abrams et al., 1987, 1994; Devanand, 2002; Kean et al., 2004).

The age of onset of the depression appears to relate to the probability of comorbidity. Patients who have early onset depression are more likely to have a comorbid personality disorder than those with late onset depression (Devanand, 2002; Kunik et al., 1994).

Those diagnosed with a personality disorder have also been shown to have a higher rate of anxiety disorders. Generalized Anxiety Disorder, the most prevalent anxiety disorder among older adults, has been shown to have a high comorbidity with personality disorders, specifically with Cluster C personality disorders (Coolidge, Segal, et al., 2000; Kean et al., 2004).

Understanding the Comorbidity

A number of hypotheses have been suggested to account for the high comorbidity rate. Each hypothesis aligns with certain theoretical orientations to psychopathology and suggests, accordingly, what might be the appropriate treatment (Devanand, 2002).

The "predisposition hypothesis" posits that one condition (either the Axis I or Axis II condition) predisposes the individual to develop the "other" condition. This corresponds well to theories of genetic loading, or diathesis, with regard to the development of psychopathology.

The "subclinical or prodrome hypothesis" posits that the personality disorder is a prodrome of the Axis I disorder, both of which share a common biogenetic substrate—having a personality disorder puts the individual selectively at risk for developing an Axis I condition. A possible flaw with this hypothesis relates to a temporal concern. How can we account for the presentation of a mood or anxiety disorder in childhood, before the Axis II condition becomes evident?

The "life events hypothesis" suggests that stressors early in life (e.g., attachment insults or trauma) lead to the development of both Axis I and Axis II disorders, especially mood disorders. This is consistent with a psychodynamic orientation.

The "scarring hypothesis" suggests that, with severe and recurring Axis I episodes, a scarring of the personality occurs, which results in the development of a personality disorder.

Again, this raises a temporal concern. Current diagnosis criteria require the personality disorder to be established by adulthood, and many individuals with a personality disorder do not have an Axis I episode until later. Have we missed identifying earlier Axis I episodes—specifically, symptoms of mood and anxiety disorders in childhood or adolescence?

Perhaps, the hypothesis with the greatest support (at least anecdotally) is the "modifier/pathoplasty hypothesis." This suggests that, with the high comorbidity rate of Axis I and Axis II disorders, each one modifies the expression of the other. This hypothesis recognizes the bidirectionality and the interrelatedness (not causality) of both types of clinical conditions, albeit this process is not yet well understood. This hypothesis also supports the likelihood that Axis II personality disorders and Axis I clinical disorders share common aspects of psychopathology (Shea & Yen, 2003).

Treatments and Therapies

Treatments and therapies can include somatic treatments, psychotherapy, environmental engineering, psychoeducational interventions, communication training and skills-development programs.

Somatic Treatments

In this section we examine biologically based interventions and discuss potential applications and issues with older adult patients.

Electroconvulsive Therapy
Electroconvulsive therapy (ECT) has been a highly controversial intervention for many years, but it is the treatment of choice for severe recalcitrant depression, which has not responded to psychological and pharmacological approaches. Electroconvulsive therapy may also be used in cases of severe depression where treatment must work quickly and when it

cannot wait for drug therapy to become effective (e.g., with the catatonic or suicidal patient). There have been a number of studies of ECT with patients with Borderline Personality Disorder, but not specifically in older patients (DeBattista & Meuller, 2001). Electroconvulsive therapy is generally found to be a good, effective treatment that appears to treat the depression but which does not have a significant effect on the underlying personality disorder condition. Another study has suggested that those with comorbid personality disorder have a poorer outcome, especially those with a Cluster B personality disorder, and have a higher relapse rate of the depression (Sareen, Enns, & Guertin, 2000). Although there are some well-supported benefits of ECT, its use is especially problematic with older adults because some common side effects of the treatment with older adults include falls, confusion, and cardiovascular problems (Sackeim, 1994). Electroconvulsive therapy also can produce memory problems, and there is controversy about whether these effects are more serious and chronic among older adults. Caution is advised due to the chance of accentuated cognitive problems among older people treated with ECT.

Pharmacotherapy

The purposes of pharmacotherapy are twofold: (1) to reduce selective maladaptive signs and symptoms of the personality disorder and (2) to treat any comorbid psychopathology. Drugs are not used to directly treat the underlying personality disorder.

Medications are often used adjunctively to other forms of treatment and are aimed at specific targets, including anxiety, depression, agitation, impulsivity, affective lability, and transient psychosis.

Among the challenges to pharmacotherapy with this population is the likelihood that the prescribing physician may not know that the patient has a personality disorder, what this means, and what effect this might have on their treatment. In addition, there are special and significant challenges to the pharmacotherapy of older adults with personality disorders, which reflects our understanding of personality disorders and old age. First, it is generally acknowledged that there is likely an underlying biologic vulnerability to personality disorders (Cloninger, Surakic, & Przybeck, 1993; Siever & Davis, 1991). We also recognize that brain changes occur in old age, which increase the brain's vulnerability. Therefore, the older adult with a personality disorder may be selectively at risk for the expression of psychopathology. Second, those with a personality disorder may not be as compliant, or reliably compliant, with medication regimens, which may also be true for older adults in general who have more conditions for which medications are prescribed. Third, there may be cognitive and fiscal concerns further compromising their compliance. Fourth, there is also the risk of polypharmacy and synergistic drug interactions with older adults taking multiple medications. Finally, age-related changes in the pharmacokinetics and pharmacodynamics make prescribing complex and challenging.

Specific personality disorders can be expected to present specific challenges to the prescribing clinician. For example, someone with Dependent Personality Disorder might not adequately question the doctor, or seek a second opinion, even when one is indicated. Someone with Obsessive-Compulsive Personality Disorder might be overly demanding, seeking more information than is necessary, and might rule out potentially helpful medications. Those with Paranoid Personality Disorder might be excessively suspicious about why the medication was being suggested; who was engineering this, and why?

Cluster B presents its own special challenges. For example, among individuals with Narcissistic Personality Disorder, their propensity toward specialness and special sensitivity could result in reporting peculiar or excessive side effects to medications. Others may do doctor shopping, and not be forthright about what drugs they use or the providers with whom they are involved. This could lead to unintentional polypharmacy or intentional drug abuse and self-harming behaviors (Kean et al., 2004).

Effectiveness of Pharmacotherapy

Pharmacological studies have examined the efficacy of atypical antipsychotics, selective serotonin reuptake inhibitors (SSRIs), and antiepileptics (Markovitz, 2004). There have been few controlled trials conducted, and most trials have focused on the Cluster B disorders, usually Borderline Personality Disorder, with scant representation of older adults.

In general, the conclusions of these studies suggest that (a) drugs can be helpful for the reduction of certain symptoms and behavioral traits (e.g., aggression or impulsivity); (b) comorbid Axis I conditions (e.g., depression, anxiety) can be helped with appropriate medications, and (c) combinations of drugs are likely indicated and will achieve a better treatment outcome.

The message is, that while drugs can help the symptom expression of a personality disorder, there is no evidence that they can directly treat (or cure) the personality disorder. However (and this is an important point), if the expressions of a personality disorder are ameliorated, the response by others to the individual will be altered, and therefore the patient's life will be altered and the quality of life improved. This indirect effect often justifies drug (or any) therapy.

Psychological Treatments

Few studies have addressed the efficacy of psychological treatment where personality disorder pathology is the main focus, and fewer still have included significant numbers of older adults in the samples. Most often studies have focused on personality disorder with a comorbid Axis I condition, using mixed ages with older adults underrepresented or not represented at all. There are a number of ways this can be understood. Younger adults with a personality disorder are typically more florid and more acute in their presentation; they present for mental health treatment more readily than older adults; they do not have the medical confounds that older adults present in terms of multiple medical conditions, taking multiple medications, and thus are "cleaner" subjects to study. In the following sections we describe several popular psychotherapeutic approaches to personality disorders and identify challenges with older adult patients.

Psychodynamic Psychotherapy

Long-term psychodynamic psychotherapy has historically been the mainstay treatment for the more severe personality disorders, with poor response overall. This has not been shown to be especially effective in the treatment of personality disorders. Many individuals with a personality disorder are not able to tolerate the intervention mainstays of analytically based treatments. For example, confrontation and interpretation could be experienced as a paranoid threat by those in Cluster A, as a threat of narcissistic injury or of abandonment for those in Cluster B, or as intimating rejection and withdrawal of support for those in Cluster C.

In general, those older adults with a personality disorder are also not well suited to the stage-appropriate tasks of life review and self-reflection (Solomon, Falette, & Stevens, 1982). They have great difficulty identifying or tolerating affect; they are prone to acting it out or in rather than being able to bring affect to conscious awareness and to consider it objectively. Also, the individual often has had a long history replete with failure and conflict, so encouraging a deep and meaningful review may be harmful rather than helpful.

Cognitive-Behavioral Psychotherapy

Cognitive-behavioral therapy perhaps is the most appropriate treatment for older adults with personality disorders (Goisman, 1999). Primarily, this is because it does not target the characterological infrastructure but rather focuses on the symptoms and goals jointly arrived at by patient and clinician. The cognitive aspect can help the individual get past a fixed, egocentric point of view, thereby enabling an expanded repertoire of behavioral options (DeLeo et al., 1999). For this to occur, a therapeutic alliance, which is often an elusive goal with this population, needs to be established. The probability of it being successfully achieved, among other factors, relates to the agreement on therapy goals and acceptance of a partnership (working alliance) to meet those goals. Patient strengths are identified and used to effect positive change. Cognitive-behavioral therapy techniques have been shown to be effective in the treatment of anxiety, depression, impulsivity, aggression, and affective lability conditions and behaviors, which often accompany the personality disorder.

Interpersonal Psychotherapy

Interpersonal psychotherapy (IPT) is a directive treatment model that uses dynamic, cognitive, and behavioral techniques to modify maladaptive relationship patterns. Interpersonal Psychotherapy was developed as a short-term treatment model for depression, and has been shown to be effective with this clinical population. The model has recently been adapted specifically for older adults (see Hinrichsen & Clougherty, 2006). However, it has not been studied as a treatment modality for older adults with a personality disorder, with or without comorbid depression. One study reported on an adaptation of IPT for use with young adults with Borderline Personality Disorder, which suggested some success (Weissman, Markowitz, & Klerman, 2000). The focus with IPT is on the interpersonal context, at the juncture at which most problems (and stress) occur; this is especially problematic for the individual with a personality disorder. The adaptation for use with Borderline Personality Disorder adds to the original protocol an additional focus on self-image.

Dialectical Behavior Therapy

Dialectical behavior therapy (DBT) has received considerable attention and has been shown to be an effective treatment for personality disorder, specifically for Borderline Personality Disorder (for a thorough review, see Robins & Chapman, 2004; also Scheel, 2000). Its efficacy with older adults is beginning to get research attention. Dialectical behavior therapy is a cognitive-behavioral treatment model based on biosocial theory with the premise that personality disorder symptoms reflect biological irregularities (Shearin & Linehan, 1994). The treatment is multi-focused and uses individual and group modalities. Dialectical behavior therapy incorporates problem-solving strategies, stress reduction techniques, and attention to the relationship between the individual and the environment.

The DBT model teaches and coaches problem-focused techniques and includes skills training for the purposes of reducing or eliminating maladaptive responses and replacing them with more adaptive responses. Boundaries, including clinical boundaries, are clearly delineated and protected. The training is hierarchical and progressive, consistent with behavioral models in general.

As noted, most of the DBT studies have focused on younger personality disorder populations. Ongoing research studies (Lynch, Morse, Mendelson, & Rubins, 2003) are evaluating the efficacy of DBT with older adults with a personality disorder and comorbid depression. Findings to date have shown DBT to be more effective than treatment as usual, typically pharmacological treatment, in a number of ways including improvement in adaptive coping, decreased reactivity, decreased self-critical behavior, and decreased feelings of hopelessness. Dialectical behavior therapy is a skills-based approach, and as such, there is no reason to think it should not apply well to older adults.

Countertransference

Countertransference refers to the emotional responses of a clinician to a patient. These responses have their origins in early relationships, most usually in relationships with one's parents, and which responses promote the reactivation of primitive defenses. Countertransference reactions are neither inherently bad nor good; they just are. Recognition and consideration of the countertransference offers clinical utility in a number of ways.

Countertransference can contribute significantly to the diagnostic refinement. The feelings and behaviors evoked in the clinician by the patient can be used to suggest and clarify a clinical diagnosis. Consider the "feeling" of being scrutinized, of being suspect, which is often evoked through interaction with an individual with Paranoid Personality Disorder.

The countertransferential experience enables insight into the phenomenology of the individual. How the clinician feels when with this individual, often reflects (mirrors) what the patient feels. For example, it is not unusual to feel the incipient rage of a person with Borderline Personality Disorder when they are talking about a relationship that triggers their anger dyscontrol.

Countertransference can serve as a microcosm of the patient's universe. As is true for all therapies, the therapy session represents and reflects the experiences the patient has outside of the session. This can help clarify the diagnosis. For example, the individual with Dependent Personality Disorder will act out the dependency in the session and the countertransference reactions might initially include feelings of competence and power, but develop over time to feeling drained and, ultimately, even useless and helpless.

The countertransference can suggest treatment options. It is the wise and experienced clinician who is able to identify the countertransference reactions, to utilize these diagnostically to better understand the phenomenology of the patient, and to choose the type and goals of the treatment based, at least in part, on the countertransference. For example, the individual who increasingly receives home care services, and feels distressed by the lack of control, can be coached and supported in adaptive ways to engage and interact with the helpers.

Managing the countertransference in clinical work with those with personality disorders is known to be exceptionally challenging. The countertransference reactions are characteristically reactive and intense. This is because individuals with a personality disorder often present clinically in crisis and with a history of frequent crises. They often demand urgent or excessive attention from the clinician and often lack awareness or respect for the feelings of others, including the clinician. When their needs are not adequately or promptly met, their symptoms and maladaptive behaviors are likely to escalate and intensify.

Countertransference feelings can be positive or negative. On the positive side are feelings of protectiveness, heightened self-esteem, specialness, and omnipotence. Negative feelings might include feelings of frustration, rage, depletion, or helplessness. These can contribute to considerable stress in the therapist and might result in the therapist acting out—behaving in a way that is a departure from his or her usual way of functioning as a clinician. The countertransference can impact the therapy in significant ways, including the development of a therapeutic impasse, a breach of the therapeutic alliance, and premature termination of the therapy.

Managing the countertransference in clinical work with personality disordered patients is a challenge, and supervision and consultation is highly recommended. Certain problem areas frequently emerge in work with the patient population and require clinical management attention.

Distance regulation refers to the clinician's ability to maintain an appropriate distance in the clinical relationship for the treatment to be effective. Personality disorders make maintaining this distance difficult. For example, the aloof and arelational stance of the Schizoid Personality Disorder interferes, and often precludes, the establishment of a therapeutic alliance. In another example, the affective lability of the Borderline Personality Disorder often is mirrored by a "distance lability" in relationship with the clinician, vacillating between becoming too close or too far apart.

Boundary management refers to the challenges to the clinician's ability to maintain the boundaries of the treatment. For example, the patient delays leaving the treatment room at the end of the session or contacts the clinician repeatedly between sessions. Clinical boundaries are frequently challenged, and sabotaged, by patients with Cluster B personality disorders, and also by those with Dependent Personality Disorder who seek excessive direction and reassurance.

Professional perspective is addressed through ongoing education around treatments which are best suited to which patient, keeping up with current thinking in the field, and awareness of what are (or are not) clinically realistic expectations of treatment. Supervision is mandatory in managing countertransference, especially in work with personality disordered patients. The clinician's personal therapy is also valuable.

Care of the care provider cannot be overemphasized. The more difficult the patient, the more the clinician's usual way of practicing clinical work is challenged by the patient's psychopathology and the more self-care is indicated.

Guideposts for Treatment Planning and Goal Setting

One general guidepost is that the more severe the personality pathology and the more poorly the individual is functioning, the more appropriate it is that the therapy/intervention be directed at the level of the environment. The obverse also bears stating. The more intact and highly functioning is the individual, the more appropriate are therapies directed at the deeper level of the individual, including the more psychodynamic therapies.

When considering treatment planning, a seminal question is: *Where in the individual or the system can I anticipate the least resistance and the greatest openness to positive change?*

The assessment of personality disorders was addressed in Chapter 9. To summarize, the basic elements need to include: chart review, clinical interview of the patient, interview with informants (e.g., from the family or the setting), and standardized assessment measures (e.g., personality inventories and structured interviews). Assessment rules of thumb lead to the diagnosis of treatable conditions, determination of the baselines of the patient's usual level of functioning, highest level of functioning, and the trajectory and rate of change.

Goal setting determines the course for the treatment and informs the options to be considered. In thinking about treatment goals, the critical questions include: Whose goal is it? Does the patient support the goal? Does the patient support how the goal is to be reached? Is the goal feasible for this patient at this time? How will the clinician and patient know that the goal has been reached? Will reaching the goal expose another problem?

Understanding the Phenomenology of Personality Disorders and Helping Guide Treatment

These thoughts are offered as creative guidelines to help the clinician better understand the experience of the individual and to aid in the selection of treatment options.

Patterns of Attachment

Four patterns of attachment have been described which typify the individual's usual position in relationship with others.

Secure Pattern

This pattern takes the form of the individual valuing both himself and others positively. It is suggested as being consistent with a normal, healthy personality.

Fearful Pattern

This pattern takes the form of the individual valuing herself and others negatively. This is suggested as being consistent with Paranoid, Schizotypal, and Obsessive-Compulsive Personality Disorders.

Preoccupied Pattern

This pattern takes the form of the individual valuing himself negatively and others positively. This is suggested as being consistent with Avoidant, Dependent, Histrionic, and Borderline Personality Disorders.

Dismissive Pattern

This pattern takes the form of the individual valuing herself positively and others negatively. This is suggested as being consistent with Narcissistic, Antisocial, and Schizoid Personality Disorders.

Inside and Outside Feeders

Another way to understand the phenomenology of the individual is by identifying the dominant source of self-confirming sustenance. The parameters of this hypothetical continuum denote, at one end, individuals who are predominantly self-confirming (inside feeders), and, at the other extreme, those who are predominantly dependent on external confirmation (outside feeders).

Inside feeders require and prefer little feedback from outside themselves. They tend to be discomforted by too much connection or regard; they tend not to seek it and often resist it. If it is pressed on them, their maladaptive expressions can be expected to become worse. The notion of inside feeder is suggested as being consistent with Paranoid, Schizoid, Schizotypal, Avoidant, and Obsessive-Compulsive Personality Disorders.

Outside feeders need a great deal of feedback, direction, and confirmation from others (the outside). This is suggested as being consistent with Histrionic, Narcissistic, Borderline, Antisocial, and Dependent Personality Disorders. When they are denied or limited in this source of sustenance, the maladaptive expressions of the personality disorder can be expected to become worse. This is often the response to frequently occurring events in old age, such as retirement and the need to move into assisted housing, among other changes, which reduce the amount of feedback they can receive.

Rules of Personality Disorders

Actual rules to govern the expression of any personality—disordered or not disordered—do not exist. However, those with personality disorders often behave as if there were such rules. The behaviors are especially challenging to clinical work. Identifying these rules can help in treatment planning and in the anticipation of resistances and therapeutic openings:

Rule 1: The personality disorder is ego-syntonic. No matter how adaptive or maladaptive, the individual's personality feels right—it "feels like me." The notions of homeostasis and constancy are in support of the ego-syntonic quality of the personality.

Rule 2: The problem is externalized. The sources of distress resulting from the Axis II condition emanate from a referent outside of the individual. The world or others are problematic, not "me."

Rule 3: The response repertoire is closed to change. The individual with a personality disorder has difficulty experiencing himself as an agent of change. His or her response repertoire (i.e., feelings, cognitions, and behaviors) is narrow and inflexible.

Illusion of Uniqueness

In contrast to a patient being more open to recognizing and accepting an Axis I diagnosis, the personality disorder is so much a part of the fiber of who an individual is (i.e., the pattern is ego-syntonic) that there is great resistance to acknowledging it as psychopathology. Each individual experiences him- or herself as unique. It is a challenge to be able to take an individual's personality as object, and subject it to clinical diagnosis and treatment, especially so for the older adult with a personality disorder.

Among the most challenging patients to diagnose and treat is an older individual with a personality disorder who, in some cases, had a relatively quiescent phase at midlife. As noted, the personality pathology can be expected to become exaggerated as the individual faces the many challenges of aging (Sadavoy, 1987, 1996) and the individual's core vulnerabilities revealed. The hallmark of a personality disorder is the difficulty people have as they are in a close relationship with others, or as they avoid such relationships. In older age, people need to be able to establish and maintain connections with others to increasingly permit and enable mutual interdependence. How successfully this is accomplished often informs whether the personality is experienced by others as a disorder or rather as the individual's distinctive style. This important distinction, and its implications for treatment are addressed in Chapter 11.

The "Goodness of Fit" Model and Its Implications for Treatment

There exists an important distinction between a personality style and a personality disorder. A personality style does not cause significant distress nor does it interfere generally with occupational or social functioning, whereas a personality disorder does have these effects. We can consider personality disorders according to a categorical or dimensional perspective. The categorical perspective posits that the disorder is either present or absent in an individual. That is, even if certain criteria are present in an individual, unless a threshold number of criteria are met and for the prescribed period of time, the disorder cannot be diagnosed, and thus is not present. The dimensional model of personality alternatively suggests that personality traits are, in and of themselves, neither adaptive nor maladaptive; neither are they normal nor pathological. Rather, these traits are presumed to be possessed by everyone, albeit differing in expression or degree and reflecting the synergy of multiple traits. The difference in whether a composite of traits, or trait profile, defines a *style* or a *disorder* often depends on variables that exist outside the individual. The dimensional model of personality allows each trait to be envisioned as lying along a continuum, which assumes its presence and describes its relative quantity. Although personality as a construct implies compelling stability, the profile of individual traits, its expression, and whether it becomes identified as a "style" or a "disorder" is informed by an equally compelling capacity for change. This potential for flexibility has significant and special relevance to the care of individuals with personality disorders.

Stage models of psychosocial development consider the context in which the personality is expressed. Developmental theorists additionally have emphasized the relevance of stage-related tasks—what the individual is being asked to do at specific stages of psychosocial development (see Erikson, 1982; Kegan, 1982; Levinson, Darrow, Klein, Levinson, & McKee, 1978). Successful adaptation can thus be defined as the successful negotiation of the psychosocial tasks required at each life stage. Using context and tasks, including roles and relationships, as referents, an individual may be diagnosed with a personality disorder at one stage in life, yet not be so diagnosed while at another stage, *even as he or she exhibits the same personality trait profile.*

The individual with a personality disorder, because of a limited response repertoire and lack of response flexibility, often has great difficulty in negotiating novel tasks. This is especially relevant to the older adult. For example, the loss of a spouse may mean that the individual needs to learn and perform tasks that the lost spouse had historically performed. Someone with a Dependent Personality Disorder might become overwhelmed and flooded with anxiety at the prospect of doing things alone without support and direction. Conversely, the move from one's home to a more institutionalized setting (e.g., an assisted living facility) can mean being freed from assuming responsibility for certain instrumental activities of daily living. Control is a reciprocal of responsibility. Assuming responsibility is threatening to the dependent personality, whereas loss of control is threatening to the obsessive-compulsive personality.

A change in the individual's context provides a novel frame for the expression of his personality traits. He will be asked to be successful at new or different tasks and can be expected to meet them in a way that is usual for him, consistent with his personality style. Or she will be asked to perform different roles, and will also do this in a way that is usual for her, consistent with her personality style. The prevailing directives here are those of *homeostasis* and *self-constancy.*

Homeostasis refers to the tendency of the individual to return to a baseline of functioning, to what feels right and comfortable to him or her. It is the process of reequilibration toward an individual's center. This process is naturally upset when an individual is thrown off his or her center by a change perceived as significant, whether the change required is initiated from in or outside the individual.

Older adults are called on to make many changes in response to changes in their health, functional status, and social and occupational domains. These many requirements for change have been referred to as the vicissitudes of old age as well as the meaning of the slogan "old age is not for sissies." However, also in older age, an individual's ability to regulate, self-correct, and re-center is also challenged. Resources such as energy, money, and time might become limited. On the other side of the equation are the qualities of wisdom, including the strength of survivorship and the ability to draw from and generalize from past experience. Well-functioning, psychologically healthy individuals at any age have a "deep bench"—a broad repertoire of responses to apply to novel situations—as well as *the ability to choose and apply those which are most appropriate.* Those with personality disorders, however, have both a narrow repertoire of responses and also are impaired in their ability to identify appropriate responses. These deficiencies are reflected in problems with affect regulation, distance regulation, core vulnerabilities, and reliance on primitive defenses (discussed earlier in Chapter 10).

Self-constancy refers to the need, throughout life, to do whatever it takes to continue to "feel like me." This need to feel like oneself is a response to the question raised often by frustrated care providers or others in close relationship with the individual with a personality disorder: "If he sees how angry he makes people by being that way, and how they avoid him, why doesn't he stop doing that?" We offer two responses to this type of inquiry. First, if what an individual "does" (i.e., thinks, acts, or feels) does not achieve what it is intended to, the tendency is for him or her to do it again and again, but louder, faster, and/or harder. Second, even if the behavior is met with an objectively negative response, it is the response that an individual usually gets and therefore it "feels like me" and reinforces their self-constancy, which is especially needed during times of change.

Intimate relationships with others both reflect and affect the expression of personality pathology. Any change or loss of others who have performed significant functions for the individual with a personality disorder is likely to be reflected through an exaggeration of his or her maladaptive traits. Having functioned as "auxiliary selves," these significant others attenuated the expression of the personality disorder in three major ways. First, they may have served to *bind* the expression of pathology (e.g., by distracting an individual from acting out his distress). Second, they may have served as a *buffer* between the individual and others, thereby reducing the opportunity for the display of pathology. This function offers a secondary gain of reducing the feedback (reinforcement) of the maladaptive traits. Third, they may have served to *bolster* the individual's more adaptive traits, thereby selectively inhibiting the expression of the reciprocal maladaptive ones (see Chapter 10 for an elaboration on these functions).

"Goodness of Fit" Model

"Goodness of fit" (GOF) is suggested here as describing the relationship between the patient (i.e., client or resident) to the care provider or context of care. Four premises are proposed as underlying the GOF model:

1. Each personality trait lies along a continuum where, by its point on this continuum, it can be identified as suggesting a personality style or a disorder.

2. The composite of these traits establishes a personality trait profile, or template, which can be identified as suggesting a personality style or a disorder.

3. The clinician or care provider, or context of care, favor certain personality traits and devalue certain others. Those that are valued are moved along the continuum toward the style pole, whereas those that are devalued, or negatively regarded, are moved toward the disorder pole.

4. The GOF between the individual and the provider or context of care affects whether a person is diagnosed with a personality disorder and the type of treatment offered.

Trait Template

Table 11.1 offers the trait template as a means to understand goodness of fit.

As can be seen in the template, an opportunity is provided for the clinician to list the personality traits that he or she values and the traits that are particularly valued by the system of care in which the patient participates. The second and third columns provide space for describing traits of the clinician's ideal patient(s) and traits of difficult patient(s). When using the trait template, consider the following issues:

- List the dominant personality traits that are valued by your system of care or self.

- List the dominant personality traits that describe your (the system's) favorite patients.

- List the dominant personality traits that describe your (the system's) most difficult patients.

- What do you recognize about the GOF between these two templates?

The examples that follow illustrate how the template works at the levels of the institutional system and the individual.

Table 11.1   **The Trait Template as a Means to Understand Goodness of Fit**

Trait Template

Traits Valued by the Institutional System or Clinician	Traits Describing Ideal (Favored) Older Adult Patient(s)	Traits Describing Difficult Older Adult Patient(s)

Institutional Example: A Prototypical Skilled Nursing Facility
Three dominant personality traits are suggested as being central to what defines the ideal nursing home resident. These traits address (a) the degree of the resident's characteristic dependency; (b) how much he or she reflects what is "usual and expectable" for a person of that age, gender, and location; and (c) how comfortable that person is functioning as a member of a highly interactive community.

The "fit" to that system can be identified by first noting where along each trait continuum the individual would be expected to fall (marked by X) and then noting where along the continuum the trait is most valued by the system (marked by Y). The alignment of X and Y indicate the "goodness of fit" between the individual and the system:

Autonomous......................X...............Y............Dependent
Individualistic..XY ...Conventional
Private..................X.....................................Y ...Public

In this example, the resident (X) would likely be a reasonable fit with the system. However, certain problems might be anticipated. For example, he might need more privacy than the institution generally provides and his need for autonomy and self-control may also not be adequately met. His tendency toward conventional ways of thinking and being would be highly adaptive to the system as this trait is one that is highly valued.

The clinician's individual psychodynamics also affect the movement of the patient between personality style and disorder. This is addressed in countertransference especially to those with difficult personalities. These emotional responses raised in a clinician by a patient have their origins in early relationships, most typically with one's parents. These responses become reactivated and then are reflected in what we "do" (i.e., think, act, or feel) in response to the encounter. These reactions can be positive or negative, but, either way, they affect how we respond to and treat the individual. Examples of positive countertransference include parental and protective feelings, heightened self-esteem, a feeling of specialness, and the development of rescue fantasies. For example, the feeling that we can be the one to help a dependent personality take more responsibility for her actions and achieve greater courage of her convictions is satisfying. We *feel* that we can repair the characterological fault line where others before us could not, even when we *know* we cannot. Additional confounds in treating the older adult with a personality disorder are the emotional reactions evoked in us because of the patient's age. Professionals are not immune to ageist contributions to countertransference.

Examples of negative countertransference with difficult personalities are legend, including feelings of frustration, fear, powerlessness, rage, and the engendering of fantasies of retaliation and escape. As with treating younger people with personality disorders, the mental health clinician is especially likely to experience powerful reactions to the personality disordered patient of any age because powerful reactions are engendered in the patient. The key here is to recall that the reactions evoked in us are often pathognomonic of the personality disorder itself. The manifestation of the personality disorder requires a referent, whether this is task, context, or relationship, and the clinician provides the opportunity for an intimate relationship. Powerful feelings are one way to diagnose the disorder, as are the experience and performance of our professional work in ways that are a departure from our norm.

Consider the "pull" of the individual with a dependent personality for us to go beyond suggesting ways in which she might help herself to actively coaching and directing her every step of the way. Consider the "pull" of the hostile narcissistic personality to deny him the attention and feedback he desperately seeks. It is very difficult to express positive regard when we feel vengeful. Finally, consider the unusual level of worry and concern experienced about the individual with Borderline Personality Disorder who is hinting at self-harm or possibly suicide.

Individual Example
Whether the system of care refers to an individual or to an actual system, the underlying premise of GOF remains the same. That is that each "system" favors certain personality traits and

devalues others. For example, a visiting nurse is assigned home visits to an elderly man with brittle diabetes. The nurse is responsible for evaluating him and for designing his treatment plan, monitoring the responses, and making any indicated changes. Her patient is "managing his levels" with outstanding attention to detail, thereby making her job very easy. He is fastidious with his record keeping, the recording of his diet, time of his meals, time and dose of all medications, as well as noting the effects of any changes in the regimen. He is clearly likely to become a favorite patient of this nurse. However, if this same man were to become a resident in a skilled nursing facility, his appraisal may be very different. He could be expected to micromanage the staff at every turn. No institution could be so unvaryingly precise in the timing of medication distribution or in attention to the intricate details of his status and responses. At best, he would be perceived as an annoyance by staff. He would likely come to be regarded as "difficult" when his anger and anxiety escalated in response to his lack of control and the institution's inattention to detail, which had historically served to inhibit his internal experience of distress and outward expression of pathology. In time, he likely would be diagnosed with Obsessive-Compulsive Personality Disorder.

Utility of a Personality Trait Model

Next, we offer several uses of the personality trait model, especially in predicting problems an individual may have, understanding these problems, and guiding intervention strategies.

Predictive Value

This model calls attention to the probability of problems occurring for a given individual in a specific setting or situation. Consider an older man who is extremely needful of privacy and intolerant of interpersonal closeness (a schizoid personality). He finds himself in a rehabilitation facility, sleeping in a room with multiple other patients, dining in a large communal dining hall, having physical therapy with many others around him, and being required to participate in group sessions. It can be anticipated that he will appear more pathological—the degree of his personality disorder will increase.

Interpretive Value

This refers to the value of the model in being able to increase an understanding of why certain expressions of an individual's personality are maladaptive in a specific context or relative to a specific task (i.e., a less "good fit"). For example, an older woman with Avoidant Personality Disorder would feel put at risk if forced into a new group setting. Her dominant traits include an aversion to public exposure, resulting in the feeling that she is being judged and will fail the scrutiny of others. It is understandable that any way she perceives being asked to perform or reveal herself would be toxic to her, and she would likely experience even greater distress.

Planning Value

This refers to the utility of the model to inform and guide treatment and care plan options. For example, the individual who thrives on considerable attention from others (and acts out if he or she doesn't get it) would likely do better (i.e., appear less disordered) in an environment where his or her behaviors were observed and affirming feedback was liberally given. Unlike the dependent personality who requires continual feedback for reassurance and direction, and unlike the schizoid personality who avoids such feedback, the narcissistic character thrives on this and needs this to reinforce his or her sense of self.

Implications of the Goodness of Fit Model for Designing a Treatment Plan

As we have highlighted in earlier chapters, older adults with personality disorders in general are likely to have problems fitting into formal institutions such as hospitals, rehabilitation facilities, and skilled nursing facilities. Generally, the more formal the institution, the more rigid the template defining the personality traits of those favored by the system. The staff working in these institutions also reflect this template for *them* to be valued by the system. Thus the GOF model can be conceptualized as one of parallel processes, identifying the favored/devalued worker as well as the favored/devalued patient (resident).

Informal systems, by comparison, are generally better able to tolerate greater deviance in the template than are the formal systems. This allows the patients (residents) more degrees of freedom before they are diagnosed with pathology. These informal systems (e.g., church groups, neighbors, or kinship networks) are thus less likely to identify a personality disorder in favor of accepting the individual's personality style.

The goals for treatment include what should be included as well as what should not be included. What should not be included is a goal to restructure the individual's personality. What should be included, generally, is whatever it is that can be anticipated to ease his or her way at this point in life and, more specifically, whatever it is that can be anticipated to enable him or her to secure and accept what help is indicated.

The purposes of treatment include the relief of symptoms, the accommodation of necessary change, the tolerance of interdependence, and the support of healthy narcissism. To conclude this chapter, we offer several guiding questions for psychotherapeutic work.

The first question to guide the treatment plan is: *Where is the pain?* For the older adult with a personality disorder, the pain often lies between the individual and the system (or individual) providing care.

The next guiding question is: *Where might we enter the system to maximally reduce distress (pain) and minimally meet resistance?* How might the system be asked to accommodate the patient (resident), and how might the patient (resident) be asked to accommodate the system? This is not suggesting an adversarial stance. Rather, the goal is to relieve distress, which is being experienced by both.

The next question is: *What is the smallest movement, amount of change, required to reduce the distress?*

The final question is: *How would this change be recognized?*
To address the guiding questions, consider these possible treatment/intervention options:

- *Change the demand on the individual to be more congruent with his style.* For example, can the system be flexible in changing the demand that "men must wear ties and jackets in the dining room" so that the individual(s) whose identity is "a casual guy" or someone who challenges dress codes on principle will not get into a regular struggle with staff at mealtime? Can the physical therapy department allow the individual with strong privacy needs to do her exercises in her room or in the PT room when others besides the therapist are not around?

- *Put the dominant, positive traits to work.* It frequently appears that difficult older adults become more difficult when their dominant traits become "unemployed." The intervention then suggests putting these traits back to work in an adaptive way or, at least, in a less maladaptive way. Recall the man with Obsessive-Compulsive Personality Disorder being cared for at home by a visiting nurse. His dominant traits were put to work in that setting and the "fit" was excellent. This changed when the man was placed in a facility where these same traits were now tolerated and became unemployed resulting in a poor fit in that setting. The message is, where possible, to put the dominant traits to use in a positive way.

- *Inhibit the expression of the negative traits.* This can be accomplished in two ways. One way is to avoid "fanning the flames" by what is done, or not done, to provoke the individual. This refers to the strong reactions individuals with personality disorders can induce in us, indeed in entire systems. The use of supervision and consultation can be helpful for purposes of processing and assisting our self-monitoring so that we are less likely to act out their psychopathology or to punish them for it.

- *Provide what "went missing" and has been identified as the precipitant in the escalation or worsening of their condition.* Often this harkens to the loss of someone in their life who had served the functions of buffering, bolstering, or binding for them. The interventions suggested then are to address the loss and to resupply the function in some way that fits the current situation.

REFERENCES

Abrams, R. C., Alexopoulos, G. S., Spielman, L., Klausner, E., & Kakuma, T. (2001). Personality disorder symptoms predict declines in global functioning and quality of life in elderly depressed patients. *American Journal of Geriatric Psychiatry, 9,* 67–71.

Abrams, R. C., Alexopoulos, G. S., & Young, R. C. (1987). Geriatric depression and DSM-III-R personality disorder criteria. *Journal of the American Geriatrics Society, 35,* 383–386.

Abrams, R. C., & Horowitz, S. V. (1996). Personality disorders after age 50: A meta analysis. *Journal of Personality Disorders, 10,* 271–281.

Abrams, R. C., Rosendahl, E., Card, C., & Alexopoulos, G. S. (1994). Personality disorder correlates of late and early onset depression. *Journal of the American Geriatrics Society, 42,* 727–731.

Aday, R. H. (2003). *Aging prisoners: Crisis in American corrections.* Westport, CT: Praeger.

Agronin, M. (1994). Personality disorders in the elderly: An overview. *Journal of Geriatric Psychiatry, 27,* 151–191.

Agronin, M., & Maletta, G. (2000). Personality disorders in late life: Understanding and overcoming the gap in research. *Journal of the American Geriatrics Society, 8,* 4–18.

Almeida, O. P., Forstl, H., Howard, R., & David, A. S. (1993). Unilateral auditory hallucinations. *British Journal of Psychiatry, 162,* 262–264.

American Psychiatric Association. (1952). *Diagnostic and statistical manual of mental disorders.* Washington, DC: Author.

American Psychiatric Association. (1968). *Diagnostic and statistical manual of mental disorders* (2nd ed.). Washington, DC: Author.

American Psychiatric Association. (1980). *Diagnostic and statistical manual of mental disorders* (3rd ed.). Washington, DC: Author.

American Psychiatric Association. (1987). *Diagnostic and statistical manual of mental disorders* (3rd ed., rev.). Washington, DC: Author.

American Psychiatric Association. (1994). *Diagnostic and statistical manual of mental disorders* (4th ed.). Washington, DC: Author.

American Psychiatric Association. (2000). *Diagnostic and statistical manual of mental disorders* (4th ed., text rev.). Washington, DC: Author.

Ames, A., & Molinari, V. (1994). Prevalence of personality disorders in community-living elderly. *Journal of Geriatric Psychiatry and Neurology, 7,* 189–194.

Bachman, D. L., Wolf, P. A., Linn, R., Knoefel, J. E., Cobb, J., Belanger, A., et al. (1992). Prevalence of dementia and probable senile dementia of the Alzheimer type in the Framingham Study. *Neurology, 42,* 115–119.

Bagby, R. M., & Farvolden, P. (2004). Personality Diagnostic Questionnaire-4 (PDQ-4). In M. Hersen (Editor-in-Chief) & M. Hilsenroth & D. L. Segal (Vol. Eds.), *Comprehensive handbook of psychological assessment: Vol. 2. Personality assessment* (pp. 122–133). Hoboken, NJ: Wiley.

Beck, A. T. (1992). Personality disorders and their relationship to syndromal disorders.

Across-Species Comparisons and Psychiatry Newsletter, 5, 3–13.

Beck, A. T., Freeman, A., & Associates. (2003). *Cognitive therapy of personality disorders* (2nd ed.). New York: Guilford Press.

Black, D. W. (2001). Antisocial personality disorder: The forgotten patients of psychiatry. *Primary Psychiatry, 8,* 30–81.

Black, D. W., Baumgard, C. H., Bell, S. E., & Kao, C. E. (1995). A 16- to 45-year follow-up of 71 men with antisocial personality disorder. *Comprehensive Psychiatry, 36,* 130–140.

Bouchard, T. J., & Loehlin, J. C. (2001). Genes, evolution, and personality. *Behavior Genetics, 31,* 243–273.

Brodaty, H., Harris, L., Peters, K., Kay, W., Hikie, I., Boyce, P., et al. (1993). Prognosis of depression in the elderly: A comparison with younger patients. *British Journal of Psychiatry, 163,* 589–596.

Burns, B. J., Wagner, H. R., Taube, J. E., Magaziner, J., Permutt, T., & Landerman, L. R. (1993). Mental health service use by the elderly in nursing homes. *American Journal of Public Health, 83,* 331–337.

Butcher, J. N., Atlis, M. M., & Hahn, J. (2004). Minnesota Multiphasic Personality Inventory-2 (MMPI-2). In M. Hersen (Editor-in-Chief) & M. Hilsenroth & D. L. Segal (Vol. Eds.), *Comprehensive handbook of psychological assessment: Vol. 2. Personality assessment* (pp. 30–38). Hoboken, NJ: Wiley.

Butcher, J. N., Dahlstrom, W. G., Graham, J. R., Tellegen, A., & Kaemmer, B. (1989). *Minnesota Multiphasic Personality Inventory-2 (MMPI-2): Manual for administration and scoring.* Minneapolis: University of Minnesota Press.

Butler, R. N., Lewis, M. I., & Sunderland, T. (1998). *Aging and mental health: Positive psychosocial and biomedical approaches.* Needham Heights, MA: Allyn & Bacon.

Carstensen, L. L. (1987). Age-related changes in social activity. In L. L. Carstensen & B. A. Edelstein (Eds.), *Handbook of clinical gerontology* (pp. 222–237). Elmsford, NY: Pergamon Press.

Carstensen, L. L., Isaacowitz, D. M., & Charles, S. T. (1999). Taking time seriously: A theory of socioemotional selectivity. *American Psychologist, 54,* 165–181.

Carstensen, L. L., & Turk-Charles, S. (1994). The salience of emotion across the adult life span. *Psychology and Aging, 9,* 259–264.

Casey, D. A., & Schrodt, C. J. (1989). Axis II diagnoses in geriatric inpatients. *Journal of Geriatric Psychiatry and Neurology, 2,* 87–88.

Casey, P. R. (2000). The epidemiology of personality disorder. In P. Tyrer (Ed.), *Personality disorders: Diagnosis, management, and course* (2nd ed., pp. 71–80). Oxford, England: Butterworth Heinemann.

Cattell, R. B. (1946). *The description and measurement of personality.* New York: World Books.

Cloninger, C., Surakic, D., & Przybeck, T. (1993). A psychobiologic model of temperament and character. *Archives of General Psychiatry, 50,* 975–990.

Cohen, B. J., Nestadt, G., Samuels, J. F., Romanoski, A. J., McHugh, P. R., & Rabins, P. V. (1994). Personality disorder in later life: A community study. *British Journal of Psychiatry, 165,* 493–499.

Cohen, G. D. (1990). Psychopathology and mental health in the mature and elderly adult. In J. E. Birren & K. W. Schaie (Eds.), *Handbook of the psychology of aging* (3rd ed., pp. 359–371). San Diego, CA: Academic Press.

Condello, C., Padoani, W., Uguzzoni, U., Caon, F., & DeLeo, D. (2003). Personality disorders and self-perceived quality of life in an elderly outpatient population. *Psychopathology, 36,* 78–83.

Coolidge, F. L. (2000). *Coolidge Axis II Inventory: Manual.* Colorado Springs, CO: Author.

Coolidge, F. L., Burns, E. M., & Mooney, J. A. (1995). Reliability of observer ratings in the assessment of personality disorders: A preliminary study. *Journal of Clinical Psychology, 51,* 22–28.

Coolidge, F. L., Burns, E. M., Nathan, J. H., & Mull, C. E. (1992). Personality disorders in the elderly. *Clinical Gerontologist, 12,* 41–55.

Coolidge, F. L., Janitell, P. M., & Griego, J. A. (1994). On the relationship among personality disorders, depression and anxiety in the elderly. *Clinical Gerontologist, 15,* 80–83.

Coolidge, F. L., & Merwin, M. M. (1992). Reliability and validity of the Coolidge Axis II Inventory: A new inventory for the assessment of personality disorders. *Journal of Personality Assessment, 59,* 223–238.

Coolidge, F. L., Moor, C. J., Yamazaki, T. G., Stewart, S. E., & Segal, D. L. (2001). On the relationship between Karen Horney's tripartite neurotic type theory and personality disorder features. *Personality and Individual Differences, 30,* 1387–1400.

Coolidge, F. L., & Segal, D. L. (1998). Evolution of the personality disorder diagnosis in the Diagnostic and Statistical Manual of Mental Disorders. *Clinical Psychology Review, 18,* 585–599.

Coolidge, F. L., Segal, D. L., Benight, C. C., & Danielian, J. (2004). The predictive power of Horney's psychoanalytic approach: An empirical study. *American Journal of Psychoanalysis, 64,* 363–374.

Coolidge, F. L., Segal, D. L., Hook, J. N., & Stewart, S. (2000). Personality disorders and coping among anxious older adults. *Journal of Anxiety Disorders, 14,* 157–172.

Coolidge, F. L., Segal, D. L., Pointer, J. C., Knaus, E. A., Yamazaki, T. G., & Silberman, C. S. (2000). Personality disorders in older adult inpatients with chronic mental illness. *Journal of Clinical Geropsychology, 6,* 63–72.

Coolidge, F. L., Segal, D. L., & Rosowsky, E. (2006). *Prevalence and comorbidity of personality disorders among older persons.* Manuscript submitted for publication.

Coolidge, F. L., Segal, D. L., Stewart, S. E., & Ellett, J. C. (2000). Neuropsychological dysfunction in children with borderline personality disorder features: A preliminary investigation. *Journal of Research in Personality, 34,* 554–561.

Coolidge, F. L., Thede, L. L., & Jang, K. L. (2001). Heritability of personality disorders in childhood: A preliminary study. *Journal of Personality Disorder, 15,* 33–40.

Coolidge, F. L., Thede, L. L., & Jang, K. L. (2004). Are personality disorders psychological manifestations of executive function deficits? Evidence from a twin study. *Behavior Genetics, 34,* 73–82.

Coolidge, F. L., Thede, L. L., Stewart, S. E., & Segal, D. L. (2002). Coolidge Personality and Neuropsychological Inventory for Children (CPNI): Preliminary psychometric characteristics. *Behavior Modification, 26,* 550–566.

Coolidge, F. L., Thede, L. L., & Young, S. E. (2000). Heritability and the comorbidity of ADHD with behavioral disorders and executive function deficits: A preliminary investigation. *Developmental Neuropsychology, 17,* 273–287.

Costa, P. T., Jr., & McCrae, R. R. (1992). *Revised NEO Personality Inventory (NEO-PI-R) and NEO Five-Factor Inventory (NEO-FFI) professional manual.* Odessa, FL: Psychological Assessment Resources.

Costa, P. T., Jr., & McCrae, R. R. (2006). Trait and factor theories. In M. Hersen & J. C. Thomas (Editors-in-Chief) & J. C. Thomas

& D. L. Segal (Eds.), *Comprehensive handbook of personality and psychopathology: Vol. 1. Personality and everyday functioning* (pp. 96–114). Hoboken, NJ: Wiley.

Darwin, C. (1859). *On the origin of the species by means of natural selection.* London: John Murray.

DeBattista, C., & Mueller, K. (2001). Is electroconvulsive therapy effective for the depressed patient with comorbid borderline personality disorder? *Journal of ECT, 17,* 91–98.

DeFries, J. C., McGuffin, P., McClearn, G. E., & Plomin, R. (2000). *Behavioral genetics* (4th ed.). New York: Worth.

DeLeo, D., Scocco, P., & Meneghel, G. (1999). Pharmacological and psychotherapeutic treatment of personality disorders in the elderly. *International Psychogeriatrics, 11,* 191–206.

Devanand, D. P. (2002). Comorbid psychiatric disorders in late life depression. *Biological Psychiatry, 51,* 236–242.

Devanand, D. P., Turret, N., Moody, B., Fitzsimmons, L., Peyser, S., Mickle, K., et al. (2000). Personality disorders in elderly patients with dysthymic disorders. *American Journal of Geriatric Psychiatry, 8,* 188–195.

Dobson, K. S., & Dozois, D. J. A. (2001). Historical and philosophical bases of the cognitive-behavioral therapies. In K. S. Dobson (Ed.), *Handbook of cognitive-behavioral therapies* (2nd ed., pp. 3–39). New York: Guilford Press.

Dougherty, L. M. (1999). Determining personality disorders in older adults through self-identification and clinician assessment. In E. Rosowsky, R. C. Abrams, & R. A. Zweig (Eds.), *Personality disorders in older adults: Emerging issues in diagnosis and treatment* (pp. 119–133). Mahwah, NJ: Erlbaum.

Dozois, D. J. A., Frewen, P. A., & Covin, R. (2006). Cognitive theories. In M. Hersen (Editor-in-Chief) & J. C. Thomas & D. L. Segal (Vol. Eds.), *Comprehensive handbook of personality and psychopathology: Vol. 1. Personality and everyday functioning* (pp. 173–191). Hoboken, NJ: Wiley.

Duffy, M. (Ed.). (1999). *Handbook of counseling and psychotherapy with older adults.* New York: Wiley.

Epictetus. (1955). *The enchiridion* (G. Long, Trans.). New York: Promethean Press. (Original work published circa A.D. 101)

Erikson, E. H. (1963). *Childhood and society.* New York: Norton.

Erikson, E. H. (1982). *The life cycle completed.* New York: Norton.

Eysenck, H. J. (1960). *The structure of human personality.* London: Methuen.

Fabrega, H., Ulrich, R., Pilkonis, P., & Mezzich, J. E. (1991). Pure personality disorders in an intake psychiatric setting. *Journal of Personality Disorders, 6,* 153–161.

Fava, M., Bouffides, E., Pava, J., & Rosenbaum, J. (1996). Patterns of personality disorder comorbidity in early-onset versus late-onset major depression. *American Journal of Geriatric Psychiatry, 153,* 1308–1312.

First, M. B., & Gibbon, M. (2004). The Structured Clinical Interview for DSM-IV Axis I Disorders (SCID-I) and the Structured Clinical Interview for DSM-IV Axis II Disorders (SCID-II). In M. Hersen (Editor-in-Chief) & M. Hilsenroth & D. L. Segal (Vol. Eds.), *Comprehensive handbook of psychological assessment: Vol. 2. Personality assessment* (pp. 134–143). Hoboken, NJ: Wiley.

First, M. B., Gibbon, M., Spitzer, R. L., Williams, J. B. W., & Benjamin, L. S. (1997). *Structured Clinical Interview for DSM-IV Axis II Personality Disorders (SCID-*

II). Washington, DC: American Psychiatric Press.

First, M. B., Spitzer, R. L., Gibbon, M., & Williams, J. B. W. (1997). *Structured Clinical Interview for DSM-IV Axis I Disorders—Clinician Version (SCID-CV)*. Washington, DC: American Psychiatric Press.

Fogel, B. S., & Westlake, R. (1990). Personality disorder diagnoses and age in inpatients with major depression. *Journal of Clinical Psychiatry, 51,* 232–235.

Freud, S. (1913). *Interpretation of dreams* (A. A. Brill, Trans.). New York: Macmillan. (Original work published 1899)

Freud, S. (1928). *The future of an illusion.* London: Hogarth Press.

Fu, Q., Heath, A. C., Bucholz, K. K., Nelson, E., Goldberg, J., Lyons, M. J., et al. (2002). Shared genetic risk of major depression, alcohol dependence, and marijuana dependence: Contribution of antisocial personality disorder in men. *Archives of General Psychiatry, 59,* 1125–1132.

Gatz, M., & Smyer, M. (1992). The mental health system and older adults in the 1990s. *American Psychologist, 47,* 741–751.

Gazzaniga, M. S., Ivry, R. B., & Mangun, G. R. (2002). *Cognitive neuroscience* (2nd ed.). New York: Norton.

Goisman, R. M. (1999). Cognitive-behavioral therapy, personality disorders, and the elderly: Clinical and theoretical considerations. In E. Rosowsky, R. C. Abrams, & R. A. Zweig (Eds.), *Personality disorders in older adults: Emerging issues in diagnosis and treatment* (pp. 215–228). Mahwah, NJ: Erlbaum.

Graham, J. R. (2006). *MMPI-2: Assessing personality and psychopathology* (4th ed.). New York: Oxford University Press.

Grove, W. M. (1987). The reliability of psychiatric diagnosis. In C. G. Last & M. Hersen (Eds.), *Issues in diagnostic research* (pp. 99–119). New York: Plenum Press.

Gurland, B. J., Cross, P. S., & Katz, S. (1996). Epidemiological perspectives on opportunities for treatment of depression. *American Journal of Geriatric Psychiatry, 4,* S7–S13.

Harpur, T. J., & Hare, R. D. (1994). The assessment of psychopathy as a function of age. *Journal of Abnormal Psychology, 103,* 604–609.

Hathaway, S. R., & McKinley, J. C. (1943). *Minnesota multiphasic personality inventory.* New York: Psychological Corporation.

Heatherton, T. F., & Weinberger, J. L. (Eds.). (1994). *Can personality change?* Washington, DC: American Psychological Association.

Hinrichsen, G. A., & Clougherty, K. F. (2006). *Interpersonal psychotherapy for depressed older adults.* Washington, DC: American Psychological Association.

Hoch, P. H., Cattell, J. P., Strahl, M. D., & Penness, H. H. (1962). The course and outcome of pseudoneurotic schizophrenia. *American Journal of Psychiatry, 119,* 106–115.

Horney, K. (1937). *The neurotic personality of our time.* New York: Norton.

Horney, K. (1939). *New ways in psychoanalysis.* New York: Norton.

Horney, K. (1945). *Our inner conflicts.* New York: Norton.

Horney, K. (1950). *Neurosis and human growth.* New York: Norton.

Horney, K. (1967). *Feminine psychology.* New York: Norton.

Horney, K. (1987). *Final lectures.* New York: Norton.

Hyler, S. E. (1994). *Personality Diagnostic Questionnaire, 4th edition, PDQ-4+.* New York: New York State Psychiatric Institute.

Jackson, H. J., Whiteside, H. L., Bates, G. W., Bell, R., Rudd, R. P., & Edwards, J. (1991). Diagnosing personality disorders in psychiatric inpatients. *Acta Psychiatrica Scandinavica, 83,* 206–213.

Jensen, P. S., Mrazek, D., Knapp, P. K., Steinberg, L., Pfeffer, C., Schowalter, J., et al. (1997). Evolution and revolution in child psychiatry: ADHD as a disorder of adaptation. *Journal of the Academy of Child and Adolescent Psychiatry, 36,* 1672–1681.

Jeste, D. V., Alexopoulos, G. S., Bartels, S. J., Cummings, J. L., Gallo, J. J., Gottlieb, G. L., et al. (1999). Consensus statement on the upcoming crisis in geriatric mental health: Research agenda for the next 2 decades. *Archives of General Psychiatry, 56,* 848–853.

Judd, L., Akiskal, H., Schettler, P., Endicott, J., Maser, J., Solomon, D., et al. (2002). The long-term natural history of the weekly symptomatic status of bipolar I disorder. *Archives of General Psychiatry, 59,* 530–537.

Kean, R., Hoey, K., & Pinals, S. (2004). Treatment of personality disorders. In J. J. Magnavita (Ed.), *Handbook of personality disorders: Theory and practice* (pp. 498–510). Hoboken, NJ: Wiley.

Kegan, R. (1982). *The evolving self.* Cambridge, MA: Harvard University Press.

Kenan, M. M., Kendjelic, E. M., Molinari, V. A., Williams, W., Norris, M., & Kunik, M. E. (2000). Age-related differences in the frequency of personality disorders among inpatient veterans. *International Journal of Geriatric Psychiatry, 15,* 831–837.

Kernberg, O. F. (1975). *Borderline conditions and pathological narcissism.* New York: Aronson.

Kernberg, O. F. (1976). *Object relations theory and clinical psychoanalysis.* New York: Aronson.

Kernberg, O. F. (1996). A psychoanalytic theory of personality disorders. In J. F. Clarkin & M. F. Lenzenweger (Eds.), *Major theories of personality disorders* (pp. 106–140). New York: Guilford Press.

Kirkwood, T. B. L. (2000). Evolution of aging: How genetic factors affect the end of life. *Generations, 24,* 12–18.

Knight, R. (2004). *Psychotherapy with older adults* (3rd ed.). Thousand Oaks, CA: Sage.

Kroessler, D. (1990). Personality disorder in the elderly. *Hospital and Community Psychiatry, 41,* 1325–1329.

Krupnick, J. L., Sotsky, S. M., Simmons, S., Moyer, J., Watkins, J., Elkin, I., et al. (1996). The role of therapeutic alliance in psychotherapy and pharmacotherapy outcome: Findings in the National Institute of Mental Heath treatment of depression collaborative research program. *Journal of Consulting and Clinical Psychology, 64,* 532–539.

Kunik, M. E., Mulsant, B. H., Rifai, A. H., Sweet, R. A., Pasternak, R., Rosen, J., et al. (1993). Personality disorders in elderly inpatients with major depression. *American Journal of Geriatric Psychiatry, 1,* 38–45.

Kunik, M. E., Mulsant, B. H., Rifai, A. H., Sweet, R. A., Pasternak, R., & Zubenko, G. S. (1994). Diagnostic rate of comorbid personality disorder in elderly psychiatric inpatients. *American Journal of Psychiatry, 151,* 603–605.

Labouvie-Vief, G., & Hakim-Larson, J. (1989). Development of shifts in adult thought. In S. Hunter & M. Sundel (Eds.), *Midlife myths* (pp. 69–96). Newbury Park, CA: Sage.

Laidlaw, K., Thompson, L., Gallagher-Thompson, D., & Dick-Siskin, L. (2003). *Cognitive behavior therapy with older people.* Hoboken, NJ: Wiley.

Lair, T., & Lefkowitz, D. (1990). Mental health and functional status of residents of nursing and personal care homes. In *National Medical Expenditure Survey Research Findings, 7*(DHHS Publication No. PHS90-3470). Rockville, MD: Public Health Service, Agency for Health Care Policy and Research.

Lang, F. R., & Carstensen, L. L. (1994). Close emotional relationships in late life: Further support for proactive aging in the social domain. *Psychology and Aging, 9,* 315–324.

Lawton, M. P., Kleban, M. H., Rajagopal, D., & Dean, J. (1992). Dimensions of affective experience in three age groups. *Psychology and Aging, 7,* 171–184.

Levinson, D. J., Darrow, C. N., Klein, E. B., Levinson, M. H., & McKee, B. (1978). *The seasons of a man's life.* New York: Alfred A. Knopf.

Lewis, L., & Appleby, L. (1988). Personality disorder: The patients psychiatrists dislike. *British Journal of Psychiatry, 153,* 44–49.

Lichtenberg, P. (1998). *Mental health practice in geriatric health care settings.* New York: Haworth.

Linehan, M. (1993). *Cognitive-behavioral therapy of borderline personality disorder.* New York: Guilford Press.

Livesley, W. J. (2004). A framework for an integrated approach to treatment. In J. Livesley (Ed.), *Handbook of personality disorders: Theory, research, and treatment* (pp. 570–600). New York: Guilford Press.

Loranger, A. W. (1999). *International Personality Disorder Examination: DSM-IV and ICD-10 Interviews.* Odessa, FL: Psychological Assessment Resources.

Loranger, A. W., Sartorius, N., Andreoli, A., Berger, P., Buchheim, P., Channabasavanna, S. M., et al. (1994). International Personality Disorder Examination: The World Health Organization/Alcohol, Drug Abuse, and Mental Health Administration international pilot study of personality disorders. *Archives of General Psychiatry, 51,* 215–224.

Lynch, T., Morse, J., Mendelson, M., & Rubins, C. (2003). Dialectical behavior therapy for depressed older adults. *Journal of the American Geriatrics Society, 11,* 33–45.

Maddocks, P. D. (1970). A 5 year follow-up of untreated psychopaths. *British Journal of Psychiatry, 116,* 511–515.

Margo, J. L., Robinson, J. R., & Corea, S. (1980). Referrals to a psychiatric service from old people's homes. *British Journal of Psychiatry, 136,* 396–401.

Markovitz, P. (2004). Recent trends in pharmacotherapy of personality disorders. *Journal of Personality Disorders, 18,* 90–101.

Maslow, A. (1954). *Motivation and personality.* New York: Harper & Row.

Mayer, J. D. (2006). A classification of DSM-IV-TR mental disorders according to their relation to the personality system. In M. Hersen (Editor-in-Chief) & J. C. Thomas & D. L. Segal (Vol. Eds.), *Comprehensive handbook of personality and psychopathology: Vol. 1. Personality and everyday functioning* (pp. 443–453). Hoboken, NJ: Wiley.

McGlashan, T. H., Grilo, C. M., Skodol, A. E., Gunderson, J. G., Shea, M. T., Morey, L. C., et al. (2000). Collaborative Longitudinal Personality Disorders study: Baseline Axis I/II and II/II diagnostic co-occurrence. *Acta Psychiatrica Scandinavica, 102,* 256–264.

Mellsop, G., Varghese, F., Joshua, S., & Hicks, A. (1982). The reliability of Axis II of DSM-III. *American Journal of Psychiatry, 139,* 1360–1361.

Mezzich, J. E., Fabrega, H., Coffman, G. A., & Glavin, Y. (1987). Comprehensively diagnosing geriatric patients. *Comprehensive Psychiatry, 28,* 68–76.

Miller, B. L., & Cummings, J. L. (1999). *The human frontal lobes.* New York: Guilford Press.

Millon, T. (1981a). *Disorders of personality: DSM-III Axis II.* New York: Wiley.

Millon, T. (1981b). *Millon Clinical Multiaxial Inventory manual.* Minneapolis, MN: National Computer Systems.

Millon, T. (1983). *Millon Clinical Multiaxial Inventory.* Minneapolis, MN: Interpretive Scoring Systems.

Millon, T. (1987). *Manual for the MCMI II* (2nd ed.). Minneapolis, MN: National Computer Systems.

Millon, T. (1999). *Personality guided therapy.* New York: Wiley.

Millon, T., & Davis, R. D. (1996). An evolutionary theory of personality disorders. In J. F. Clarkin & M. F. Lenzenweger (Eds.), *Major theories of personality disorder* (pp. 221–346). New York: Guilford Press.

Millon, T., & Davis, R. D. (2000). *Personality disorders in modern life.* New York: Wiley.

Millon, T., Davis, R., & Millon, C. (1997). *MCMI-III manual* (2nd ed.). Minneapolis, MN: National Computer Systems.

Millon, T., & Grossman, S. D. (2006). Goals of a theory of personality. In M. Hersen (Editor-in-Chief) & J. C. Thomas & D. L. Segal (Vol. Eds.), *Comprehensive handbook of personality and psychopathology: Vol. 1. Personality and everyday functioning* (pp. 3–22). Hoboken, NJ: Wiley.

Millon, T., & Meagher, S. E. (2004). Millon Clinical Multiaxial Inventory-III (MCMI-III). In M. Hersen (Editor-in-Chief) & M. Hilsenroth & D. L. Segal (Vol. Eds.), *Comprehensive handbook of psychological assessment: Vol. 2. Personality assessment* (pp. 108–121). Hoboken, NJ: Wiley.

Molinari, V. (2000). *Professional psychology in long term care.* New York: Hatherleigh.

Molinari, V., Ames, A., & Essa, M. (1994). Prevalence of personality disorders in two geropsychiatric inpatient units. *Journal of Geriatric Psychiatry and Neurology, 7,* 209–215.

Molinari, V., Kunik, M. E., Snow-Turek, A. L., Deleon, H., & Williams, W. (1999). Age-related personality differences in inpatients with personality disorder: A cross-sectional study. *Journal of Clinical Geropsychology, 5,* 191–202.

Molinari, V., & Marmion, J. (1995). Relationship between affective disorders and Axis II diagnoses in geropsychiatric patients. *Journal of Geriatric Psychiatry and Neurology, 8,* 61–64.

Morey, L. C., Waugh, M. H., & Blashfield, R. K. (1985). MMPI scales for DSM-III personality disorders: Their derivation and correlates. *Journal of Personality Assessment, 49,* 245–256.

Mroczek, D. K., Hurt, S. W., & Berman, W. H. (1999). Conceptual and methodological issues in the assessment of personality disorders in older adults. In E. Rosowsky, R. C. Abrams, & R. A. Zweig (Eds.), *Personality disorders in older adults: Emerging issues in diagnosis and treatment* (pp. 135–150). Mahwah, NJ: Erlbaum.

National Center for Health Statistics. (2000). *Monthly vital statistics report, 50*(16).

Neale, M. C., & Cardon, L. R. (1992). *Methodology for genetic studies of twins and families.* London: Kluwer Press.

Nordhus, I. H., VandenBos, G. R., Berg, S., & Fromholt, P. (Eds.). (1998). *Clinical geropsychology.* Washington, DC: American Psychological Association.

O'Connor, B. P., & Dyce, J. A. (2001). Personality disorders. In M. Hersen & V. B. Van Hasselt (Eds.), *Advanced abnormal psychol-*

ogy (2nd ed., pp. 399–417). New York: Kluwer Academic/Plenum Press.

Oldham, J. M. (2001). Integrated treatment planning for borderline personality disorders. In J. Kay (Ed.), *Integrated treatment of psychiatric disorders* (pp. 52–75). Washington, DC: American Psychiatric Publishing.

Oldham, J. M., Skodol, A. E., Kellman, H. D., Hyler, S. E., Rosnick, L., & Davies, M. (1992). Diagnosis of DSM-III-R personality disorders by two structured interviews: Patterns of comorbidity. *American Journal of Psychiatry, 149,* 213–220.

Paris, B. J. (1994). *Karen Horney: A psychoanalyst's search for self-understanding.* New Haven, CT: Yale University Press.

Paris, J. (1998). Anxious traits, anxious attachment, and anxious cluster personality disorders. *Harvard Review of Psychiatry, 6,* 142–148.

Paris, J. (2003). *Personality disorders over time: Precursors, course, and outcome.* Washington, DC: American Psychiatric Press.

Paris, J. (2005). Nature and nurture in personality disorders. In S. Strack (Ed.), *Handbook of personology and psychopathology* (pp. 24–38). Hoboken, NJ: Wiley.

Perry, J. C. (1993). Longitudinal studies of personality disorders. *Journal of Personality Disorders*(Suppl.), 63–85.

Pfohl, B., Blum, N., & Zimmerman, M. (1997). *Structured Interview for DSM-IV Personality (SIDP-IV).* Arlington, VA: American Psychiatric Publishing.

Pincus, A. L. (2005). The interpersonal nexus of personality disorders. In S. Strack (Ed.), *Handbook of personology and psychopathology* (pp. 120–139). Hoboken, NJ: Wiley.

Pretzer, J. L., & Beck, J. T. (1996). A cognitive theory of personality disorders. In J. F. Clarkin & M. F. Lenzenweger (Eds.), *Major*

theories of personality disorders (pp. 36–105). New York: Guilford Press.

Qualls, S. H., & Segal, D. L. (2003). Assessment of older adults and their families. In K. Jordan (Ed.), *Handbook of couple and family assessment* (pp. 109–127). New York: Nova Science Publishers.

Qualls, S. H., Segal, D. L., Norman, S., Niederehe, G., & Gallagher-Thompson, D. (2002). Psychologists in practice with older adults: Current patterns, sources of training, and need for continuing education. *Professional Psychology: Research and Practice, 33,* 435–442.

Regier, D. A., Narrow, W. E., & Rae, D. S. (1990). The epidemiology of anxiety disorders: The Epidemiologic Catchment Area (ECA) experience. *Journal of Psychiatric Research, 24,* 3–14.

Reich, J., Nduaguba, M., & Yates, W. (1988). Age and sex distribution of DSM-III personality cluster traits in a community population. *Comprehensive Psychiatry, 29,* 298–303.

Reinecke, M. A., & Clark, D. A. (Eds.). (2004). *Cognitive therapy across the life span: Theory, research, and practice.* Cambridge, England: Cambridge University Press.

Rhee, S. H., & Waldman, I. D. (2002). Genetic and environmental influences on antisocial behavior: A meta-analysis of twin and adoption studies. *Psychological Bulletin, 128,* 490–529.

Robins, C., & Chapman, A. (2004). Dialectical behavior therapy: Current status, recent developments, and future directions. *Journal of Personality Disorders, 18,* 73–89.

Robins, L. N. (1966). *Deviant children grown-up: A sociological and psychiatric study of sociopathic personality.* Baltimore: Williams & Wilkins.

Rogers, R. (2001). *Handbook of diagnostic and structured interviewing.* New York: Guilford Press.

Rose, M. K., Soares, H. H., & Joseph, C. (1993). Frail elderly clients with personality disorders: A challenge for social work. *Journal of Gerontological Social Work, 19*, 153–165.

Rosowsky, E. (1999). The patient-therapist relationship and the psychotherapy of the older adult with personality disorder. In E. Rosowsky, R. Abrams, & R. Zweig (Eds.), *Personality disorders in older adults: Emerging issues in diagnosis and treatment* (pp. 153–174). Mahwah, NJ: Erlbaum.

Rosowsky, E., & Dougherty, L. (1998). Personality disorders and clinician responses. *Clinical Gerontologist, 18*, 31–42.

Rosowsky, E., Dougherty, L. M., Johnson, C., & Gurian, B. (1997). Personality as an indicator of goodness of fit between the elderly individual and the health service system. *Clinical Gerontologist, 17*, 41–53.

Rosowsky, E., & Gurian, B. (1991). Borderline personality disorder in late life. *International Psychogeriatrics, 3*, 39–52.

Rosowsky, E., & Gurian, B. (1992). Impact of borderline personality disorder in late life on systems of care. *Hospital and Community Psychiatry, 43*, 386–389.

Sackeim, H. A. (1994). Use of electroconvulsive therapy in late life depression. In L. S. Schneider, C. F. Reynolds, B. D. Lebowitz, & A. J. Friedhoff (Eds.), *Diagnosis and treatment of depression in late life* (pp. 259–277). Washington, DC: American Psychiatric Association Press.

Sadavoy, J. (1987). Character pathology in the elderly. *Journal of Geriatric Psychiatry, 20*, 165–178.

Sadavoy, J. (1996). Personality disorder in old age: Symptom expression. *Clinical Gerontologist, 16*, 19–36.

Sadavoy, J. (1999). The effect of personality disorder on Axis I disorders in the elderly. In M. Duffy (Ed.), *Handbook of counseling and psychotherapy with older adults* (pp. 397–413). New York: Wiley.

Sadavoy, J., & Fogel, B. (1992). Personality disorders in old age. In J. E. Birren, R. B. Sloane, & G. D. Cohen (Eds.), *Handbook of mental health and aging* (2nd ed., pp. 433–462). San Diego, CA: Academic Press.

Sareen, J., Enns, M., & Guertin, J. (2000). The impact of clinically diagnosed personality disorders on acute and 1-year outcomes of electroconvulsive therapy. *Journal of ECT, 16*, 43–51.

Scheel, K. (2000). The empirical basis of dialectical behavior therapy: Summary, critique, and implications. *Clinical Psychology, 7*, 68–86.

Schneider, L. S., Zemansky, M. F., Bender, M., & Sloane, R. B. (1992). Personality in recovered depressed elderly. *International Psychogeriatrics, 4*, 177–185.

Segal, D. L., & Coolidge, F. L. (1998). Personality disorders. In A. S. Bellack & M. Hersen (Eds.), *Comprehensive clinical psychology: Vol. 7. Clinical geropsychology* (pp. 267–289). New York: Elsevier Science.

Segal, D. L., & Coolidge, F. L. (2003). Structured interviewing and DSM classification. In M. Hersen & S. Turner (Eds.), *Adult psychopathology and diagnosis* (4th ed., pp. 72–103). Hoboken, NJ: Wiley.

Segal, D. L., & Coolidge, F. L. (2004). Objective assessment of personality and psychopathology: An overview. In M. Hersen (Editor-in-Chief) & M. Hilsenroth & D. L. Segal (Vol. Eds.), *Comprehensive handbook of psychological assessment: Vol. 2. Personality assessment* (pp. 3–13). Hoboken, NJ: Wiley.

Segal, D. L., & Coolidge, F. L. (2006). Reliability. In N. J. Salkind (Ed.), *Encyclopedia of human development* (pp. 1073–1074). Thousand Oaks, CA: Sage.

Segal, D. L., Coolidge, F. L., & Hersen, M. (1998). Psychological testing of older people. In I. H. Nordhus, G. R. VandenBos, S. Berg, & P. Fromholt (Eds.), *Clinical geropsychology* (pp. 231–257). Washington, DC: American Psychological Association.

Segal, D. L., Coolidge, F. L., O'Riley, A., & Heinz, B. A. (2006). Structured and semi-structured interviews. In M. Hersen (Eds.), *Clinician's handbook of adult behavioral assessment* (pp. 121–144). New York: Academic Press.

Segal, D. L., Hersen, M., Kabacoff, R. I., Falk, S. B., Van Hasselt, V. B., & Dorfman, K. (1998). Personality disorders and depression in community-dwelling older adults. *Journal of Mental Health and Aging, 4,* 171–182.

Segal, D. L., Hersen, M., Van Hasselt, V. B., Silberman, C. S., & Roth, L. (1996). Diagnosis and assessment of personality disorders in older adults: A critical review. *Journal of Personality Disorders, 10,* 384–399.

Segal, D. L., Hook, J. N., & Coolidge, F. L. (2001). Personality dysfunction, coping styles, and clinical symptoms in younger and older adults. *Journal of Clinical Geropsychology, 7,* 201–212.

Seivewright, H., Tyrer, P., & Johnson, T. (2002). Change in personality status in neurotic disorders. *Lancet, 359,* 2253–2254.

Serin, R. C., & Marshall, W. L. (2003). Personality disorders. In M. Hersen & S. Turner (Eds.), *Adult psychopathology and diagnosis* (4th ed., pp. 613–650). Hoboken, NJ: Wiley.

Shea, M., Pilkonis, P., Beckham, E., Collins, J., Elkin, I., Sotsky, S., et al. (1990). Personality disorders and treatment outcome in the NIMH treatment of depression collaborative research program. *American Journal of Geriatric Psychiatry, 147,* 711–718.

Shea, M., & Yen, S. (2003). Stability as a distinction between Axis I and Axis II disorders. *Journal of Personality Disorders, 17,* 373–386.

Shearin, E., & Linehan, M. (1994). Dialectical behavior therapy for borderline personality disorder: Theoretical and empirical foundations. *Acta Psychiatrica Scandinavia, 89,* 61–68.

Siegel, D. J., & Small, G. W. (1986). Borderline personality disorder in the elderly: A case study. *Canadian Journal of Psychiatry, 31,* 859–860.

Siever, L., & Davis, K. (1991). A psychobiological perspective on the personality disorders. *American Journal of Geriatric Psychiatry, 148,* 1647–1658.

Skodol, A., Stout, R., McGlashan, T., Grilo, C., Gunderson, J., Shea, M., et al. (1999). Co-occurrence of mood and personality disorders: A report from the Collaborative Longitudinal Personality Disorders Study (CLPS). *Depression and Anxiety, 10,* 175–182.

Smyer, M. A., & Qualls, S. H. (1999). *Aging and mental health.* Malden, MA: Blackwell.

Soloff, P. (1998). Algorithms for pharmacological treatment of personality dimensions: Symptom-specific treatments for cognitive/perceptual, affective, and impulsive-behavioral dysregulation. *Bulletin of the Menninger Clinic, 62*(2), 195–214.

Solomon, J., Falette, M., & Stevens, S. (1982). The psychologist as geriatric clinician. In T. Miller, C. Green, & R. Meagher (Eds.), *Handbook of clinical health psychology* (pp. 229–230). New York: Plenum Press.

Spitzer, R. L., Forman, J. B. W., & Nee, J. (1979). DSM-III field trials: Pt. I. Initial interrater diagnostic reliability. *American Journal of Psychiatry, 136,* 815–817.

Stek, M. L., Van Exel, E., Van Tilburg, W., Westendorf, R. G. J., & Beekman, A. T. F. (2002). The prognosis of depression in old age: Outcome 6 to 8 years after clinical treatment. *Aging and Mental Health, 6,* 282–285.

Stern, A. (1986). Psychoanalytic investigation of and therapy in the border line group of neuroses. In M. H. Stone (Ed.), *Essential papers on borderline disorders* (pp. 54–73). New York: New York University Press. (Original work published 1938)

Stevens, A., & Price, J. (1996). *Evolutionary psychiatry: A new beginning.* London: Routledge.

Stevenson, J., Meares, R., & Comerford, A. (2003). Diminished impulsivity in older patients with borderline personality disorder. *American Journal of Geriatric Psychiatry, 160,* 165–166.

Stone, M. (1993). *Abnormal personalities: Within and beyond the realm of treatment.* New York: Norton.

Teeter, R. B., Garetz, F. K., Miller, W. R., & Heiland, W. F. (1976). Psychiatric disturbances of aged patients in skilled nursing homes. *American Journal of Psychiatry, 133,* 1430–1434.

Thompson, L. W., Gallagher, D., & Czirr, R. (1988). Personality disorder and outcome in the treatment of late-life depression. *Journal of Geriatric Psychiatry, 21,* 133–146.

Torgersen, S. (1994). Genetics in borderline conditions. *Acta Psychiatrica Scandinavica, 89*(Suppl. 379), 19–25.

Torgersen, S., Lygren, S., Oien, P. A., Skre, I., Onstad, S., Edvardsen, J., et al. (2000). A twin study of personality disorders. *Comprehensive Psychiatry, 41,* 416–425.

Trappler, B., & Backfield, J. (2001). Clinical characteristics of older psychiatric inpatients with borderline personality disorder. *Psychiatric Quarterly, 72,* 29–40.

Turkhat, I. D. (1990). *The personality disorders: A psychological approach to clinical management.* New York: Pergamon Press.

Turkheimer, E. (2000). Three laws of behavior genetics and what they mean. *Current Directions in Psychological Science, 9,* 160–164.

Turkheimer, E., & Waldron, M. C. (2000). Non-shared environment: A theoretical, methodological, and quantitative review. *Psychological Bulletin, 126,* 78–108.

Tyrer, P. (1988). *Personality disorders: Diagnosis, management, and course.* London: Wright/Butterworth.

Tyrer, P., & Seivewright, H. (2000). Outcome of personality disorders. In P. Tyrer (Ed.), *Personality disorders: Diagnosis, management, and course* (2nd ed., pp. 105–125). Oxford, England: Butterworth Heinemann.

U.S. Bureau of the Census. (2003). *Statistical abstract of the United States.* Washington, DC: Author.

van Reekum, R. (1993). Acquired and developmental brain dysfunction in borderline personality disorder. *Canadian Journal of Psychiatry, 38*(Suppl. 1), 4–9.

Weissman, M. M. (1993). The epidemiology of personality disorders: A 1990 update. *Journal of Personality Disorders, 7,* 44–62.

Weissman, M. M., Markowitz, J., & Klerman, G. (2000). *Comprehensive guide to interpersonal psychotherapy.* New York: Basic Books.

Westen, D., & Shedler, J. (2000). A prototype matching approach to diagnosing personality disorders: Toward DSM-V. *Journal of Personality Disorders, 14,* 109–126.

Widiger, T. A. (2005). Personality disorders. In R. J. Craig (Ed.), *Clinical and diagnostic interviewing* (2nd ed., pp. 251–277). Lanham, MD: Aronson.

Widiger, T. A., Costa, P. T., & McCrae, R. R. (2002). A proposal for Axis II: Diagnosing personality disorders using the Five-Factor

Model. In P. T. Costa Jr. & T. A. Widiger (Eds.), *Personality disorders and the Five-Factor Model of personality* (2nd ed., pp. 431–456). Washington, DC: American Psychological Association.

Widiger, T. A., Mangine, S., Corbitt, E. M., Ellis, C. G., & Thomas, G. V. (1995). *Personality Disorder Interview-IV: A semistructured interview for the assessment of personality disorders* (Professional manual). Odessa, FL: Psychological Assessment Resources.

Widiger, T. A., & Rogers, J. H. (1989). Prevalence and comorbidity of personality disorders. *Psychiatric Annals, 19,* 132–136.

Widiger, T. A., & Seidlitz, L. (2002). Personality, psychopathology, and aging. *Journal of Research in Personality, 36,* 335–362.

Widiger, T. A., & Trull, T. J. (1992). Personality and psychopathology: An application of the five-factor model. *Journal of Personality, 60,* 363–393.

Williams, R., Briggs, R., & Coleman, P. (1995). Carer-rated personality changes associated with senile dementia. *International Journal of Geriatric Psychiatry, 10,* 231–236.

Wilson, E. O. (1975). *Sociobiology: The new synthesis.* Cambridge, MA: Belknap Press.

Wolf, R. S. (1998). Domestic elder abuse and neglect. In I. H. Nordhus, G. R. VandenBos, S. Berg, & P. Fromholt (Eds.), *Clinica geropsychology* (pp. 161–165). Washington, DC: American Psychological Association.

Wolff, S. (1995). *Loners: The life path of unusual children.* London: Routledge.

Young, J. E. (1999). *Cognitive therapy for personality disorders: A schema-focused approach* (3rd ed.). Sarasota, FL: Professional Resource Press.

Young, J. E., Klosko, J. S., & Weshaar, M. E. (2003). *Schema therapy: A practitioner's guide.* New York: Guilford Press.

Zanarini, M. C., Frankenburg, F. R., Sickel, A. E., & Yong, L. (1996). *The Diagnostic Interview for DSM-IV Personality Disorders* (DIPD-IV). Belmont, MA: McLean Hospital.

Zarit, S. H., & Zarit, J. M. (1998). *Mental disorders in older adults.* New York: Guilford Press.

Zweig, R. (2003). Personality disorders in older adults: Managing the difficult patient. *Clinical Geriatrics, 11,* 22–25.

Zweig, R. A., & Hillman, J. (1999). Personality disorders in adults: A review. In E. Rosowsky, R. C. Abrams, & R. A. Zweig (Eds.), *Personality disorders in older adults: Emerging issues in diagnosis and treatment* (pp. 31–53). Mahwah, NJ: Erlbaum.

Author Index

Subject Index